The Good Guys Wear Black

The Real-life Heroes of the Police's
Rapid-response Firearms Unit

The Good Guys Wear Black

The Real-life Heroes of the Police's Rapid-response Firearms Unit

by

Steve Collins

CENTURY · LONDON

Published by Century Books in 1997

Century
20 Vauxhall Bridge Road, London, SW1V 2SA

Random House Australia (Pty) Limited
20 Alfred Street, Milsons Point, Sydney,
New South Wales 2061, Australia

Random House New Zealand Limited
18 Poland Road, Glenfield,
Auckland 10, New Zealand

Random House South Africa (Pty) Limited
Endulini, 5a Jubilee Road,
Parktown 2193, South Africa

Random House UK Limited Reg. No. 954009

A CIP catalogue record for this book is available
from the British Library

Papers used by Random House UK Limited are natural, recyclable
products made from wood grown in sustainable forests. The
manufacturing processes conform to the environmental regulations of
the country of origin.

ISBN 0 7126 7728 3

Typeset by Palimpsest Book Production Limited,
Polmont, Stirlingshire
Printed and bound in Great Britain by
Mackays of Chatham Plc, Chatham, Kent

FOR JILL – THOSE EARLY MORNINGS – AND FOR SFO WIVES EVERYWHERE, WITHOUT WHOSE SUPPORT WE COULDN'T FUNCTION.

THE YOUNG DEAD COPPER

'OK, son,' and over the gun.
Come quietly now. Don't try to run.'

Born to suffer. The Young Dead Copper.
A family tradition. A life in the Force.
Born a scuffer. The Young Dead Copper.
Cut down by villains who show no remorse.

Buried with honour. The Young Dead Copper.
Buried beneath his family's wreath.
Proud of tomorrow. The Young Dead Copper.
Proud of a Force who now show remorse.

Prayers were said. For the Young Dead Copper.
Prayers of justice. Retribution and revenge.
Prayers were read. For the Young Dead Copper.
Empty words that are said for the Dead.

Born to Suffer. The Young Dead Copper.
Born to a Tradition. A Life in the Force.
Born a scuffer. The Bright Young Copper.
Buried by the force of an Unknown Source.

Laurence M. Hayes, 1996

Contents

Acknowledgements

I wish to thank the following:

Mum and Dad; my family and friends (they know who they are), for all the encouragement and support they gave me over what is probably the biggest risk I've ever taken; Jill, for driving me on and believing I could do it; Mark Booth and his team at Random House (it hasn't been easy); my agent Barbara Levy, who first saw the spark; but most of all to Black Team – thanks for the memories.

Author's Note

Due to the sensitive nature of its content, the manuscript of this book was submitted to the Commissioner of Police for the Metropolis.

At their own request the names and identifying features of some individuals have been changed.

This is the story of an extraordinary team of volunteers who routinely carry out the most dangerous tasks in the name of law and order. They are not saints but mere mortals thrown together in the most unique and violent of circumstances. As such this book contains strong language, and for that I make no apology!

Picture Credits

The plates in this book emanate from the following sources, to whom the publishers gratefully offer acknowledgement: *PA News*: 2, 3, 4; Kenneth Saunders and the *Guardian*: 5, 6; Steve Roberts: 9, 10, 14, 15, 20; Joyce Lowman: 28; *Sun* newspaper: 29, 30. The back cover photograph, 17 and 18 belong to a private collection.

The author and publishers have made all reasonable efforts to contact copyright holders for permission. We apologize for any omissions or errors in the form of credit given and this will be corrected in future printings.

Foreword

With its cracked black and white mosaic staircase, the once-grand-now-cheap West London boarding house nestled innocuously among the ramshackle buildings of Glenthorne Road.

Monday, 24 September 1996, early morning – and for the large Irish population that inhabited this part of Hammersmith, it was just like any other Monday morning. But this week would be far from normal.

In a room on the ground floor of the boarding house slept twenty-seven-year-old, red-haired and baby-faced Diarmuid O'Neill, reputed volunteer for the London-based IRA Active Service Unit.

Nothing stirred as the unmarked vans glided noiselessly to a halt, disgorging their cargo of heavily armed, black-clad assaulters. Suddenly shouts from the building as the calm is shattered by the ominous bark of gunfire.

Later, the limp body of O'Neill was dragged from the building, his blood congealing in the cracks on the floor. Another page from the history books of the world-renowned Special Air Service? Certainly the reader may be forgiven for thinking that. But it was in fact just another day in the working week of the Metropolitan Police Specialist Firearms Unit SO19.

The Men in Black.

Friday, 7 March 1997, the front page of London's *Evening Standard* pictures an SO19 Firearms Team training on the River Thames under the caption 'THIS IS HOW OUR FRIENDLY POLICE NOW WANT US TO SEE THEM. ARMED TO THE TEETH AND LOOKING SET FOR WAR IN BOSNIA.' Stirring words indeed, nevertheless SO19 remain the true unsung heroes of the Police Service, who daily wage war against armed and violent aggressors in the name of law and order. The last defence in the armoury of the Thin Blue Line.

Move over Dixon. This is their story!

1

'Where the Fuck is Surrey?'

I suppose I was destined to join the job from the start. I entered this world in October 1957, six days earlier than expected. No problem, though – I was raring to go.

Dad was present at the delivery, which took place in Nan's front room. Even today I'm no oil painting, but as the midwife dried off my pink, disproportionate shape, Dad took a step backwards. 'Fucking hell,' he said. 'Will he be all right?'

'Of course he will,' the midwife replied.

Dad's eyes scanned my body, taking in the black bags under my eyes before coming to rest, transfixed, on the large, pointed head.

I've always had a conscience, even as a kid. Values. A strong sense of what's right and what's wrong. So I suppose it came as no surprise when I finally joined up. There were really only two options open to me: go through life being constantly patted on the head in an attempt to flatten it, or paint it blue and join the Police Force. I chose the latter.

My earliest memories are of a strong family bond, not only between me and my parents but also my grandparents and aunt, with whom we lived, and who never failed to provide encouragement and support, putting food on the table and shoes on my feet even when times were hard. That small house in South London harbours the happiest memories of my childhood.

Home was the downstairs front room, converted into a bedroom that I shared with Mum and Dad. The living room and kitchen were communal, and Nan, Grandad and Aunt June lived upstairs. Yes, the accomodation was cramped, but nobody really noticed.

1

I loved to play with Grandad's old camera, and I would run to Nan when I was hurt. I can still smell the onions on her clothes. I would put my small arms around her legs and cry into her apron. And I can still see Mum, standing by the sink with her hands in a bowl of washing-up. 'You have to get your priorities right,' she would say. 'We want you to do well and have opportunies that we never got.'

I was four years old when my brother Dave was born. After recovering from the initial pangs of jealousy I was delighted to have a playmate. However, apart from playing sometimes with a young lad up the street called Micky, I was pretty much a loner. But I was a happy loner, because I had a dog – well, she wasn't really *my* dog, she had been taken in by Nan and Grandad. We would go everywhere together. Half boxer, half bull mastiff, she towered above me. Her name was Butch. Why? I don't know, she just looked like a Butch. She was the most loyal friend and confidante any five-year-old could wish for.

I can still see her almost human features, tongue lolling to one side as she charges up the garden path. She would often meet me from school, and I would walk proudly beside her or ride on her back, showing off to the other kids as I went home for lunch.

During the cold evenings we would huddle together in front of the old coke fire. Somehow oblivious to the heat, she would ignore the small pieces of red-hot ash which flew out and landed on her coat. With the smell of singed hair filling my nostrils, I would lie with my head on her chest, listening to the rhythm of her heart, my small head rising and falling with each huge lungful of breath. I would whisper my innermost thoughts and feelings into her battered and moth-eaten ear, and declare my undying love for her.

When I was seven we moved house. Mum and Dad had been allocated a flat on the Cherry Orchard Estate, just around the corner. Undeterred, I would walk from school to Nan's house every lunchtime to visit Butch. But one day she wasn't there. I knew she'd been ill, But I had no idea how bad her condition was. She had been put down while I was at school. I know they had thought it best not to tell me, but if I ever blamed my family for anything it would be that Butch had left this world and I was never given the chance to say goodbye. I had lost my best friend.

2

Now, thirty years later, not a week passes that I don't think of her with a tear in my eye and a lump in my throat.

Nan's house never felt the same after that.

On that day I changed too. I had never been a sporting child, but – fuck football, I wanted war!

After leaving school I drifted, not really knowing what I wanted to become. I was no academic and had been desperate to leave, but I was intelligent enough to realize I had to make something of myself. I got a job as a trainee salesman in the electrical department at the Co-op in Lewisham, but I soon became bored, and started to toy with the idea of joining the Army.

I had often talked for hours with my grandad Arthur, a career soldier of twenty-two years. (His medals now hang in pride of place in our front room.) A large, barrel-chested man, he had joined the Army at fourteen and seen his way through six years of war. In the latter part of his life he had had a stroke which unfortunately left him paralysed and bedridden. It broke my heart to see such a strong, proud and wonderful man wasting away. However, he kept a sound mind and memory, and often thrilled me with his stories of derring-do.

'I'm thinking of joining the Army, Grandad,' I said one day. 'But Mum doesn't like the idea of Ireland.'

He looked up from his pillow. 'Son, I've seen it all, from Europe to Africa. Your mum is right to worry; soldiers do get shot at. It's their job. But remember one thing.' He grinned lopsidedly. 'You never see the bullet that hits you.'

With a spring in my step I marched down to the Army Careers Office, but couldn't quite bring myself to walk in.

For the next couple of weeks I drifted some more. I was daydreaming of excitement and travel, but at the back of my mind there was always that small niggling doubt.

One Saturday in 1977 started, like many others, with my weaving in and out of the early-morning traffic on my motorbike. But today was different. Today, my life was to reach an important crossroad. Turn right for security and drudgery; turn left for uncertainty and excitement. I would turn left.

That afternoon the National Front were exercising their right to march through the streets of Lewisham. Anti-right-wing

3

groups, such as the Socialist Workers' Party, counter-demonstrated. What followed was a pitched battle through the streets of South London that the Thin Blue Line could barely contain.

'Bloody hell, look at that,' said Norman, one of the Co-op drivers. I followed the direction of his outstretched finger. On the street, far below my vantage point on the roof of the Co-op, stood two hatless members of the infamous Special Patrol Group. Between them they held the limp form of a long-haired youth. With an arm and a leg each, they swung his prostrate form to and fro, his head repeatedly colliding with the side of their van like a battering ram. Then, as the side door slid open, the semi-conscious offender was flung inside. All around, bricks and bottles rained down in a hail of destruction.

Truncheons drawn, small groups of police charged the crowd, their only protection dustbin lids and traffic cones hastily slipped on their arms to parry the missiles. Constantly beaten back, they retreated only to regroup and charge again.

Heart pounding and adrenalin pumping, I watched as police officers, bloodied and injured, were tended by their colleagues, makeshift barricades shielding them from yet more harm, and ambulances battled to penetrate the rag-tag army. Anything in uniform was now considered fair game to the baying pack, all reason lost in the spiralling escalation of hatred.

Never before had I witnessed violence on such a scale. But there was more: I felt excitement. And then suddenly I was overwhelmed with a sense of purpose. Fuck the Co-op – I was going to join the Police.

I stared down at my grandfather's sunken cheeks, the saliva flowing across the grey stubble of his chin and soaking into the pillow. The old man's rheumy eyes opened, a portal into that sharp brain. With a shaking hand he dabbed a handkerchief laboriously across his lips, then he smiled.

'Grandad,' I whispered, 'I want to join the Police.'

He held me in his gaze. 'Son,' he slurred, 'whatever you do I'll be proud of you. And no matter what you think, your dad will too. I look forward to seeing you in uniform.'

Unfortunately he never would, for the man I had most looked up to and admired during those adolescent years was to die soon afterwords, a welcome release from years of imprisonment in a frail, wasted body.

Ask a policeman why he joined the Force and he'll probably spout off some crap about it being a vocation or even a calling. Most people I know do it to pay the mortgage. I'll never know exactly what led me into it, but that day on the roof played a major part; it appeared to me to offer both glamour and the potential for a punch-up.

'Why do you want to become a policeman?'

I had anticipated the question and rehearsed the answer, but now I stared open-mouthed at the three senior officers sitting across the table, immaculate in their blue serge uniforms. 'Well, sir, I think it is both a demanding and important challenge, but most of all I want to help the public.'

'Oh yeah,' sneered the chairman, then become a social worker.'

'*Next*,' I heard him call as I walked dejectedly back along the hall.

Sitting on the train on the way home I pondered the day. In the canteen at Paddington Green Police Station I had watched in awe as the Security Section swaggered in, revolvers hanging loosely from their leather holsters. To see a policeman with a gun was as rare as seeing a rocking-horse shit, and I daydreamed of being in their position. But I was on the way home to Mum, and I realized it was not to be. I think she saw my disappointment, but in her heart of hearts she was probably glad. Perhaps now I would get it out of my system and get a proper job.

'There are other forces, you know,' a friend said to me down the pub one night. 'You don't have to join the Met.'

I slowly put my pint on the bar and looked at him. 'What do you mean?'

'Well, you could always join a county force and transfer back later.'

'You're a fucking genius,' I said. 'Where shall I go, then?'

'Well, try Surrey. That's near.'

'Brilliant,' I replied. 'Surrey sounds good. Where the fuck's Surrey?'

* * *

'Young man,' boomed the balding chief constable, 'I'm going to take a chance on you. But I don't want you running off back to the Met. Is it a deal?'

'That's a deal, sir.' I shook his outstretched hand.

On that day in 1978 I stared into the mirror and my gaze was held. Not by that of a twenty-year-old South Londoner, but by Police Constable Collins of the Surrey Constabulary.

I was posted to Reigate, on the eastern side of the county, where I kept my head down and worked hard. 1981 saw more rioting in Brixton, Toxteth and Leicester. Other Forces were mobilized, Surrey included, to provide mutual aid. Standing behind those flimsy shields as the missiles rained down made me remember why I had joined. Gritting my teeth, I ducked, realizing that I craved the danger and excitement. Even the fear.

The memories of those early beginnings are hazy. My short spells on CID were interspersed with the fun of the Area Crime Car.

'What's up, shag?' asked Brakey, my partner, one early morning. He was a fast car driver and thief-taker who had transferred in from West Mercia. We had worked together for the past four years. It was more than a partnership really, more of a bond; we seemed to know what each other was thinking, how each other would react. What's more, we had a hard reputation among the local villainy.

'That motor bugs me,' I said, pointing to the dark-coloured Volvo which had just passed in the opposite direction. It was 3 a.m.

'What do you want to do?' Brakey asked, glancing in his rear-view mirror.

'Let's tug it.'

Pulling hard on the handbrake, Brakey spun the steering wheel. The old Cortina's tyres screamed loudly in the deserted street as we executed a perfect handbrake turn. As he kicked down the accelerator my neck snapped back, and we took off up Redhill High Street at breakneck speed, catching up in seconds.

'That's odd,' I said, reading the number-plate to myself. 'That's a diplomatic motor. What's he doing down here?'

'Dunno,' Brakey replied, staring intently ahead. 'What do you wanna do?'

'Stop the fucker.' I picked up the handset. 'H.J. H.J. Bravo Two Zero.' I spoke clearly, giving our familiar callsign.

'Bravo Two Zero, go ahead,' came the disjointed reply.

'Vehicle check please,' I said, and read the number.

'Bravo Two Zero, Bravo Two Zero,' the voice come back, now urgent.

'Go ahead, H.J.'

'This is a diplomatic car from the Russian embassy. Is it accompanied by a Metropolitan Police vehicle? Over.'

'Negative, negative, H.J. What are your instructions? Over.'

'Bravo Two Zero, details will be passed to Special Branch. From the control room supervisor: do not, repeat *do not* stop this vehicle.'

'Well, bollocks to you,' I muttered under my breath. 'What shall we do, mate?'

'Well,' came Brakey's tense reply, 'you wanted to stop the fucker, shag, so let's stop it.'

Switching on the blue light, I pulled at the radio handset. 'H.J., Bravo Two Zero,' I shouted, 'Radio blackspot. You are breaking up. Repeat, please . . . H.J., I'm losing you. Please show vehicle stop Redstone Hill. Bravo Two Zero, out.'

The frantic cries of the operator were blotted out by the wail of the two-tone horns as the vehicle in front slowed. The blue light played off the walls and underside of the railway bridge.

Stepping out into the chilly morning air, I thought about what we would do. My mind playing tricks, I thought of the exiled Bulgarian radio presenter Georgi Markov, recently murdered by the Eastern Bloc's security service while waiting at a London bus stop.

Approaching the driver's side, I whispered to Brakey, 'Check this fucker out for any vicious looking umbrellas.'

Brakey grinned.

The electric window retreated with a faint hum. 'Gentlemen,' was the greeting from within.

I looked down, and was confronted by a middle-aged, tanned individual with a perfect though slightly clipped English accent. 'Are you lost, sir?'

'Not at all, not at all,' came the pleasant reply.

'Do you have identification, please?'

'Yes, indeed. Do you?'

'What do you mean?'

'Come, come, Officer,' he said, a hint of sarcasm in his voice. 'In this day and age one cannot be too careful. Were you genuine, you would surely have been instructed not to hinder my journey. But,' he raised his hands in mock surprise, 'here you are. No. I think first I need to see your authority – warrant card, please.'

I had started this game; it was a matter of personal pride not to back down. On the other hand I didn't want to start a diplomatic incident. Slightly gobsmacked, I unfolded the small blue case to reveal my face on the black and white photograph, strangely pale in the bright yellow stream of torchlight.

'Officer Collins,' the driver muttered to himself. 'I will look out for you.'

Fuck this, I thought. Our details will end up on some fucking Red's computer.

'Can I have your registration number, please?' he asked politely. Now I could see through his façade. He was trying to goad us.

'No, you can't have our fucking registration. This ain't Checkpoint Charlie, you know. We ask the questions! Now, as you know who we are, perhaps you'll do the honours?'

'What?'

'What is your fucking name, sir!'

Sitting bolt upright, he produced a Russian identity card complete with stamps. 'I, Gentlemen, am a colonel of the Soviet Air Force, and believe me, your superiors will hear of this.'

I studied his documents meticulously – after all, it wasn't every day I met a full-blown Russian colonel out for a drive in the country. 'One thing escapes me, guvnor,' I said, bending down, my torchlight scanning the interior of the vehicle where it picked out an open map case on the passenger seat. 'Just what the fuck are you up to?'

'Oh, nothing really,' he replied, snatching back his ID. 'Just plotting airfields.'

The car pulled away with a screech of burning rubber. Transfixed, we stood in silence and stared at each other. 'Did he just say what I thought he said?' asked Brakey.

'He did, mate,' I said. 'And he's headed for the aerodrome. Let's go!'

Jumping back into the vehicle, we sped off in hot pursuit. But it was to no avail; he had disappeared down one of the many country lanes.

Resigned to the fact that we would never see him again, we made our way back to the nick. Throwing the report in the in-tray, I wiped the incident from my mind.

'Well done, chaps,' said the superintendent a couple of months later, sitting in his spacious office.

'What for, sir?' I asked.

'That Russian you stopped a few months back – remember? When you had radio problems.'

I flushed. 'Oh, yeah.'

He continued, 'For obvious reasons this must remain confidential, but a Home Secretary's Commendation has been placed on both your files.'

I looked at Brakey, bewildered.

'The man has since been deported for conduct unbecoming his status.'

'What's that then, boss?' Brakey asked.

'That, son, is a spy. He was a colonel in Air Force Intelligence. Once again, well done.' He smiled.

'Fucking hell, mate,' I said, patting Brakey on the back as we walked up the corridor. 'Fucking spycatchers or what?'

When later I transferred, I got to see my file. I can only assume the Home Secretary had had a game of golf that day, or something equally important. Was there a commendation in there? Was there bollocks!

The years passed, and I drifted unhappily from one department to the next. I took a stab at the promotion exam, and in 1986 was made up to sergeant. It was around this time that a large number of firearms officers – 'shots' as they were known – were required for a forthcoming protection post. Termed Operation Minster, it was to involve guarding the residence of the recently married Duke and Duchess of York.

Having little or no knowledge of firearms, I found the course hard. I was certainly no natural shot, but revelled in the tactics and decision-making. My final report read: 'He shows good qualities in ability to fully assess and command situations, with total control of his actions. An officer who is quiet in manner but authoritative when required.'

I had made it.

2

Rubbing Shoulders with Royalty

I had always admired the royal family, and when I was approached to participate in their protection as part of the Minster team I was delighted.

'Bloody hell,' said Mum. 'Rubbing shoulders with royalty. Whatever next?'

The silence of the control room was shattered by the persistent *wee wah, wee wah* of the gate's electronic bell.

The property stood in its own grounds in picturesque countryside just outside Egham. A large, imposing building, it sported a long driveway, a pool, servants' quarters and, in the grounds, a small detached bungalow which ideally served our purpose as a self-contained control centre. We were told that the property was leased from the Queen by King Hussein of Jordan. He in turn permitted the recently married Duke and Duchess to live there when not in residence. It was obviously an arrangement that worked, and gave the young couple seclusion and privacy from the rest of the family, although with Windsor Great Park a mere stone's throw away Mum and Dad often popped in.

Wee wah. I put down my copy of the *Sun*. 'Everything all right, Pat?' I called to the controller.

'There's someone at the gate he said, but I can't pick them up on camera.'

I made my way to the cramped control room.

Pat, the tactical advisor, sat surrounded by banks of small video monitors. 'Can I help you?' he called into the gate's intercom system. The crackled reply was unintelligible and punctuated by the *wee wah* of the bell. 'Go out and have a

11

look, Steve.' Pat squinted at the screen. 'Can't see a bloody thing. Probably someone mucking about.'

In recent weeks, as the location had become common knowledge, a number of pressmen and curious locals had become constant callers; one night a drunken intruder had even been arrested at gunpoint.

Closing one eye, I peered intently through the spyhole.

'What you got?' Pat's disembodied voice crackled in my earpiece.

'Can't really see,' I said, trying to focus my watering eyeball. 'Sun's too bright. Looks like some geezer on a horse and cart – what's he want?'

'Fucking hell,' said Pat. 'Get the bloody gates open, it's the fucking Duke of Edinburgh.'

I fumbled with the large bolt. Drawing it slowly back, I pulled open the large black rusted gates. With a groom alongside him, flat cap on his head and blanket across his knees, I was confronted by the duke. With whip in hand he spurred the team of horses through the gate.

'About fucking time,' he fumed, looking down at me as he passed. I stepped back as the large carriage wheels narrowly missed my toes. He wasn't exactly known for his patience.

The gates were wide open in good time when he left. I even stopped the traffic.

But after a few weeks I was no longer in awe, and the job began to get boring. I wanted to be a firearms officer, but on the other hand I needed to be active. The Royalty Protection Officers seemed in general to be happy to take any amount of abuse, but it was really pissing me off, bowing and scraping to people who treated you like shit.

The job wasn't so bad during the summer months, when most of my day was taken up wandering around the grounds on perimeter patrol. I'd often meet the Duke of York in the woods, where he walked his small Jack Russell dog, Bendicks, a present to the duchess from her dashing sailor, apparently an old Naval tradition. When the dog had first arrived Fergie had been constantly worried about his state of health – he was often sick and he refused to eat.

One day, as I sat in the control room reading the paper,

a flicker of movement caught my eye. 'Hello boy,' I whispered.

The dog was sitting there, staring. Following his hungry gaze, I spotted a half-eaten corned beef sandwich. 'Come on, then.' Removing the filling, I knelt down. His small nose twitched cautiously as he sniffed the offering and then gently pulled it from my fingers.

'Great,' came a soft voice from the doorway. 'You've got him to eat.'

Somewhat startled, I took in the flame-red hair. 'Yes, ma'am,' I replied courteously.

'How do you do that? I've tried everything. He even refuses duck pâté.'

'Well, ma'am,' I replied, 'puppies are like babies.' I looked down. Bendicks, oblivious to the conversation, wolfed down the last of the meat. 'Give them anything rich and they'll bring it up. I'm not surprised he won't eat pâté.'

As if reminding me of my place, she scooped up the puppy in her arms, turned on her heel and left the room. From that day on, keeping a simple diet, the dog had no more problems, and throughout the summer became a regular visitor to the control centre. A triumph indeed for that great British institution, the corned beef sarnie.

'Well, I don't fucking like it!' I heard as I entered the room. 'It's got to go!'

Up to that point I'd only ever seen the Duke of York in full flow once before; that was with his hapless protection officer, who had stood with his hands behind his back like some naughty child. I remembered thinking that if somebody spoke to me like that I'd fucking fill him in.

Now the duke slammed his palm down on the desk and stormed out.

'Good-morning, Your Royal Highness,' I smirked as he passed. Red-faced, he glared in my direction and slammed the door on his way out. 'What's that all about?' I asked Pat.

'He's got the fucking hump with the camera by the pool,' he said. 'Reckons he's going to sort it out.'

I looked down at the bank of bright screens. In the heat of the midday sun the bikini-clad duchess lounged at the poolside.

'He thinks it's an intrusion of his privacy,' Pat continued. I could see his point of view; unfortunately he refused to see ours. We were responsible for his safety, and that of his wife, so we had to balance their need for privacy with our need for security.

Two days later the phone rang. The controller answered. 'Yes . . . Yes, fine . . . Thank you . . .' Replacing the handset, he looked up. 'Stand to. The duke and duchess are going to the pool.'

Watching the monitors, I charted their progress from the house to the chalet, disappearing from one screen and appearing on the next. Flopping on to a reclining sunlounger, Fergie began to apply copious amounts of suntan lotion to her pale skin. Andrew meanwhile strode over to the hated camera and stared directly into the lens so that his face dominated the small screen. Then the image flickered and died.

'Bastard,' muttered the controller, pushing buttons on the console with no effect. The screen stared blankly ahead.

'What's up?' I enquired.

'He's had a fucking override button fitted to the camera.'

'That's fucking great,' I said. 'What do we do now?'

'No problem.' The controller smiled up at me. 'For God's sake, don't let the protection blokes know about this. If the duke finds out he'll go fucking ballistic.' And pressing a concealed button below the control panel he said, 'Fuck you, smartarse.'

The blank screen suddenly blinked into life, revealing the duke and duchess, oblivious to their hidden audience, canoodling on the lounger.

Rather you than me, I thought. 'How did you do that?' I asked.

'We thought he'd do something after his outburst the other day,' the controller replied. 'So we had our own override built in. Stand down now, mate,' he added, staring at the screen.

I pulled up my gunbelt and stepped out into the bright sunlight. I'd had enough of the royal family. I decided they wouldn't last five seconds in the real world – half of that in a South London boozer – they simply had no respect for the common man. Compounding my frustration was the fact that I was bored; and interestingly enough the Met were advertising for sergeants.

3

Enter Fifty Fucks

'Whilst you're here you have certain rights,' I heard myself say for the umpteenth time that evening. The job was custody officer, every sergeant's nightmare: repetitive, thankless and boring, but none the less important. I looked up from the custody record into the eyes of the prisoner.

'Fuck you,' he said.

I had been posted to Croydon, where I'd thrown myself into the job. Compared with Surrey I found the pace fast-moving and furious. However, I hated these postings that took me from the streets.

'As you're a juvenile,' I continued, 'Your parents will be informed of your arrest.'

'Fuck you.' The fifteen-year-old hard man attempted to fix me with his most terrifying thousand-yard stare.

'Sign here, please,' I said, offering my pen. He held me in his gaze. 'Son,' I said, bored, 'I have shits that are harder than you. Chuck him in the detention room, Andy,' I called to the jailer, 'While I phone Mummy.' The boy's lip quivered in defiance as he was led away. 'What a fucking night,' I said to myself.

I went to the canteen and bought a coffee. Fucking hell, I need a break, I thought. And I've only been here three hours! Everybody else is out scouring the streets and estates. Me, I'm here.

A flicker of movement caught my eye, and looking up I saw a dark shadow through the frosted glass door. It drew closer and began to take shape. The door creaked open, and in strode a lone figure. A black beret adorned his head, worn at a jaunty angle, its once silver badge now blackened against the light. His heavy Goretex jacket enveloped his body armour and blue coveralls,

15

its collar turned up against the wind. On his right hip he wore a leather holster, thumb break clipped tight against the sinister black butt of the Glock 9 mm self-loading pistol.

I nodded. He took in my rank. 'All right, Sarge?' he said.

'What's going on, mate?' I asked.

'Oh, nothing really, Sarge. We're just a PT17 security patrol.'

'Got any jobs for sergeants?'

'Funny you should say that. I think they're advertising soon for Level Two.'

'What's Level Two?'

'Well,' he started, pulling off his beret and flopping in the chair opposite, 'our department has two levels of response, graded Level One and Level Two.'

This was a totally new concept to me, having come from a small force where the one team did everything. 'What's the difference?'

He looked at his watch. 'Level Two do the day-to-day work, early morning dig-outs, robbery plots, that sort of thing.'

'Dig-outs?' I asked quizzically.

'Yeah. Early-morning raids, firearms warrants, that sort of stuff. Then if you pass the course you move up to Level One.'

'What's that entail?'

'Level One are all instructors. We change on a regular basis between ops and training.'

'Yeah, great,' I replied, 'but what do you actually *do*?'

'Our definition is criminals with exceptional firepower, hostage rescue, and armed besieged criminals. That may involve terrorists.'

'I'm Steve Collins.' I offered my hand.

'Alan Ball.' He gripped it firmly. 'Come outside and meet my skipper.'

Pushing open the swing doors, I stepped into the yard and shivered as the cold night wind cut through my thin cotton shirt. Parked in the corner, engine running, was a dark-coloured Senator. Falling into step behind my new-found friend, I sauntered over, and the driver's window opened with a faint electrical hum. Alan passed in two cups and climbed into the back, where he engaged in conversation with the front-seat passenger. Unblinkingly, the driver stared directly ahead.

'So you want to join us?'

16

Ducking down, I sought the location of the voice.

The passenger leaned across the driver's lap and smiled. 'I'm John.' His small, lean frame was swamped by a massive jacket, and he sat with a Heckler & Koch MP5 across his knees. 'Sargie here wants to join the department,' John said to the unsmiling driver.

'Oh, yeah. Who doesn't?'

'This is Chris,' said John. 'Level Two. Hates wannabes.'

'World's full of 'em,' said Chris, turning to face me.

Smug fucker, I thought and smiled as I took in his hard features, short blond hair and stocky frame.

'Can't hang about all night, buddy,' he said in his faint southern accent. 'See you around!' And he gunned the accelerator.

PT17 sounds a good crack! I thought as I pushed my way back through the security door. Here I was, hot, sweaty, honking and deskbound. Out there they patrolled, weapons ready.

Crash! I was jerked to my senses as the custody door to the yard flew open.

'YOU FUCKERS, I'LL KILL YOU!'

Out of the darkness appeared a spittle-coated, long matted beard, attached to a wild man who dived headlong through the door and came to rest at my feet. I looked down at the prone figure surrounded now by his captors, shirts torn and tieless.

'Fucking hell, Sarge, he's crazy!'

The prisoner looked up and growled, his face contorted with rage. He appeared totally without reason.

'All right,' I shouted. 'Let's have some calm. Andy, we'll get his details later. Put him in a cell and search him.' The jailer nodded.

With a growl deep in his throat, the wild man leapt from the floor. 'I'll kill you. I'll kill you,' he screamed.

I stepped back as he disappeared, lost from sight under four uniformed bodies. With arms and legs thrashing wildly he was dragged across the floor and tossed into the cell, his rage suddenly silenced by the slamming door.

'What the fuck's going on?' I asked the torn and bleeding uniforms.

'He's fucking mad, Sarge,' said one. 'Went crazy, just jumped out in front of the van screaming, took four of us just to hold him down. He should be fucking deemed.' (The admittance of a

17

criminal to a mental hospital for assessment – this was possible under the authority of an inspector in consultation with the local police surgeon.)

'Sarge, Sarge!' Andy's frantic cries from the cell block. 'The prisoner's trying to set fire to himself!'

'Oh, for God's sake.' I screamed. Slamming my paperback on the desk, I ran towards the smoke-filled room. 'You silly fucking bastard!' I threw the naked prisoner a pair of paper overalls as his heaped clothes smouldered in the corner. Standing on one leg, the wild man eyed me suspiciously before slipping on the thin garment. 'Now,' I said, jabbing my finger in his chest, 'I don't want any more fucking trouble from you. *Understand?*' I slammed the door on the staring face.

'Fucking hell, Andy, what's going on? I told you to search him properly.'

'I did, Sarge,' the hapless jailer stammered. 'But he had a box of matches stuffed up his arse.'

I looked down at the crumpled box, gripped tightly in my hand, and stormed off to the washroom.

It was while I was drying my hands I heard Andy's faint cries: 'Sarge, quick! The prisoner's trying to strangle himself.' I hit the panic button with a clenched fist as I ran past. Fumbling with the huge bunch of keys on my belt I heard the door outside slam against the wall, sounds of running feet. Throwing open the cell door, I quickly scanned the small room. Naked again, the wild man lay in the far corner, his face grey and swollen, tongue lolling grotesquely from his mouth. Around his neck, the paper suit was somehow fashioned into a makeshift noose. With an end grasped tightly in each hand, he was attempting to strangle himself – and by all accounts he was making a fucking good job of it.

Anger welled inside me. I pulled a switchblade from my pocket and leapt on to the foul-smelling body, hacking at the soft material. It separated, slowly at first, then quickly as the knife bit deeper. Suddenly his Adam's apple flicked excitedly as air surged into his tortured lungs, his chest heaving to satisfy the craving for oxygen. The blade retracted with a sharp snap.

'You tosser,' I said. 'I ought to kill you myself, you are giving me the right fucking arse.' Rising to my feet, I surveyed the shocked faces filling the doorway. 'Andy, he's having nothing till we can get rid of him, understand?' The jailer nodded. 'Good. Now hurry that bloody doctor up and let's get rid of this crank.'

As I made my way wearily back to the office, I passed the detention room. Muffled banging sounds were coming from inside, kicks raining down on the heavy wooden door. Standing to one side, I pulled it sharply open mid-kick, and the juvenile hard nut fell forward on to the stone floor. Grabbing his collar, I jerked him upright, spun him around and kicked him up the arse and back through the doorway. 'Sit down and shut up!' I shouted, slamming the door.

I looked at my watch. 'Two forty-five and all's well!'

For some reason I couldn't seem to get PT17 out of my mind. I recalled lying on a beach in Portugal, where I had picked up the previous day's *Sun*. THE EQUALIZER! was emblazoned across the front page, together with a large photograph of a Browning self-loading pistol. With a pang of jealousy I'd read how a lone PT17 officer had engaged three armed robbers at the abattoir in Woolwich. In the ensuing gun battle all three went down. Unscathed, the officer was hailed a hero. Gripping stuff! Arriving back at Heathrow from another holiday some years later, I'd found they'd been at it again, this time shooting and killing notorious South London villain 'Crazy' Kenny Baker, and wounding another member of the gang. Had the men I met tonight been there? I wondered. I was soon to have an answer. Little did I know I had already crossed paths with The Equalizer.

'Go get a cuppa, Steve. I'll stand in.' The inspector pulled up a chair.

'Oh, cheers guv,' I said. I studied him hard. Young to be an inspector, I thought, trying to place his age. About thirty, I guessed, but a decent enough bloke.

He flicked his lighter, ignoring the red NO SMOKING signs posted on the walls. Smoke curled from the small, brown, foul-smelling cheroot that jutted firmly from the corner of his mouth. Coughing, I rose and headed for the canteen.

Ten minutes later I was back.

'Put that cigarette out!' I heard the inspector tell the hard nut, who sat with a grin on his face and a fag in his mouth, while his bewildered parents eyed him cautiously. I'd seen it all before: older people with a young son of whom they lived in fear.

'Fuck off,' came the now familiar reply.

'I'll tell you one more time,' said the guvnor, chewing his cheroot, 'put that out. You can't smoke in here!'

'You are.'

'Yeah, but it's my nick.' He looked towards Mum and Dad for support but was met merely with a timid stare. 'OK,' the guvnor said, rising. 'Have it your way.' And he left, slamming the door.

Two minutes later he marched in again, still puffing the cigar, a blank expression on his face, holding out a standard grey metal Metropolitan Police litter bin. I was enthralled. What the fuck was he up to?

The young hard nut began to blow smoke rings in the air in a gesture of defiance.

Splash! Without bothering to empty the rubbish, the guvnor had filled the bin with water, and now he had thrown the entire contents over the young offender.

The youth sat sobbing, a damp dog-end hanging from his trembling lips, empty crisp packets adorning his soaking head and clothes.

In stunned silence the parents stared at their now not-so-hard hard nut. Wading across the custody office floor, the guvnor thrust a form beneath their noses and politely offered them his pen. 'Sign here, please.'

Then I watched as the bedraggled youngster was led to freedom, shoulders hunched, all the fight knocked from him. Maybe the little bastard will think twice next time, I thought, smiling inwardly.

'Sarge, Sarge!' Andy again. Fuck it I thought, heading back for the cells. 'This had better be fucking good!'

For what seemed like the hundredth time that night I found myself looking down at the pink nakedness of the wild man, his cat-like eyes wide with fear and panic as he tried to choke himself with toilet paper.

'That fucking does it,' I said. 'Out! *NOW!*'

He rose meekly.

'Right. You've proved to me that you're not to be trusted; there's only one way I can keep my eye on you.'

Padding barefoot through the guvnor's fast-spreading water-course, the wild man was led by Andy to the bench in front of the reception desk. Reaching into my belt, I laid him flat and handcuffed his hands round one leg of the bench, securing his feet with string at the other end. Looking down at my handiwork, I nodded. At least now I could watch him.

Sitting down at my desk I sighed, and attempted to get the evening's paperwork into some semblance of order. But my train of thought was soon interrupted by the harsh ring of the telephone.

I picked it up. 'Custody Officer.'

'Hello, Sarge,' came the pleasant reply. 'Front office here. I've got two lay visitors to inspect the cells . . .' I never heard his last words. Dropping the phone I surveyed the scene of destruction. On one side a huge, unsightly puddle of sopping rubbish, on the other, Jesus Fucking Christ Superstar!

Alan had been true to his word. Applications to join PT17 had been invited from suitably qualified sergeants – 'a knowledge of firearms desirable, but not essential'. I fitted the bill and applied immediately.

In the weeks preceding the assessment I dug into the history of the department, which came into being shortly after the horrific murder of three unarmed officers in Shepherds Bush by the small-time villain Harry Roberts. Then, it was known as D6. Later, after some internal restructuring, it would be called D11, the 'Blue Berets'. And now it was PT (Personnel and Training) 17.

The initial assessments were to take place over a two-day period. The successful candidates would then be invited to attend 'selection'. The two days would be gruelling, designed to test both physical and mental toughness.

All ten sergeants selected after a paper sift were competing for a chance. We were never told how many vacancies would arise. Each instructor possessed a scoring sheet, on which he would chart your progress in Agility, Shooting Skills, Physical Fitness, and Command Tasks. The assessment would culminate in a ten-minute lecture on a subject of your choice. Prepared in advance, this was to test your IT (or Instructional Technique) and future ability to teach.

*　　*　　*

Lippitts Hill Camp is the firearms training establishment of the Metropolitan Police. A National Firearms Centre, it is responsible for (among many other things) Bodyguard and Firearms Instructor courses. It also houses the the ASU or Air Support Unit, the Met Police's helicopter section. To me it was a grand-sounding place, situated as it was in the heart of Epping Forest. Never having been there before, it conjured up a romantic, almost cinematic image: James Bond visits Q; in the background, the crash of explosions as men experiment with new weapons, gunshots filling the air as recruits forward roll across the screen practising unarmed combat . . .

No such bleeding luck. In reality, Lippitts was a former army camp, converted during World War Two to house prisoners of war, much resembling Stalag 13. A preservation order ensured that the wooden barrack blocks could not be altered; hence 'home' to those on courses was nothing more than a draughty Nissen hut shared by eleven other men, with no private facilities for ablutions.

Speaking to a fellow candidate I was lucky enough to discover a timetable for the first day (or what I naively thought was a timetable – after all competition was tough), the first lesson being PE in the gym. With this in mind, and wishing to create a good impression, I arrived that morning wearing a track suit and carrying an immaculately pressed uniform under my arm. I was determined that this would be my day.

But upon opening the classroom door I was confronted by nine sergeants, who sat with light glinting off the fine metal thread that comprised the stripes sewn on the arms of their best uniforms. We were supposed to be prepared for a talk from one of the department heads. Panic rose in my throat. I looked at my watch. Bollocks – too late now to change. I sat and awaited my fate.

Two minutes later, dead on nine, the door burst open inwards. For a split second all light was lost as a large frame was silhouetted in the doorway. This was a tall, ruddy-faced, bushy-eyebrowed superintendent affectionately nicknamed 'Fifty Fucks' because of his frequent outbursts. He was also known not to suffer fools gladly. Peering beneath his huge eyebrows, he surveyed the room.

'Morning, gentlemen.'

I relaxed.

'Firstly, what I'd like to know,' he said quietly, then built into a crescendo, 'is why there are nine men in uniform and only one in a fucking *track suit*!'

I hesitated. 'Well, sir,' I mumbled, clearing my throat and glancing at the smugly smiling face of the bastard that had given me the 'timetable', 'I was reliably informed that PE was first on the agenda. Isn't that right?'

His red face shook with anger. '*NO!*' he screamed. 'That ain't fucking right, and your fucking informant wasn't that fucking reliable, was he?'

'No, I suppose not. Sorry, sir.'

'Sorry! Fucking sorry! I'll be fucking watching you,' he yelled, slamming the door on his way out.

This little incident had got me noticed all right, and part of me felt like chucking the towel in there and then – but I was soon to learn that it was all a façade with Fifty Fucks, and he actually liked 'characters'.

I put a lot of effort into the next two days, did well in the PE test, and obtained a Marksman classification on the Smith & Wesson .38 Model Ten revolver, the standard Metropolitan Police firearm. The mile-and-a-half run presented no problems, and as I passed the finishing line I was met with an encouraging 'Well done, Mr Collins.'

At the end of the second day I sat in class with the rest of the hopefuls. 'Right, lads,' shouted Fifty Fucks, 'you've put a fucking lot of effort into the last two days, but all it has done is shown us whether we think you have the potential to become a member of this department. To be quite frank, some of the shooting was not up to it.' He glanced around the room at various offenders. 'And you'll know who you are. Some of you are not going to make it. If you do, then the next stage will be an interview. We'll be in touch. Now, fuck off!'

Sipping a pint of lager in the garden of the pub opposite the camp, I squinted against the bright sunlight and looked at the four other prospective candidates who'd joined me. 'What do you think of that, then?' I broke the silence.

'Fucking awful,' one of them said. 'This is my second go at it!'

My mind wandered back to the lectures. Mine had gone

smoothly enough: 'The History of the Rottweiler'. Presented at a time when the so-called Devil Dogs were prevalent in the public's mind, I had delivered an informed and what I considered well-balanced argument in favour of the breed. Catching Fifty Fucks' eye, I had even received what amounted to a nod of approval.

When I had first been called for an assessment I had racked my brains for a suitable subject. Having a keen interest in history, I thought I'd found the answer. 'The Battle of Rourke's Drift and the Zulu Wars'. However, I was to have that subject matter kicked well and truly from under my feet. Croydon Police Station is one of a handful in the Metropolitan Police area that sports a range. I'd often seen the firearms instructors huddled in the corner of the canteen, a breed apart from the normal uniformed officers in their blue training gear and 'Instructor' flashes. I'd smile in amusement at the way their trousers were tucked into the tops of their boots. Not many fucking snakes in here, I'd think with a twinge of envy. Having learnt that I'd applied for the department, I was invited across by a tall, slim, ginger-haired chap in his mid-thirties who introduced himself as Tony. 'Come and have a chat.' I'd learnt a lot from Tony about the make-up of the unit, and through him was now on nodding terms with many of the staff, although some still remained wary. I had sought advice from an instructor on my forthcoming assessment, only to find myself lectured on its harsh realities. 'For God's sake, don't do anything on firearms. They'll rip you up for arse paper.'

'I was actually thinking of "The Battle of Rourke's Drift",' I bleated, somewhat deflated, as I'd already started the research.

He slapped his forehead with an open palm. 'For fuck's sake don't do anything racist.'

'That's not racist!' I protested.

'No, maybe not, but it's about Zulus, and one of the teams slotted a spade on a post office job last year – and lastly, don't do anything sexist. That is one big no-no.'

I looked at him squarely. 'Fucking brilliant. With the three most interesting subjects gone, what's left?'

He grinned inanely.

*   *   *

24

I tried to push the assessment to the back of my mind and take one day at a time, but it was hard. Mundane crimes, mundane hours. I'd almost given up hope when, three weeks later, I was congratulated: 'Well done, Steve!' said the guvnor, tugging me in the corridor. 'I've just received confirmation. PT17 have invited you for an interview.'

'Sit down, please, Sergeant Collins.'

I sat in the small, neat office. Black and white photographs of men in coveralls and guns decorated the walls. A gaunt, somewhat scruffy chief inspector shuffled through a sheaf of papers. He looked up suddenly as if only just aware of my presence. 'Won't keep you a minute. Just waiting for the superintendent.'

The door closed quietly behind me. I resisted the urge to turn around and sat stony-faced, staring ahead. I'd been on plenty of boards in the past and understood their protocol: sit still, don't fidget, keep your hands on your knees, don't gesticulate – and think about the question before you answer.

'Morning, Mr Collins,' boomed Fifty Fucks, pulling up a chair opposite.

'Morning, sir.' I nodded.

'Cheer up,' he said, sifting through my file. 'Now then, you're here today as the second part of an assessment. As you probably realize, a sergeant on a firearms team has a tremendous amount of responsibility. Not only to his team, but also and more importantly to the public we protect.' He paused, then continued. 'Sergeants, for the most obvious of reasons, require interpersonal skills. We're here to judge those characteristics and your eligibility for further training.'

Blimey, I thought. A whole sentence and not a single 'fuck'.

'Let me give you an example of what you might be up against. You're in charge of a team on a robbery plot. You ambush the villains and one of your team shoots and kills a blagger going across the pavement. All eyes are on you!'

'Well,' I said carefully, trying to remember PIP (Post Incident Procedure) as laid down in the Association of Chief Police Officers' *Manual of Guidance on the Police Use of Firearms*. 'The first thing to remember is safety. Once the firearms team is happy the scene is secure, they can hand it over to the scene commander or senior investigating officer. I've obviously never been involved in one before, but I think it would need to be treated like any crime scene.'

'Crime scene?' The chief inspector looked up sharply.

'Well, yes, sir,' I affirmed. 'By that I certainly don't mean we've committed a crime, but the scene must be kept sterile for the investigation that will subsequently follow.'

'Ensure the integrity of the forensic evidence is maintained.' He nodded as he quoted the book.

'Absolutely, sir,' I agreed.

'OK,' interrupted Fifty Fucks. 'One of your men is standing there with a smoking gun. What are you going to do with him?'

'Well, firstly I'd make sure he was both physically and mentally OK. He's obviously been through a traumatic experience, but it will affect different people in different ways. I'd have him taken from the scene and make sure one of the team stays with him.'

'Why can't you just tell him to give up his weapon and go sit in the car?' demanded Fifty Fucks testingly.

'I personally wouldn't let him give up his weapon until he does it in front of the Scene of Crime Officer, when it's unloaded and bagged for examination. Secondly, I would never leave him alone – who knows what he might do? Also, it's important that he remains a member of the team and isn't ostracized.'

'That's fine,' said the chief inspector, 'but what other support can you think of that you might need?'

I thought hard. 'I'd make sure that our senior officers were informed along with the Fed Rep.'

'Anyone else?' enquired Fifty Fucks.

'I suppose we could contact the FME.'

'FME?' He looked at the chief inspector in bewilderment.

'Police surgeon.'

'Oh.' He nodded.

'Forensic Medical Examiner, sir,' I said confidantly, the bit between my teeth.

'Would you let him ring his wife?'

'I'd let him ring anybody from a welfare point of view – but it would probably be a better idea to send somebody round to her, perhaps a friend. After all, we wouldn't leave him on his own, so why her? In effect she's a victim herself.'

Fifty Fucks nodded. 'Yeah.'

'All right.' The chief inspector decided to go off at a tangent. 'Are you aware of what weapons PT17 have at their disposal?'

'I've made enquiries, sir,' I said meekly, 'but people really don't want to talk too much about it. I suppose they think they might be giving something away.'

Looking up, he tutted. 'Well, you only had to phone here to find out,' he said sarcastically. 'What do you think we use?'

'I'm given to understand that the standard firearm is a Smith & Wesson Model Ten revolver, but that you'll shortly be changing to the Glock SLP.'

'Anything else?'

'The Heckler & Koch MP5 Carbine for containments.'

'What's that, then?'

'I don't know much about it, sir, but I believe it's a single-shot carbine.'

'What calibre?'

'Nine mil?'

'What do you understand by carbine?'

'Well, it's a short rifle.'

'So, it's a rifle is it?'

'Well, sir, a carbine is a shortened rifle once used by the cavalry,' I stammered. It was obvious he was trying to tie me in knots.

Writing furiously, he looked at Fifty Fucks and nodded. 'OK, Mr Collins,' he said. 'Thanks for coming. We'll be in touch.'

Back at Croydon, I checked my in-tray daily for news. I didn't have to wait too long. Coming in for a late turn one afternoon, I pulled open the correspondence drawer, and this time it was there! A single brown envelope sat in the middle of the tray. With a trembling hand I removed it, slowly turning it over to examine both sides for any clues, then I tore at the seal, and from inside retrieved a white sheet of paper. Unfolding it, I quickly scanned the typewritten script. Fifty Fucks' final conclusion hit me like a train: 'PS Collins gave some good answers, and although others were preferred I would like to make him first reserve.' I re-read the paragraph. What the fuck is first reserve? Had I passed or not?

I ran up the stairs, taking them two at a time, and knocked on the guvnor's door. 'Come,' came the muffled reply.

'Excuse me, sir!' I said to the smiling face. 'I've just had this from PT17.' I handed him the report. 'Can you tell me what it means?'

'Well, it's very ambiguous,' he said finally, 'but it means what it says. You've failed. Sorry, Steve, I know this meant a lot to you.'

Snatching back the report I turned and left the room. Failed, I thought. I've never fucking failed at anything in my life!

For the next week I was an automaton, with one thing only on my mind. Failure! And it was eating me up inside.

'PT17.' The young lady's voice answered sweetly. I hesitated. I simply had to phone, unable to stand the suspense any longer – either I was in or out, but I had to check for myself.

'Hello. Sergeant Collins from Croydon here. I came for a Level Two board three weeks ago and have now been told I'm first reserve. What does that mean exactly?'

'Oh, you'll have to speak to an inspector. Hold the line, please.'

'PT17,' the gruff voice snapped.

For the second time I found myself going through the entire story.

'Hang on, mate!' The phone went dead.

By now I was getting severely pissed off with the runaround. Inspector or not, when he came back on the line I would be ready for him.

'Hello, mate.'

'Yes,' I demanded aggressively.

'We were actually going to write to you. One of the current candidates has dropped out. Your course is in February . . . Hello?'

Dumbstruck, I replaced the receiver. By the skin of my teeth I had been given a chance!

Day one, lesson one: the Glock 17 9 mm self-loading pistol. Developed in Austria, this revolutionary handgun had undergone strict and rigorous testing. With its light durable polycarbonate body and its seventeen-round magazine capacity, this robust weapon was to replace the old six-shot Smith & Wesson

Model Ten .38 revolver, and was now standard issue to both Level One and Level Two PT17 teams.

In my experience, all courses start the same; with each student and instructor giving a potted history of his career. 'Hi, I'm so-and-so and this is my experience.' But I've always found that it is during the social 'down time' of the evenings that friendships are made, often over a pint, when with a relaxed tongue others can weigh up your particular traits and characteristics.

Sipping on an ice-cold lager one evening soon after the start of the course, I studied my companions: Big Len, weightlifter and ex-Royalty Protection Officer; four ex-Marines; one RAF; and an ex-inspector from Hong Kong who (even at this early stage of the game) had been nicknamed 'Posh'. The only other anomaly came in the form of the dark, polished features of Mas, who now sat to my left sipping his Coke. Mas was the first member of an ethnic minority to be admitted into the department. Of Indian origin, he was strictly teetotal – partly because of his religion, and partly because he hated the taste of beer. Short and muscular, he was a far cry from your archetypal Indian and resembled more a Polynesian islander. He soon became known as 'The Fijian' or 'Strangely Brown'. I liked Mas – and although our backgrounds were totally different, in years to come we would form a firm bond of friendship.

After a few days we were split into teams. The 'honeymoon period' was now over and we would be expected to work – and work hard – on both the physical and tactical aspects associated with 'high risk' firearms operations. Although each man would be highly trained in his own right, a marksman on all weapons, physically fit and mentally alert, we were also training to become part of a team – and any maverick unable to gel would be a liability not only to himself but also to those reliant on his support.

As a supervisor, all eyes were in my direction. Team leaders are expected to be able to make fast and accurate assessments, often with very little information. Devise a plan and deploy a team safely and with minimal risk to the public – the main priority of any firearms operation. My team consisted of Len, Mas, Stevie (an ex-Territorial Support Group officer) and two of the ex-Marines, Roy and Keith.

Running his hand through the shock of grey curly hair that

would later earn him the nickname 'Mr Pastry', the sergeant called for hush. 'OK, lads. You've been split into two teams. This is not a competition, more of a friendly rivalry. We just need to assess how you operate in a team environment, and – ' he looked in my direction and winked – 'how the sergeants take control.' I raised my eyebrows, 'Don't worry, Steve – I know what it's like in at the deep end.'

Passing out sheets of paper, he added, 'We'll do a tabletop exercise first and see what you come up with as a team.'

With a scrape, chairs were dragged to opposite sides of the room, each team huddling down and whispering quietly in an effort not to divulge the tiniest portion of their plan to the opposition. I read quietly from the typed script.

> You are part of a firearms team called in to support the Flying Squad. Information has been received that three known armed robbers will today attempt to commit a blag on a Cash in Transit vehicle. All have access to firearms, although the type and calibre is unknown. It is anticipated that a surveillance team will take them all off from their home addresses. If possible, they are to be arrested prior to the commission of an offence, should the scene commander believe there is justifiable evidence to support a prosecution. For the purposes of this exercise, you have at your disposal as many men and vehicles that you require.

Ten minutes later the sergeant called a halt. 'OK, Steve,' he said quietly from beneath his greying moustache, 'what have you come up with?'

I looked down at my handwritten scrawl. 'From what we were told, there not being a static plot, the only thing we could think of was to act in support of the surveillance. I would deploy two men to the back of each squad vehicle, ready to be called forward and to effect an ambush if required to do so.'

'Yes. We call those "gunships",' he interrupted calmly. 'How many would you need?'

'I'd think about four. If you had a ten-man team, the other two could perhaps tag on the end with a couple of support dogs.'

'Good idea, but we don't normally use them on robbery plots. What about comms?'

'Yeah, we've got that, compatible with the squad. Also each vehicle should carry a first-aid kit.' I screwed up my face. 'Sorry – with such a fluid plot there's not a lot more we could come up with!'

He nodded, deep in thought. 'Not bad. I had a job very similar once, and – you're right – there's not really a lot you can do.' Pulling up a chair, he seemed to regress into the past. 'I'll never forget it. A combined Level One and Level Two job – in fact, just the role you're training for. I had a new inspector with me. The Chief Super had told me. "Whatever you do, don't let him out of your sight, and for God's sake don't let him get hurt."

'The squad believed that at least two villains, Ronald Easterbrook and Tony Ash, were going to commit a robbery in Woolwich. In the game of cat and mouse that followed, we got up behind them in "gunships". For reasons I won't go into, the robbery came off but we were unable to put in an attack. The next thing I knew, we were at the change-over point near some garages. Easterbrook was carrying a nasty piece of kit which he was more than prepared to use, a Smith & Wesson .357 Magnum, stainless steel with a six-inch barrel . . . As a matter of fact we have it in the museum. I'll show you later.'

Must have thought he was Dirty Harry. I smiled to myself.

'A challenge went in from our side but they opened fire,' the sergeant continued. 'In the ensuing gun battle they used their vehicle as cover. One of the lads opened up with a ninety-three. I don't know if it was the angle or what, but the rounds hit the boot of the car and stopped – never seen anything like it. Then the inevitable happened. With a blood-curdling scream the new guvnor hit the ground, blood pissing from a leg wound. Up to our necks in muck and bullets, I looked at him and knew I was in the shit – face all contorted and that. I'll never forget it. Ash was wearing a raincoat. As he lifted his arm and pointed the gun in our direction, one of the Level Two guys got off a shot.' He paused, looking around the class. 'Brilliant shot with a Model Ten – the round travelled straight up his sleeve and entered through his armpit. Killed him stone dead.' I listened, enthralled. 'Easterbrook was wounded and gave up. God, I've never seen so much hate in a man's eyes. Sounds easy in the classroom, doesn't it? But what I'm trying to say is that no matter how well you plan and brief a job, things can still go to rat shit. It's at that point you must pick up the pieces and – even if colleagues are injured – be professional enough to carry on. After all, who else is there?'

We sat in silence. 'Well,' the sergeant said, hand slapping an imaginary object, 'that's enough of swinging the old lamp. Any questions?'

We shook our heads.

'Get some grub, fellas.' Mr Pastry grinned happily. 'Evening input: back here with Kev for a lesson on Passive Night Goggles.'

'Night-vision goggles,' said Kev, the youngest member of staff. 'Not issue kit to Level Two teams at the moment, but nevertheless something you should all be aware of and able to use.' He held up what resembled a pair of binoculars with a single front lens. 'Made by Pilkington, these PNGs can be used at sieges, for recces, and building searches. A terrific piece of kit which enables you to see in total darkness by drawing on any ambient light source, it can also be used in conjunction with an infra-red filter fitted to a streamlight.

'What's that, Staff?' I asked.

Smiling, he fitted a black cover over the lens of his torch, flicking the switch. 'This torch is actually on, though you'll never see the beam, even in pitch darkness – unless of course you're wearing PNGs, in which case it will light the area like a normal torch. Compatible with the standard S6 respirator, PNGs can be hand-held or head-mounted. Pass these round, Paddy,' he said, handing the glasses to the other sergeant. It seemed almost ironic; nearly everybody now had a nickname except me.

The room darkened. Peering through the inky blackness, I could barely make out the shapes opposite.

'Turn 'em off now, Paddy,' Kev said, switching on the light. 'All right, chaps, I've explained to you what a wonderful piece of kit these are, but there are some drawbacks. The biggest that immediately springs to mind is that you could move from darkness into light without realizing it.'

'But, Staff!' interrupted Len. 'Wouldn't you get a blinding flash of light?'

'Only in films, Len,' came the reply. 'Which is the second drawback; somebody could turn on the light and you wouldn't realize it. Apart from being well on offer, you'd look a complete wanker tip-toeing round the room with this lot on your head. The opposition would probably die laughing.' Len feigned a hurt look, and we laughed.

'Right, Steve,' Kev said, turning in my direction. 'Let's try the head-mount, and I'll show you what I mean.'

Pulling sharply on the straps, I tightened the PNGs. With the counterbalance weight at the rear they felt more like an instrument of torture than a modern technical aid. Clipping the goggles to the top of the mounting plate, I slowly lowered them over my eyes and secured the bottom bracket clips. The room went black. Feeling for the switch, I turned the setting to One. It clicked into position and my vision suddenly went green, and I experienced for the first time the thrill of something new. I looked around the assembled room. The screens inside the goggles seemed to emit some strange, almost ethereal glow. As I'd been instructed, I clicked the setting to Two. This would in effect switch the power to the image intensifier, which in turn would allow the IR light-emitting diode to do its job. The image flickered brighter. Checking the room, I could now quite clearly see the assembled teams. Stretching out my hand, it entered my field of vision strangely detached and unreal, almost like virtual reality.

'Edd the Duck! It's Edd the fucking Duck!' I jerked around sharply. Mas was folded up to my left, tears running down his face as he clutched at his ribs. 'Edd the Duck,' he continued to chirp hysterically.

Turning the switch to Off, I raised the goggles thirty degrees from my face. That bastard Kev had switched on the light! Oblivious to the change in conditions, I had continued to scan the room. The straps securing the mount on either side of my head had left my hair standing up in a blond Mohican; that, coupled with the large 'beak' and the jerky movements, had sparked Mas into a frenzy. Unable to draw breath, he pointed. 'Edd the Duck,' he cried, cupping his face in his hands.

'Fuck off!' I grinned.

I had a nickname!

'The Heckler & Koch MP5 A2 Carbine.' The instructor spoke in a high-pitched voice that had years ago earned him the nickname Squeaky.

Hoisting the sinister-looking short-barrelled weapon aloft, he continued. 'Now standard issue to both Level One and Level Two teams. When you take this out consider it your primary weapon; the Glock will be carried as a backup.'

I suppressed the urge to grin like a kid in a toy shop. Now they had brought out the big guns I felt we were really getting down to business.

Squeaky continued: 'Made by Heckler & Koch in Oberndorf, Germany, since the 1960s, and carried by most major counter-terrorist teams worldwide. MP5 refers purely to the model number.' With an open palm he slapped the black polycarbonate butt. 'A2 is the fixed stock model. The A3 version, which Level One carry, has a retractable stock which makes vehicle work and concealment much easier; in fact it cuts down the length from twenty-seven inches to nineteen.

I raised my hand. 'Excuse me, Staff, but why don't Level Two carry those?'

'Fuck knows, Sarge. Probably because the stocks cost about a hundred and fifty quid each,' he squeaked. 'These weapons are nine millimetre, taking the same bog-standard round as the Glock. To the media and many other people, these are often referred to as sub-machine-guns; we, however, have replaced the selector lever and adapted them to fire single shot only.' He paused to draw breath. 'However, other rapid-fire and silenced versions are available to us. With its unique design this weapon unloaded weighs only 5.59 pounds; with a thirty-round magazine capacity, it is accurate to well over fifty metres but, make no bones about it, fellas, the nine millimetre round we use in this and the Glock is more than capable of ripping through skin, tissue and bone at that distance. And with its jacketed soft point, hopefully it will dump its energy and not over-penetrate. Don't ever underestimate your weapon or ammunition.'

He pointed to an exploded-view wallchart opposite. 'Exams next week, fellas. I suggest you study and learn part names and specifications – it will be in your interests, if you get my gist.' He returned to the table. Picking up the weapon, he retracted the cocking lever and with a metallic *snap* it slipped into place, opening the breach, which he showed to the class, announcing, 'This weapon is clear!'

The day continued. With each progression I became more bamboozled with facts, figures, specifications and drills.

'Reload,' announced Squeaky. The ex-Marines amongst you will know this – or had better.' (Squeaky had confided earlier in the course that he himself was an ex-Bootie, and with a sense of belonging had taken the others under his wing.)

'Cock, lock, remove mag, change mag, de-cock, and carry on,' Roy rattled off.

I looked at him in amazement. What the fuck was he talking about? I'll never get my fucking head around this lot, I thought. He might just as well talk in Chinese.

'Not bad.' Squeaky seemed to have a hint of admiration in his voice. 'Cock, lock, look, remove and change mag, *look*, and carry on. Where should your finger be, Sarge?' He shot me a glance.

I stared in silence. 'Off the trigger, I suppose.' Cautiously.

'Right,' he nodded. 'Selector on fire – after all, if you have to reload after thirty rounds you're in the shit. Large.'

Wandering back to the relative warmth of the billet, I dived onto the rickety bed and studied the handout in a daze. What I'd originally thought would be fun and exciting was rapidly turning into stress and bewilderment.

As the weeks progressed the weather got colder and colder. Snow settled on the ground and buildings, giving the camp a festive feel – but as pretty and picturesque as it may be it certainly didn't help with the relentless round of exercises performed in the open: tactical use of cover, open country searching, effecting ambushes from vehicles and, most importantly, CTR (Close Target Reconnaissance) – the ability to lay up and TI (Target Indication) a building.

Next came the roles and responsibilities that were maintained within a firearms team, but were alien to anything I'd previously been taught. We learnt all about the 'shield man', whose responsibility was to lead the team into any potential hazard, covering them from behind the safety of the large, heavy ballistic shield; and the 'stick man', who, weapon holstered, would arm himself with a three-foot stave, moving in on anybody that was unwilling to comply with the commands of the team. Then came the MOE or Method of Entry man. An art in itself. His job was gaining access to premises as quickly as possible and using any method at his disposal. And so it went on: 'cover man', 'prisoner reception', and finally my role – 'team leader' – whose responsibility was to get the best out of the other men.

One day it snowed and snowed hard. 'There's an exercise this afternoon, fellas,' Kev announced over breakfast. 'A Level One team are doing an assault on the Field Craft house. As you're doing resi (respirator) work this evening you can play the hostages. Don't eat too much.' He grinned. 'You'll only bring it up later.'

'I have control. Standby, standby. *GO, GO, GO!*'

The raised voice of the team leader could be heard clearly through the earpiece of the safety officer. In the eerie darkness of the upstairs room I huddled further into the corner, feeling the comforting hardness of the walls. 'Fuck being a real-life hostage,' I thought.

BANG, BANG, Hissss.

Outside, the team shotgunner had fired 'Ferret' through the window to initiate the assault, and in a split second the room began to fill with the CS irritant contained within the load. Closing my eyes tightly, I tried to fight the effects of the mixture as it fought its way through every mucus membrane. In the swirling haze of the room I heard the sound of rapid gunfire below and felt the floor shake from the terrific concussion of the multi-burst stun grenades. My chest pounded, frantic to suck clean air through my chemical-seared lungs. I had never experienced anything so frightening, my head unable to respond to any reasonable thought apart from 'Get me out of here!' I nearly coughed my heart up in the corner, my eyes and nose streaming uncontrollably. I'd heard it said that CS affects different people in different ways; I found out the hard way that I'm extremely susceptible. All I wanted was freedom from the choking fog.

CRASH! The door imploded, smashing loudly against the wall. Through tunnel vision I focused on the small, round, black object that bounced into the room. Too late.

BANG!BANG!BANG! I closed my eyes and ears against the blinding light and din of the pyrotechnic device. Suddenly, hands grabbed me roughly, pushing my face against the wall. I sobbed uncontrollably, glancing around the small room at the figures in black, their breathing laboured through the confines of their gas mask filters. What's the hold up? I thought as the plasticuffs bit tightly into my wrists. Please get me out of here!

Others before me were bundled quickly from the room, then it was my turn. I was thrown bodily from man to man down the stairs. Sunlight streamed through the open door. Oblivious to anything apart from the pain, I was thrown roughly to the ground and the welcoming wetness of the freshly fallen snow.

'Sarge, Sarge!'

I looked up, disorientated, at the grinning face of Kev, camera in hand. *Snap*. 'Cheers,' he said brightly, leaving me trussed up on the deck.

'Your clothes are contaminated. Do not rub your eyes, do not wipe your face,' the voice commanded, snipping off the plasticuffs. In an involuntary reflex my hands went straight to my face. He was right – the pain in my eyes was excruciating. To think that two small pellets could create such mayhem. I looked at my choking colleagues, some bent double, others throwing up in the bushes.

'OK. End-ex, End-ex,' came over the radio. I blinked furiously in an attempt to stem the pain. The whole exercise had lasted only three minutes; to me it seemed like three hours.

'The trick with CS,' we had been told, 'is to leave it alone to dissipate. If later you shake your clothes in the billet you will re-circulate the irritant.'

'How you doing, Sarge?'

I looked up in an attempt to locate the voice. Standing over me was a member of the assault team. Gripping the front of his resi he pulled it over the shock of ginger hair, and smiling down at me was Tony, the instructor from Croydon.

'All right,' I sobbed, rubbing my nose.

He grinned affably. 'Thought I'd leave you in there till last – give you a taste of what it's all about!'

'Bastard,' I moaned at his back as he strode away.

'Do you know him?' said Stevie at my side.

I nodded. 'He's an instructor I met at Croydon. Why?'

'No reason,' he said. 'Only he's the one the papers call The Equalizer!'

37

4

The Equalizer

'"The Equalizer" – I hated that headline,' Tony casually remarked. But the fact was that, as both the first and the second man in PT17 to fire shots 'in anger', on active service rather than in training, when confronted by armed and dangerous aggressors, he had become something of a celebrity within the department.

I listened, spellbound, to his accounts of the operations that had forced him into the public eye, sat through many of his presentations, and worked through numerous archives.

This is the story I've pieced together.

He joined the Met in 1975, where he served for five years at Lewisham and earned himself a reputation as a 'good copper'. It was this that later ensured his transfer to the élite (if slightly controversial) SPG (Special Patrol Group). Although a keen private weapons enthusiast, Tony knew little of the then D11 Force Firearms Unit.

'I remember I'd been with the SPG about three years,' he recalled in one conversation. 'We were sent to Lippitts Hill for an anti-terrorist exercise. I'd never been there before. As we drove in through the gates the whole place was swarming with little SAS guys running around in kit. Believe it or not, it was the role of the SPG to search for nuclear devices. There I was, sneaking around the camp in green wellies and holding a Geiger counter, looking for atomic bombs.' He grinned. 'As the exercise concluded I was sent on "Perimeter Patrol" round the back of the Field Craft house to stop the press or locals from having a look. Being the nosy bastard I am, I stuck my head through the door and saw two men in the kitchen dressed in coveralls, dripping with stun grenades and MP5s. [As early as 1976 the then Labour Home Secretary had authorized the purchase by the Metropolitan Police of four SDs (suppressed/silenced fully-automatic MP5s) and two standard A3s (MP5s with collapsible stocks). The A3 was to be used for training purposes so as not to burn out the baffles on the silenced version. The SD, however, could be used for 'live' operations. The thinking of the day presumably was that, if no shots were heard, they could totally deny the presence of sub-machine-guns in the hands of the civilian police. The four original SDs have now been converted to single shot and, are still, in use by the teams today.] Tony continued, 'One of these guys turned towards me, beret at a jaunty angle. As I stood there, Geiger counter in hand, looking a total wanker, he smiled. "Hello Tony." It was Clive. We'd served together at Lewisham. "Why don't you join this lot?" he said. "It's the dog's bollocks."'

Tony later passed the course. Of some two hundred applicants, twelve were selected; of the twelve, four passed the six-week ordeal.

D11 or, as I have always termed them, the Lippitts Hill Gentlemen's Shooting Club, was made up mostly of ex-military personnel selected as far back as 1967. They were veterans of the Spaghetti House and Balcombe Street sieges; most had also been at the Iranian Embassy. (When I joined the department some eight years after Tony, I was struck by the arrogance. Being an easygoing sort of guy, I found it hard to take their strutting around like peacocks, reminiscing about this siege and that siege as if it were yesterday, rather than ten years ago. To hear them talk you'd think some of them had single-handedly assaulted the fucking embassy themselves.)

In the two years following the Steven Waldorf 'Yellow Mini' saga of January 1983 (when plain-clothes surveillance officers had shot and then pistol-whipped an unarmed man, thinking him to be the wanted and violent criminal David Martin), and the senseless and evil murder of a young policewoman, Yvonne Fletcher, D11 operations increased in intensity. Conscious now of the poor image of police officers with guns, more agencies were calling the 'professionals' rather than going it alone.

Christmas 1985, season of goodwill to all men – but not women, apparently. Errol Walker, a violent criminal, went to visit his common-law wife at her friend Jacqueline Charles's flat in Poynter Court, Northolt. During a violent argument with his wife he produced a kitchen knife and, in the frenzied attack that followed, repeatedly stabbed and killed Jacqueline. In the wild confusion of the attack his wife escaped, managing to alert the police to the fact that her own child (Walker's daughter) and Jacqueline's daughter, four-year-old Carlene, were still inside the flat.

By the time the police arrived, Walker had dumped the bloody and broken corpse of Jacqueline on the balcony and had quickly started to fortify his 'stronghold'. The siege that followed was to last twenty-nine hours. Its dramatic end would be witnessed by millions of Christmas TV viewers across the country.

'Sitting at home on Christmas Day I watched,' Tony told me. 'It was obvious that it would go on for some time. Although I was not on call, I wasn't at all surprised when the phone rang. As I arrived at the Old Street base in the early hours of Boxing Day, the mixture of Blue and Green teams had wearily dragged their kit from the shelves. The weather was bitter! Freezing cold and exposed, particularly for the officers on containment and the young Asian PC who on the previous day had started negotiations. He did a magnificent job and quickly secured the release of Walker's daughter, but Carlene still remained.'

To date, every protracted siege dealt with by the wing had ended peacefully with a negotiated surrender. So they had no reason to believe that this case would not have the same result – after all, one hostage had already been released, and it was only a knife, wasn't it? But the only way to reach out and stop him from stabbing the girl was with a gun!

The scene commander, however, had placed certain restrictions on the sniper. If, for instance, Walker were to come out on to the balcony and hold a knife to the girl's throat saying, 'She dies in ten minutes unless I get a car,' it would have been unlawful for the sniper to slot him because there was no immediate threat. That was the sort of twisted logic they were up against. And if Walker were to stab the girl, then again the sniper couldn't shoot because Walker would already have committed the act – and it would be a shot in revenge. In effect it would be murder!

The on-scene commander handed control to the suits to negotiate a peaceful surrender. Trouble was, this guy would never surrender. He was a psycho.

While these negotiations were going on, Tony pulled his Browning from the rack, automatically checking the breech and the action – second nature to any firearms officer. He was about to load the magazine when he stopped mid-way. No, he thought, there's no suggestion he has a firearm in the flat, so firepower is out. Besides, the 9 mm Full Metal Jacket round used in the Browning Hi-power at that time was more than capable of over-penetrating its target at short range. If the worst-case scenario developed, the round could quite easily pass through the suspect and into the girl, or for that matter another member of the team. What Tony really needed was something that would dump the psycho on his arse! Returning the weapon to the rack, he examined the firing pin and action of a Smith & Wesson .357 Magnum revolver. Satisfied, he booked it out and loaded it with six 158 grain .38 Special JSP (Jacketed Soft Point) rounds. Securing it in his holster, he took a further twelve rounds for a re-load, although he knew full well that at short distance – the width of a room, perhaps? – the soft-point ammunition would give him the stopping power he desired.

Inside the flat, Carlene screamed. Then her frantic cries were cut short by the plastic bag secured over her head. (Tony would later learn how the condensation trickled down the inside as she feverishly tore at the bag fighting for air, fighting for her very life!) In their wisdom, and as a gesture of goodwill, the police negotiators had provided Walker with a PR (Police Personal Radio) with a large, heavy battery at one end and a two-and-half-foot lead connecting it to the microphone. It was fully intended (and God only knows why!) that Walker could monitor police activity. However, he found another use for it. As little Carlene, lungs bursting, drifted slowly into unconsciousness, he helped her on her way. Standing back and holding the PR, he lifted the heavy battery in the air, and repeatedly beat the four-year-old around the head until she was senseless. Not satisfied with the outcome, he then brought the carving knife to bear, slashing her small exposed arm so severely that the white of bone shone through. Then in a fit of bloodlust he dangled the lifeless toddler out of the window some three storeys up, until the blood drained from her tiny veins on to the tautly held blankets and faces of the firefighters that held them far below.

41

Then he pulled the cord off an electrical appliance, bared the wires, and plugged it into the mains, threatening to electrocute her.

The negotiators took advice from some jobsworth in green overalls with a tool-box who was putting up screens to shield the scene from view. 'Ah that's right,' he said. 'If he does that he'll short the whole place out, won't he?' Much relieved, they decided that there was no real danger in him electrocuting her because he wouldn't kill her!

'It was a total clusterfuck,' Tony recalled. 'Outside, we never even had a clue this was going on. Red Team, the team we had relieved, had been standing men on each side of the door with the negotiators; the ER [Emergency Reaction Plan] if the wheel really came off was to flash crash the windows each side, or simply reach through and shoot him point blank. At the same time, as a distraction, a shotgunner at the rear would blow out the windows with birdshot.'

'What about Ferret?' I asked. This is a term for a shotgun cartridge containing a CS irritant which bursts on impact, dispersing its load.

'Well, we questioned their decision at the time,' Tony replied. 'But they said they were worried about the little tot's susceptibility and lasting damage caused by the CS, as if the poor little cow hadn't been through enough.'

In the hours that followed, the team stood to, ready to deploy on a hostage rescue at the drop of a hat. But things were about to change and events would quickly overtake themselves.

Happy in the assumption that the incident was nearing a peaceful end, the negotiators banned all movement by the team in the vicinity of the flat. By doing so they had in effect split the team in two: one half located in a flat at the far end of the balcony, their only view of the 'stronghold' through the door's security spyhole; the second half (including Tony and his partner, Rick) stuck at the opposite end of the balcony, in the stairwell.

'The balcony resembled a battlefield,' Tony explained. 'Littered with debris, old riot shields from the first units on scene, pieces of old furniture, and blood-soaked bandages from the woman.'

As the siege dragged on, and with a no movement order, Walker was getting bolder and bolder, even so far as to come right out on to the balcony to drag in anything that would help fortify his position.

The team hatched a plan. It was more than feasible to rush him and cut off his escape route back into the flat, should he venture far enough along the balcony. With no hostage there, he could then be safely dealt with.

The commander listened to the plan. 'And you think the plan's feasible?'

The stairwell team nodded in unison.

'No.' He shook his head. 'Don't like the sound of that.' Retreating, he issued an order: no direct action was to be taken under any circumstances.

CRASH! The door flew open and Walker suddenly emerged, cradling the battered body of the child, sitting her on the balcony, her legs dangling over the edge.

He jeered at the baying crowd below. Racial tension was beginning to run high. Many of the three-hundred-strong crowd that had rushed to the scene were black. They had seen enough: a black man had cold-bloodedly hacked to death a black woman and taken hostage and tortured a black baby. And what were the police doing about it? 'Jack Shit!' was the answer. Every plan the team had put forward had been firmly kicked into touch.

'This is fucking ridiculous,' Rick said. 'Every moment that child is in that maniac's hands she is in danger of her life!'

Tony elaborated: 'The negotiators were actually joking with Walker. He even squirted water at them from the sink. By now he was seriously taking the piss, with the teams just sitting there like morons.'

Anyway, some bloke who Tony had never seen before, but who was obviously part of the negotiation team at the top of the stairs, had heard Rick's comment.

'Well, it's all a matter of perception, isn't it, officer? You obviously perceive it as a thinly veiled threat, that he's actually going to drop that child over the balcony. But if you study the man's body language then you will clearly see that he has his arm around the child in a protective manner, and he's actually creating a protective barrier between himself, the child, and the outside world. No. I feel sure that this man has a very strong love bond between himself and this child, and he won't harm her in any way, shape or form.'

Within minutes of this strange conversation Walker emerged from the flat in a manner never seen before – it could almost be described as 'tactical'. Ducking low, he crept along the balcony, keeping below the frosted glass screen. With wild eyes he looked about, holding in his hand a large kitchen knife, then at a crouch he sprinted away from the flat towards Tony and Rick's position.

'Fuck me, he's going for it!' screamed one of the team in the flat at the end of the balcony, to the sergeant our course was later to dub 'Mr Pastry'.

TV cameras below recorded the commander in a news interview, vowing to the press that the police would take no 'forcible action'.

'*GO! GO! GO!*' screamed Mr Pastry.

'What's that, then?' asked the news reporter, pointing to the flat in the background as armed officers charged on to the balcony, screaming.

Walker in the meantime had reached his objective. Grabbing a discarded riot shield that had been propped against the wall, he turned and fled back towards his sanctuary, back towards the team. Reaching the open doorway at the same time as the lead man, Walker quickly and violently struck out with the shield, knocking his pursuer off balance, and slammed the door behind him.

Now it had gone too far. Keeping the momentum of the assault in full flow, and fearing for the safety of the child, the team continued to carry on the initiative, oblivious to the smouldering looks of the commander on national TV far below.

On reaching his 'stronghold', Walker immediately set to work on fortifying his makeshift position by propping barricades against the door. Cries of 'Get the Meanie, get the Meanie!' echoed along the balcony (team slang for the then green stun grenade dubbed a 'Green Meanie'); in his haste to get to the door, Clive had left it in the flat.

'I heard a commotion,' Tony told me. 'Rick and I peered round the corner and saw the team reaching the door. What the fuck's going on? I thought, breaking into a sprint and drawing my weapon with my right hand. I put the pin of a flash crash under my right thumb so all I'd have to do was pull it with my left hand. It was fucking chaos. The team were shouldering the door, it was a right shambles. I looked at Clive who by now had a meanie in his hand. Our eyes met. You first, you bastard, I thought, I haven't got a clue what's going on! I knew when he pulled that pin I'd do the same, because by then we were game on!

'That's it!' Walker had screamed from inside the flat. 'You've done it now! She dies, she dies, she dies.' And suddenly all vision through the frosted glass door into the flat was obliterated, as an internal door reinforced the barricade.

Having now lost sight of their man they could only assume the worst. Senses at an all-time high, they pushed on. This was for real!

The radio crackled. 'Go back, go back,' screamed the man who had earlier told the sniper not to shoot because he would not be in possession of all the facts; having not heard Walker's threats he was now in the same boat.

Ignoring the radio and holding his Browning in one hand, Mr Pastry smashed the window, enabling Clive to lob a flash bang into the bathroom. Tony threw his through the shattered kitchen window. Rick followed up, attacking the flimsy door with a sledgehammer. *CRASH!* The sledgehammer impacted the glass but its head became wedged in the wire mesh. Try as Rick might to retrieve the tool, it was stuck!

BOOM! BOOM! The concussion shook the balcony as two grenades exploded in unison, hurling smoke and debris from every opening.

'Window, window, window!' Tony screamed. Their primary objective (the door) now baulked, so it was imperative they gain access through the secondary entry point.

Screams emanated from within; had he reached the baby? S.A.S. – Speed, Aggression, Surprise. Surprise now lost, it was imperative they maintain speed and aggression.

Hitting the floor with both feet, Tony peered through the inky darkness, all light blotted out by the thick black all-enveloping smoke. With Rick at his shoulder he searched the blackness, found the door and reached for his torch. 'Bollocks,' he cried. His torch was stuck between the unyielding layers of cloth of his Goretex over-trousers.

'I had a revolver in one hand and no fucking torch,' he told me. 'The whole thing was a total fuck up!'

45

Locating the living room, Tony and Rick quickly found their objective.

'He was lying on his back on the settee with the girl pulled defensively across his body. It was pitch black. I remember only three things. Her eyes, staring straight ahead lifelessly, his eyes and teeth, and a large kitchen knife held over her. I couldn't even make out where her body finished and his begun it was so dark. We all know action beats reaction, and I had to act before him – if I didn't I knew she would die! I could just make out his shoulder where he held the knife. Without shooting her it was the only part I could be certain of hitting. I was about four feet away when I brought the revolver up in both hands. I searched for a sight picture but it was too dark, so I made a conscious decision there and then.'

BANG BANG! Two shots rang out in quick succession as Tony levelled the weapon and double tapped the suspect.

'The knife came down almost as I fired,' Tony remembered. 'The first round went through the fabric of his shirt and lodged in the settee, the second hit the muscle underneath his arm. I saw the knife plunge into the girl. It was fucking awful.'

Having been hit, Walker involuntarily shied away and turned his head. In doing so he presented Tony with an ideal target. *BANG!* The third round left the barrel in excess of nine hundred and forty feet per second. The soft-nosed bullet impacted Walker's shoulder. The round ricocheted off the bone and into his temple, where it entered his brain.

'His eyes just rolled back into his head and he flopped back on to the settee. I thought: End-ex. You've done it now, Tony. You've fucking killed him.'

Suddenly the flat was alive with activity. Rick, Clive and other members of the team flooded the room, guns drawn and ready, but it was too late. As the curtains were ripped down light filtered into the smoke-filled room, and it was then they saw the knife jutting from the young girl's chest. Tony acted first. Scooping her up with both hands, he fumbled for a field dressing. Bollocks! They were with his torch!

Later Tony said, 'It was almost as if my training had taken over. I'd recently developed a shoot scenario under similar circumstances. From the drawn weapons position [handgun drawn and held at waist level facing the target] you had one and a half seconds to fire a pair into the body, assess the damage, then put one in the head. On the day in question I did exactly that. It's important we train hard and have the discipline. I hated that man with every fibre of my body, but I didn't fire more. I desperately wanted to empty my gun into him, but thought, No, you've done enough. End of shoot. The knife fell out. I picked her up – she was lifeless, not crying or anything. I thought she was dead. It crossed my mind that I might have shot her,' he added sadly.

As the team ripped frantically at the barricade, Tony cradled the child against his chest, then sprinting across the balcony he fled the nightmare scene.

'I thought, Fuck me, she's got another knife sticking in her neck. How did I miss that? As I reached the stairwell I skidded on a pool of her mother's own blood. It was only later, after I'd passed her to the ambulance crew and seen the TV news footage, that I realized what I'd thought was a knife was actually the barrel of my gun. I still had it in my hand. At that stage I was at such a loss, I didn't know if she or the suspect were dead or alive.'

Turning on his heel, Tony had started back to the control room, desperate for more news from the scene.

The radio in control buzzed. This was indeed something new. Apart from putting down the odd cow or two that had escaped from abattoirs, D11 had never fired a shot in anger since its inception in 1968. Also, the unwritten understanding had always been, if you did fire a shot, then bye bye.

Needless to say, this weighed heavily on Tony's mind. Sticking some sausages in the pan, he started to cook the boys some breakfast to keep himself busy.

There were many heroes that day: Tony, Clive and Rick – and let's not forget Mr Pastry, who made that momentous decision to go, to save face and end the débâcle, to put his career on the line against all odds and to have the balls to call on an attack that undoubtedly saved a young girl's life.

Carlene later made a full recovery.

Errol Walker survived the bullet that entered his head, but it left him with stroke-like symptoms and partial paralysis down his left side. Sentenced to life imprisonment for murder, he is still serving time.

And what of Tony? Contrary to the unwritten rule, he remained within the department.

In the months that followed Northolt, the police were to come under a great deal of pressure. More than one team should have been present and a 'sniper group' on hand; more importantly, there should have been proper liaison between the team and the negotiators. It was now obvious that properly formulated plans for both an ER (Emergency Reaction) and a DA (Deliberate Action, a deliberate assault on the team's terms, properly planned and initiated, rather than a reaction to some act committed by the suspect) should have been made. It wasn't that D11 were unfamiliar or untrained in such responses, it was just that the internal politicians and senior officers had not allowed them to do their job.

In 1972, three years before Tony joined the job, the world had been shattered when fanatical members of the infamous Black September Palestinian terrorist group took hostage and murdered eleven members of the Israeli team at the Munich Olympics. The Western world now had to sit up and take stock of its own counter-terrorist measures, and it soon became clear that local police forces were way out of their league when it came to such matters. As the result of a meeting by European heads of state, it was decided to upgrade their response. In September 1972, Germany implemented a specialist paramilitary counter-terrorist team, and GSG9 (Grenzschutz Gruppe 9) was born. Little over a year later, France followed with the inception of a similar team, GIGN (Groupment d'Intervention de la Gendarmerie Nationale). In the UK, the SAS (Special Air Service) was the obvious choice, and in the same year they developed their own CRW (Counter Revolutionary Warfare) Wing, whose role would be to train the SP (Special Projects) teams.

However, by the SAS's own admission, it would take at least six hours to respond to a terrorist threat in London – a city which housed the most obvious of targets. As a result, the Home Secretary decided that the Metropolitan Police should have some form of counter-terrorist response. With the image of the good

48

old British Bobby in everyone's mind (they convieniently chose to forget that Dixon of Dock Green had been shot to death), a paramilitary unit was immediately ruled out. The police orignally looked at the SPG before deciding to give the role to D11 firearms instructors, whose primary objective was after all the training of all other firearms users (such as those engaged in royalty or airport protection duties). As a result, the government was able to deny the existence of any SWAT (Special Weapons and Tactical) team. No. They were merely making the most of their resources!

During the long years of a Labour government, D11 was not permitted to train with the SAS at Hereford, even though they may eventually have to work alongside each other (as they did at the Iranian Embassy and Balcombe Street sieges). This rule was later rectified and they were reinstated in 1983. Now they certainly had the capabilities – and yet the unthinkable had still happened: they were unprepared, and a single man with a knife and a hostage had left them with egg on their faces.

Thus it was now apparent that they had to come away from the 'containment' role and train more specifically for CQB (Close-Quarter Battle, or 'room combat') and hostage rescue scenarios. After all, not all sieges involved terrorists. To relieve the workload of the instructors, an alternative really had to be found and, as a result, Level Two teams were born! From an early stage it was decided that three additional units of six men – Black, White and Grey teams – would supplement the existing Level One teams of Red, Blue, Green and Orange. The new teams would relieve the existing ones of the burden of some of the 'lower grade' operations. Their team leaders (sergeant tactical advisors) would be drawn from Level One.

Now free to fulfil their instructional role, Level One teams would still have the responsibility of hostage rescue and facing criminals with 'exceptional firepower'.

Between winter 1986 and summer 1987, No. 9 RCS (Regional Crime Squad), working out of an office in East Dulwich, were up behind a particularly nasty and violent gang of robbers who were believed to be responsible for a string of armed robberies in South London and the Home Counties. Their trademark was to discharge their weapons needlessly at the scene of the crime, causing mayhem, panic, and fear.

Tony had been training one day during that period – nothing out of the ordinary – but as he pushed his way through the door of Old Street he found John, his team leader (the small sergeant I would meet years later in the yard at Croydon), babbling on about some job coming off with the rumour of bombs, Armalites and armour-piercing rounds. It was believed that a gang of four to six white males proposed to rob a Securicor van delivering wages to the RACS (Royal Arsenal Co-operative Society) meat-packaging factory located in the old abattoir, Plumstead, south-east London. An inside agent (possibly a friend or relative) could also be involved and acting as a 'third eye' (surveillance speak for look-out).

The plot had been described as ideal: situated just off a residential street, the factory could be reached only by a dirt track in Garland Road. As you approached the large concrete hardstanding, you were confronted by a semi-glazed loading bay with adjoining office. To the north and west of the plot was woodland two hundred yards deep, and to the south lay open farmland. To a switched-on gang such as this, it proved the perfect rural setting for an ambush.

The Armalite was a fearsome weapon. If deployed using armour-piercing rounds, it could for example shoot into he cab of a truck and frighten the driver into opening up. There was also the possibility of an IED (Improvised Explosive Device) for strapping to the guard, and hand grenades. It was believed that the robbers were to lay in wait in the wooded area, that they had access to a stolen car, that they possessed a 'scanner', a device for monitoring police radio frequencies, and that they would possibly escape along a farm track which exited a mile and a half away in Shooters Hill Road, where there was a padlocked gate. It was suggested that if the gate's lock had been 'cropped' the night before it was a good indication they were game on. Apart from the duty officer (inspector), local officers would be unaware of the operation. (Police officers are by nature nosy people; if they were told in advance it was inevitable that somebody would pitch up for a look-see and either blow the job or get in the way.)

Tony and the others were told that the robbers were especially surveillance conscious, so they had to be careful. Aerial photographs were taken, and John carried out a quick plain-clothes CTR (Close Target Reconnaissance) by walking one of his dogs through the woods. They were to arrest the robbers on the hardstanding, prior to the commission of the offence, and to this end they drilled holes in the side and back of the 'horse' (Trojan horse; with 'Trojan' being the callsign of PT17 – as the department was now known – a Trojan horse was any covert vehicle used to secrete a team on a plot from which they could deploy). In this instance it happened to be a Luton hire van, which was to be parked in the delivery bay.

John had a plan whereby the team would have eyeball on the villains as they moved from their LUP (lying-up point) on to the plot. That's when they would strike.

John outlined the plan. Group D (the PT17 attack team), an inspector, a sergeant and five PCs in the 'horse' would operate in coveralls, berets and body armour, supported by two PT17 dogs and handlers, and an RCS radio operator hiding above the cab in a bullet-proof compartment.

Group C – George, a new Level Two man – would act as cut off, approaching down the farm track from Shooters Hill Road in an armoured Land Rover.

Group B was the RCS surveillance team, working in support of a CROPS (Covert Rural Observation Post) man, who would lay up on the golf course and watch the approach. CROPS is a highly specialized and very often dangerous form of surveillance. Much like a sniper, a CROPS officer may be required to lie up and be self-sufficient for days on end, reporting back to his team. DC John Fordham, a CROPS officer with the Metropolitan Police, was once keeping observation from a hide in the grounds of a house owned by one Kenneth Noye, a millionaire businessman who was believed to be smelting gold from the multi-million pound Brinks Mat bullion robbery. After being found by Noye's Rottweiler dogs, he was stabbed to death. Noye was later aquitted of murder.

Group A would be the OIC (Officer in Charge). Also involved were the ASU in case of 'runners', the London Ambulance Service in case of casualties, and two RCS drivers in white hats and coats. They would drive in and position the 'horse', then head for the manager's officer to keep the staff away.

51

The plan looked good. On paper!

Following the tactical brief, the unit moved to Eltham, where a more complex briefing took place. There they were given the identity of some of the possible players, who, it was believed, had been involved in a number of armed robberies. On one occasion a security guard had been shot and wounded, and police officers had been shot at as they pursued the gang.

This concluded, the team moved to the yard, where they practised jump-offs from the 'horse'. To ensure the success of any operation, the team will always rehearse the order of the stick leaving the van. This ensures there's no clusterfuck at the back with everybody wanting to leave first, and can be compared with Paras leaving a plane in an orderly file.

From Eltham, the team was driven nearer to the plot, to Shooters Hill and their FUP (Forming-Up Point). At this stage they all dived out for a last-minute nervous piss.

Tony didn't know why, but this job had a feel about it. They were told that the padlock had been cropped on the Shooters Hill Road gate, and that a car had been stolen. It was definitely shaping up nicely.

At about seven, the team were moved once again by the RCS drivers. They now parked up on the hardstanding at the old abattoir, with the rear roller shutters facing the loading bay. This was now designated the FAP (Final Assault Position). Apparently it had been agreed with a Co-op supervisor (who was unaware of the extent of the operation) that all delivery trucks would be parked at the far end of the bay, in order to keep staff at a distance from any forthcoming action, and to feed the Securicor van into the gap next to the 'horse'.

Tony looked through a hole they'd drilled in the rear shutter, and couldn't believe their bad luck. Parked right behind them was a Co-op lorry. The driver had got in late, so he hadn't seen his supervisor. As an OP they were stuffed.

Suddenly the radio crackled into life. They started to get a lot of broken radio traffic from the surveillance team and CROPS man. India One (the main suspect) had been spotted in the woods having a look-see. He was then joined by India Two and they embarked on a long conversation. After a while India Three appeared, carrying a 'happy bag' (police slang for a bag or holdall containing firearms, balaclavas, etc.). Things were really looking good in the van. They were looking around, giving each other nervous grins and the thumbs up. (The team were later to learn that the suspects had actually walked over the top of the CROPS man's OP. He turned out to be a credit to his training.)

Now things were really moving. India Four had been spotted in the stolen car, and looked to be sweeping the plot (driving around in an effort to locate any police activity). All the players had arrived!

But there was no sign of the Securicor van.

By now the dogs were getting restless. It was a boiling hot day, and they were panting like fuck – but they never made a sound. They were marvellous.

Then, from his spyhole position in the van, Tony gave the thumbs up.

The Securicor van reversed into the bay and out of sight, and the getaway car manoeuvred into position, facing the road. For the four main players – Michael Flynn (24), Nicholas Payne (29), Derek Whitelock (24), and driver Richard Parfett (24) – there would be no going back.

Tony had stuck his eye against the hole in the shutter. All of a sudden he saw a blur of movement from right to left, a sort of beige colour. This had to be it. With no information from outside he had to make the biggest decision of his life. Should he give the go or not? Bollocks!

'*GO, GO, GO!*' he screamed. *WHACK!* The heavy shutter recoiled, just as rehearsed. Sunlight flooded into the rear of the small van. He squinted. Nobody there. Not a fucking thing.

The rest of the team looked at him, thinking, What the fuck have you done, Tony? You've fucking lost it! With the heavy ballistic shield on his left arm and a Browning in his right hand, Tony dived from the van, stumbling as he hit the pavement.

The team followed. Tony advanced round the front of the parked lorry, his Browning held out straight, using the shield as cover. As he exited the other side he was confronted with the ideal training scenario. (These were the days before video; they used slides superimposed on a screen to shoot at, and that's exactly what this was. Totally frozen.)

Four metres to Tony's right stood Flynn, a short man with his back to Tony, wearing dark clothing and a balaclava. He was standing on tiptoes and holding a long-barrelled stainless-steel handgun (a Smith & Wesson 686 .357 Magnum revolver). It was pointed into a small grilled hatch behind the driver's door of the Securicor van, and he was craning his neck, presumably in an effort to see the guard inside. 'Open this fucking van,' he shouted.

At the rear of the van was a similar grille, located just in front of the rear wheels and above the money chute.

Payne, similarly kitted out in a balaclava, also with his back to Tony, was holding one of the most devastating weapons yet encountered by the wing: a Franchi SPAS (Special-Purpose Automatic Shotgun); with a pistol grip and folding stock, it also had a special function selector, enabling the weapon to revert to pump-action mode. It was pointing at the stomach of a terrified security guard.

With his elbow, Payne was hammering on the side of the van, demanding cash. Beyond him, Whitelock was facing Tony! He was armed with a sawn-off Browning self-loading shotgun held to the head of the guard, who was between him and Payne.

Between the Co-op lorry and the Securicor van there was a space no more than four or five metres wide. And Tony was in poll position.

From somewhere behind him he heard John call, *'ARMED POLICE, ARMED POLICE!'* through the loud-hailer attached to his waist. All of a sudden everything was moving.

Flynn started to turn. Tony looked right into his eyes. He'd once read some old soldier's autobiography. Talking about the war, the writer said something like: 'If you go into an armed situation, and one of your opponents starts to react, shoot him first. Because simply by reacting he has become dangerous!'

CRACK, CRACK! Tony fired. The two 9 mm soft-point rounds left the muzzle of the Browning in quick succession and found their mark. Striking Flynn in the back no more than two inches apart, they severed his spine, and he dropped, totally out of play. Payne started to spin with the SPAS. But instead of bringing his weapon to bear from his left side he took the longer route, spinning in towards the side of the van.

Tony bought the Browning up. *CRACK, CRACK!* A second pair found their mark, the first round entering Payne's right shoulder and ricocheting off bone before entering his chest cavity. With a crunch of shattered bone the second round found Payne's chin; it started to break up as it deflected downwards and into his heart. With no more than a quick cry, he fell forward across the front of the guard.

Whitelock moved quickly and in self-preservation. Ducking behind the horrified guard, he started a run.

CRACK! Tony did consider a pair, but it was too tight: with the guard in the way it wasn't feasible.

Disappearing behind the van, Whitelock emerged on the far side in a state of panic, to face two of the team carrying Remington 870 pump-action shotguns. The villain threw his hands in the air, screaming, 'Don't shoot, don't shoot!'

Tony in the meantime had darted across the front of the van. Peering from behind the shield he saw Whitelock's hands go up, and it suddenly dawned on him that the man wasn't holding a gun! He talked him to the ground while the others covered, but all the time he was thinking, Fuck, fuck, fuck. What have I done? What have I done?

Since Tony's original incident at Northolt (some eighteen months previously), no shots had been fired. Now he had three men down with two possible fatalities. This time it was serious shit! But he carried on regardless.

Ditching the heavy shield, he attended Whitelock. Rolling him over, he applied plasticuffs. The robber was moaning about something but Tony wasn't taking any of it in. Pulling off his balaclava and gloves, Tony placed them on the floor as evidence. Then he ran around to the front of the van, where he was confronted by a scene of carnage.

Team members were hunched up around the still forms of the two downed suspects. Tony looked at Flynn. From his appearance it seemed that he didn't have long to live. His eyes were rolling around in their sockets.

Tony asked if Payne needed cuffing.

'Don't bother, Tony,' one of his team-mates said, shaking his head. They knew he was dying.

Returning to Whitelock, Tony pulled him to his feet and placed him against the side of the van. The man was still moaning.

One of the team approached Tony, scuttling up to him like a little schoolkid. 'Brilliant shooting, Tony. Brilliant shooting!' he cried.

Tony said, 'Don't fucking worry about that! Go and see what weapons they had!'

'You've shot me, you've shot me,' mumbled Whitelock.

Tony looked down. Lying next to his feet was a shotgun. He was ecstatic: that was at least one gun accounted for!

The team man emerged. 'Tony, brilliant news. We've got an SPAS and a Magnum round the other side.'

Tony relaxed. 'I knew I'd been right,' he said.

Whitelock groaned.

'Sorry, mate. What did you say?' asked Tony.

'You shot me,' he whined.

Tony pulled up his shirt. On the right side was a neat entry wound. (Tony was later to learn from the autopsy report that he had in fact achieved six hits with five rounds. Apart from the rounds to the shoulder and chin, Payne was hit through the lower arm as he dropped in front of the guard. The round passed through his arm and into Whitelock's side.)

The whole incident had lasted two and three-quarter seconds.

Meanwhile, the getaway driver came nose-to-nose with the cut-off team, and went through them like a knife through butter. A chase had ensued, with the bandit vehicle stacking it against a wall. In an almost comical manner, the arrest of India Four was finally made in a little old lady's garden. She was later interviewed for the TV: 'I came out into my back garden,' she said. 'And I saw three very large policemen sitting on top of a man. They all had guns. "What's happening?" I asked. "We've arrested him," they said. "Oh," I said. "Would he like a cup of tea?" "No," they replied, "but we would." So I went and put the kettle on.'

'She wrote me a lovely letter,' Tony recalls, 'Dear PC – If people go out with guns then they must expect to get shot. All of the people round here think you did a marvellous job. Thank you very much for looking after us.'

At the inquest, despite threats to his life, Tony was refused permission to give evidence from behind a screen. He was publicly named in the national press.

After the eight-day hearing, the jury took four hours before returning a unanimous decision on Payne and a seven-to-two majority in favour of lawful killing on Flynn.

Feelings in South London, however, ran high. Tony was a marked man.

Whitelock recovered from his injuries. The bullet had lodged near his spine. He was later found guilty of robbery and jailed for thirteen years. Parfett never did get his cup of tea, and was later sentenced to eight years for his part. In a strange twist, Whitelock's brother-in-law, who had worked at the factory since leaving school, was quizzed for eight hours. No basis for charges was ever found.

In the months that followed, Tony returned to instructional duties. At the end of our course, he summed up: 'Remember, fellas: if you go into a firearms situation with no sort of plan about what you're going to do when confronted by an armed suspect, you're going to lose, because it's too late by then to come up with one, on the spur of the moment. The thing that strikes me over and over and over again, when I speak to guys who've been involved in a shooting for the first time, is, no matter how switched on you think they may be, they all say, "I couldn't believe it was happening." Now, to my mind, that simply echoes a man who hasn't taken his training seriously. When we do room combat, we know the targets are cardboard, or falling plates. But if you don't throw yourself into it one hundred per cent – if you don't imagine what it would be like to shoot somebody when the bullets are coming back at you, when real bodies are falling down – then when it does happen for real, you'll be the loser!' He grinned.

Tony never did receive the recognition he deserved. For some reason the management always kept him at arm's length, although his professionalism did more for the department than any other single member could hope for.

Five years later, under a Policy of Tenure, he was forced to find a role back on the streets, and left the department.

5

Just Another Dig-Out

The pain in my head was awful, like two men with cricket bats were pounding at my skull. I opened one eye cautiously. The light seared into my already battered brain. Strange, I thought. The ceiling appeared to be closing in on me. Never again, I thought. I'll never touch another drop!

Peeling my tongue from the roof of my mouth, I smacked my lips. 'God, I'm thirsty.'

Faint laughter. I looked to my right and a thunderbolt of pain shot through my temples. 'Fucking hell, was there a dog in here last night?' I called to nobody in particular.

'Course not. Why?' came Mas's voice from opposite.

'Well, if there wasn't, it must have been one of you bastards that shit in my gob, that's why!'

Mas laughed as only he could do.

Lying on my back I didn't want to get up. I knew full well it would be unbearable; the end-of-course piss-up had gone on all night. Through a haze I focused on a photo of the Queen. 'Where'd that picture come from?'

'You nicked it out of the senior officers' canteen,' said Mas. 'Don't you remember?'

'No.' The truth of the matter was I couldn't remember anything. I tried to sit up slowly but found I couldn't move.

Click. Whirrr. A faint noise.

I tried again, panic setting into my alcohol fuddled brain. 'Fucking hell, I'm paralysed! I've turned into a raspberry overnight.' ('Raspberry ripple' – police rhyming-slang for cripple.) Laughter – louder now – from across the billet. 'What the fuck's going on?' I called, for try as I might, I couldn't move.

58

Mas appeared by my side – at least, his head and shoulders did.

I looked down. My entire bed had been cocooned in abseil rope, until I resembled one of those silent movie stars, lying across a railway track. 'You bastard!' I screamed. 'I was so pissed I could have choked on my own vomit!'

He smiled. 'That's if the fall didn't kill you first.'

It suddenly dawned on me, peering cautiously over the side, that Mas was actually standing. No wonder the ceiling looked so close. My entire bed was balancing precariously on the backs of two chairs. I was four foot from the ground! 'Have I been here all night?'

Mas nodded. 'You were unconscious. We could have done anything to you,' he beamed.

'Well don't feel fucking hard done by!' I screamed. 'All I need is a shower, so for fuck's sake get me down!'

'Please,' Mas said.

'What?'

'Please!'

'All right. Please, for fuck's sake, get me down.'

He grinned. 'Pretty please.'

'You bastard.' Swinging to my right, I lunged at his throat, and the bed collapsed in a tangled heap.

'How do you feel, Edd?' Mas asked cautiously from across the breakfast table.

I squinted, eyes focusing. My mouth was chewing on automatic pilot, but I felt so rough I simply couldn't swallow. 'Fucking awful,' I said slowly. 'How do I look?'

Mas studied me hard, then shrugged his shoulders. 'Fucking awful.'

'Cheers.'

'Do you think we've all passed, Edd?' he asked.

'No,' I said, scooping more beans into my already over-crowded mouth.

Mas looked shocked. 'Do you know something? Do you know who's failed?'

'Can't say,' I said, sipping my coffee in an effort to lubricate my throat. 'But I've got my doubts about some of them,' I continued, swallowing hard. I smiled as I studied his worried features. It was pay-back time. 'I could tell you,' I slurred, 'but it would be un-ethnic-al of me to do so. But we'll find out soon enough, won't we?'

Kev jerked me back to reality. 'OK, fellas. When you've had grub, line up in the corridor outside the class. Course dispersal and critique – with the superintendent. It's make or break time.' He looked directly at me. Fighting to swallow a particularly stubborn piece of bacon, I grinned inanely.

In all honesty I really thought I'd done enough to pass, but at this late stage it was in the lap of the gods – or God, to be precise, because Fifty Fucks was on camp for the final day!

'We'll have the skippers first,' Kev announced from the door-way. 'In you come, Paddy.'

I leant against the wall, fighting the urge to vomit. I shouldn't have had that last bit of bacon. Still, at this rate it should all be over by lunchtime, leaving time for some hair of the dog before heading home. 'Fancy a pint later?' I asked.

Mas laughed. 'For fuck's sake, Edd, where do you put it all?'

Click. The handle turned and the door swung inwards. Taking a deep breath, Paddy emerged, tears filling his eyes. 'Four fucking weeks of hard work dine the pan,' he choked in his broad Irish accent.

Failure. Nobody really knows what to say. 'I'm sorry mate' simply isn't good enough, but what can you do?

Despite the slaps on the back and muttered outrage, the other students are really quite glad to see the back of you. It's as if you're some sort of infectious disease that needs to be cut out before it reaches the rest of the course. I instinctively knew that, when we got back to the billet for final dismissal, Paddy would be long gone, yesterday's man, almost as if he'd never existed in the first place.

'OK. Edd, let's have you,' Kev called from inside.

Mas slapped my back. 'Good luck, mate.' I knew he meant it.

In I strode, a ridiculous grin on my face. It was the most formal setting I'd seen since starting the course. In the centre of the room stood a single empty chair, flanked on each side by the staff, immaculate in their training blues and berets. At the head table sat Fifty Fucks, staring at me from beneath those dark bushy eyebrows. To his right, the course director, to his left, Mr Pastry. I staggered for the chair, feeling very much the condemned man.

'Fucking hell,' Squeaky beamed. 'Can you see through those eyes?'

I nodded. 'Perfectly, Staff,' I slurred.

'Sit down, Mr Collins,' boomed Fifty Fucks, eyeing me up and down. 'I've been watching you!'

Oh God, I thought.

'And I fucking like what I see,' he continued. 'We are all in agreement that you handle a team well, and I like your attitude. As you know, with changes in the pipeline, this is the last ever Level Two course. So far we've had no sergeants that have passed. Apart from you. Congratulations!'

I sat in stunned silence.

'Well done, Steve,' said Mr Pastry, as the full extent of what I'd just been told fought its way through my alcohol-fuddled brain.

'Thank you, sir,' I muttered. 'Thank you all.' I nodded around the room.

'We've also marked you down for potential as an instructor,' Fifty Fucks added. 'So fuck off and keep your nose clean. We'll be in touch.'

With a spring in my step I left the room. '*Yesss*,' I grinned, giving a thumbs up to the ten silently staring faces that greeted me outside.

'Well done, mate,' they cried, slapping my back. I had broken their duck. I had passed! Now all I had to do was wait.

Three months later I was invited to join the department.

'These fit where they touch,' I whined to the storeman, pulling on the baggy blue coveralls. 'And there's a hole in the knee. They're second-hand!'

'They're clean,' he said, ticking off the item on his kit list.

'Well, haven't you got any new ones?'

'New?' he asked indignantly. '*You're* new. You'll have to prove yourself first. After all, you may not be here that long. Holster,' he said officiously, handing me a tatty leather object. 'Haven't got any belts. You'll have to make do.'

I turned it over in my hand. 'But this is a left-handed holster,' I said, somewhat bemused.

'Yes.'

'But I'm right handed,' I protested shaking my hand in his face.

'Out of right-handed holsters. You'll have to make do!'

'How the fuck can I make do? My gun will be on the wrong side,' I bleated.

'Look, I'm not only a storeman, you know, I happen to be a senior staff instructor.'

I'd never heard of a senior staff instructor, but guessed it was some self-imposed title to boost his already overinflated ego. A new tack was required. 'Well then,' I stated, 'you of all people should know how difficult it is.'

'Difficult? It's not difficult,' he said incredulously. 'If the shit does hit the fan, draw it with your left hand, then swap it over into your right. Simple.'

I slapped my hand over my face and peered out through my fingers. Then I pointed down at the sergeant's stripes on my epaulettes. 'You're a PC, right?'

'Wrong!' he said indignantly. 'I'm a – '

'Yes, yes. I know, you're a senior staff instructor,' I said, getting off on the wrong foot. 'Well these ain't fucking laundry marks, you know.' I jabbed at the stripes. 'Now give me some kit.'

'I can't give you what I haven't got, can I?'

I scanned the storeroom, shelves stacked to the gunnels with goodies. 'Well, what's this lot then?' I enquired, getting the right arse.

'Well, they're my stores,' he said seriously. 'You can't have those. They're for storing. If they were for issue, they'd be called issues, wouldn't they?'

Gobsmacked, I scooped up my kit and left, two seconds short of filling him in!

The door flew open with a crash. In strode Chris, a familiar figure, dressed in coveralls, with his body armour hanging loosely from his stocky frame. He carried an MP5 in one hand. His eyes scanned the room. 'Anyone got the keys to the armoury?' he scowled in his faint southern accent.

'Base room,' Mas answered. He had filled in since our course, and I'd been assigned on to his team. 'Get him?' he asked.

'Course we did. Black Team always get their man,' Chris growled.

'Why? You all fucking Mounties, then?'

He glowered at me.

I nodded. 'Steve Collins. We met a while back, in the yard at Croydon.'

'Oh aye!' He nodded, looking me up and down. 'The only bloke I remember was a fat little sergeant.'

Since our initial meeting I'd 'done' a couple of stone. 'Not so much of the little,' I grinned.

'Great!' he said, rattling the keys. 'Just what this department needs most. More fucking sergeants!'

I stared at his back as he walked from the room. I'd never been a strict disciplinarian, but this department took the biscuit! 'Says a lot, doesn't he?' I said to Mas.

'Yeah. Chris, Black Team,' he smiled. 'Been here a while, lot of experience. Don't worry, you'll get used to him.'

I grinned evilly, already hatching a plan. 'Or he'll get used to me.'

'You must be a fucking jinx, Sarge,' said Mick, a large, outspoken member of the team. I'd never really hit it off with him from the start. 'We haven't had a job since you've been here. How you supposed to prove yourself?'

I stared at him intently, already rattled by Chris's attitude. 'What? I don't need to prove fuck all to you,' I snapped.

'Yeah, but you're ex-counties, aren't you?' he said goadingly. 'You've only been a real copper for two years. Where was it? Sussex?'

'Surrey,' I barked, well pissed off.

Apart from Mick and Mas, the team was really quite a mixed bunch from varied backgrounds. Colin, a small, extremely fit athletic type, came to the department from the DPG (Diplomatic Protection Group). He was always drumming his fingers and singing heavy metal songs. Mark and Paul were ex-fire brigade. Two other members of the team, Nigel and Neil, were currently on an instructors' course and were covered by men from the 'spare' team. Clive, the team leader, on the other hand, was a different kettle of fish. Short and stocky, with a large bushy moustache, he immediately struck me as a very serious character. Joining the department as a PC early in service, he'd been promoted to sergeant and retained by the wing. A keen outdoorsman, I was later to learn that he maintained extremely close links with members of both the SAS and SBS (Special Boat Squadron).

The phone broke the silence. I picked it up. 'Crewroom.'

'Yeah, reserve here, Sarge,' said the baseman from next door. 'We've got a siege going on in London.'

I replaced the receiver as the information sunk in. 'Fucking great. My first job, and it's a siege. 'Where's Clive?' I called frantically, now well out of my depth.

The shrill scream of the siren cut through the din of the heavy lunchtime traffic, as the bulky marked carrier plotted a course for Lincoln's Inn Fields. Information was still coming in over the net that a lone gunman had taken hostage a young female solicitor. Patrolling ARVs were quickly on the scene, and had closed down the inner cordon to one specific building. But because of the outer road closures necessary for the scene to remain sterile, traffic was at a standstill. 'Get out of the way, you fucking wanker,' our driver screamed at a dumbstruck pedestrian.

Finally, after a harrowing twenty-minute drive, we arrived at the scene. Snapping the blue and white plastic incident tape, the uniformed PC beckoned us through.

Clive wound down his window. 'PT17, mate. Where's our control?'

The PC pointed to an ARV parked down the road.

'Get kitted up, fellas – caps and Bod [body armour]. Come with me, Steve.'

Trotting along behind him, we quickly made our way to control. 'What you got?' Clive asked curtly.

'Well, Sarge,' said the uniformed officer, eyeing the new guy up and down, 'some of our blokes are inside, where we have him trapped in the boardroom.'

'Standby, Standby.'

The uniform cupped his ear with his palm and listened intently to his radio. 'I have a Level Two team here . . . Is that confirmed? The hostage has been released?' Nodding his head, he turned in our direction. 'The hostage, a female solicitor, has just been released, but we have confirmation that the gunman's still inside, with a small, black handgun.'

Clive nodded. 'OK. Show me the plans.'

For the next two minutes the controller illustrated the positions of his men around the building, which consisted of a large number of office blocks forming a rough quadrangle.

'Entry point's at the back?' asked Clive.

'We've got a ladder up through the window.'

'OK,' Clive agreed. 'It's not over yet. We'll bolster your men and see if we can get some sort of OP opposite.' We turned.

'Oh, just one thing, Sarge,' smiled the controller. 'He's doused himself in petrol!'

At a trot we worked our way around the rear of the building – a motley crew in ragged jeans and T-shirts, MP5s at the ready. Ducking beneath a cordon, we sprinted across the open expanse of pavement until we reached our objective. Fire crews and ambulances stood to by a precariously placed ladder, balanced between some railings and an upper window which was to be our entry point. Clive climbed first, sitting half in and half out of the window in an attempt to stabilize the platform. Jumping on to the railings, I tested the rickety construction for weight and looked down. Bollocks, I thought. Fall off here and it's a thirty foot drop straight down. And these fucking railings don't look too clever either. I've never been one for heights.

Throwing the team my MP5 I started cautiously up the steps. I was half-way up when I heard a shout. 'You take that picture, and I'll stick that camera right up your arse,' Clive called to a reporter.

Brilliant, I thought. Here I am dicing with fucking death, and all he's worried about is whether they've captured his best side! (As it turned out there was a huge colour photograph in next morning's *Sun* of Clive's face and my arse. 'Not a bad match, really,' I had grinned at him.)

Clive dragged me through, and I landed heavily on the floorboards. I surveyed my surroundings. It was immediately apparent that I was in some sort of anteroom, an outer chamber to the main offices. There was a faint hum of voices from the other side of the connecting door. Holding my breath, I reached for the handle with my left hand, MP5 now tucked firmly into my right shoulder, ready to react to whatever lurked on the opposite side. The handle turned silently, until: *creak!* Shit. The noise sounded deafening in the small confines of the room.

Light poured in through the crack in the jamb. Directly

outside stood Paul, one of the ex-Marines from my course, who had previously clambered through the window. Wearing uniform and body armour, he was crouching in the hallway, his MP5 covering the corridor ahead. He had heard the noise but remained still, focusing on the threat area.

I leaned over him. 'Fuck me, don't we look smart?' I whispered.

'Bollocks,' he said.

Behind me, I heard the rest of the team slipping in quietly through the window. Paul looked ahead. 'It was chaos when we arrived, he said. Nobody knew what the fuck was going on. We managed to set up a control outside and establish an armed perimeter cordon, I've been here an hour now.'

'Don't worry,' I hissed, 'I'll spell you in a minute. What's the score? Control didn't know too much.'

'From what I can make out,' he whispered, 'this guy called Steve comes down from up north, something to do with bankruptcy. He asks to see the woman solicitor dealing with the case, produces a handgun and holds her hostage. One of the locals has been trying to negotiate,' he added, nodding towards an unarmed PC ten feet from the door. 'Anyway, he eventually lets the woman go. She's seen the gun, but now the tosser's doused himself in petrol and is threatening to torch himself.'

I nodded. 'What about evacuation?' I asked, mentally running through what we'd just been taught.

He shook his head. 'Can't do it, Edd.'

'Why not?'

'He's holed up in the boardroom with a clear view of the square. He'd see what was going on. I think some of the building's clear, but only this part is shut down.'

I tapped his shoulder. 'Cheers, mate. Two ticks!' Darting back into the room, I gave the team a quick resumé of what I'd been told.

'Fuck,' said Clive. 'All we can do is reinforce the containment and continue to negotiate. Although he doesn't have a hostage, the whole building could go up if he torches himself. Besides, I've been on the trumpet. A Level One team is being scrambled.'

I sighed. My first real job and it was going to be nicked off us by Level One. Bollocks!

Pecky piped up. Pecky was a White Team member, strapping with us for the day. A Tony 'prodigy', he had considerable experience and was very switched on. Although only about five foot seven and skinny with it, the little Welshman was extremely agile, and a tough little fucker to boot. 'I've got an idea, Clive,' he suggested. 'We've only got a containment round the outside. Nobody's actually got eyeball on the suspect. I've been having a look at the plans, and I reckon I could get round the other side and into the church bell tower right opposite.' We looked at the plans, Clive nodding as Pecky continued, 'From there I'd have the ideal sniper position.'

Clive pondered this for a moment. 'Go. Take somebody with you, and let control know when you're in.'

Creak. I opened the door. Paul hadn't moved. I bent down and whispered in his ear. He nodded and moved forward a couple of feet, his weapon continually trained on the door. Clive and I silently filed past.

'Control.' My earpiece crackled as Pecky's voice broke the silence. 'I'm in position. Tell Clive I nearly killed myself on all this pigeon shit; but if you look through the window at the tower, I'm the other side of the stained glass, about twenty-five feet opposite the suspect.'

'Well be careful,' I interrupted. 'That stained glass is expensive.'

My nose twitched. 'What's that smell?'

'Petrol,' said Clive.

'No, not that. I can smell something else.'

'OP, OP,' Clive called to Pecky. 'Can you see what he's doing at the moment?'

'Dunno. He was fiddling with something earlier. Standby, standby!' he whispered urgently. 'He's coming over to the window.' *Click.* In his perch opposite, Pecky silently thumbed the safety catch from his MP5 and stared down the sights. Had he been spotted?

The radio jumped into life. 'Clive, he's eyes about, repeat eyes about. Keep movement to a minimum. He's looking down into the square. Confirm a small black automatic in his right hand!'

'Gas,' I said.

'What?'

'Gas. Can I smell gas?'

'Oh, for God's sake,' Clive said. 'If he's got access to the mains he could take the whole building out.'

Yeah, and what about the muzzle flash from an MP5. I said, thinking out loud.

Clive looked up thoughtfully. 'Hang fire, Steve. I'll speak to the brigade.'

I tensed as he moved off; with Clive away I was in charge.

Twenty minutes later I relaxed as he returned. 'Level One are here,' he announced. My heart sank. I had really wanted to be part of this, but now it looked like we'd be fucked off. 'The brigade reckon a nine mil could well ignite the fumes,' Clive continued. 'I've agreed with the guvnor that we'll do containment while Level One do any assault. The pressure's really on – the whole of the City is at a standstill because of this, and they want it resolved.'

We'd been there two hours when I heard a now-familiar voice. A hand grabbed my shoulder. 'How you doing, Sarge?'

I turned. 'Tony. Fancy seeing you here!'

'I've come for a look,' he said. 'They want a quick ER in case this bloke goes too far. Where's the sniper point?'

I nodded out of the window towards the church. 'Pecky in the bell tower.'

He moved silently across the floor, a sinister-looking figure clad from head to toe in the dark kit, making no sound. Paul shifted as the thin leather combat glove touched the handle. 'Wait for it, wait for it!'

I smiled to myself. The door opened inwards without a sound, I shook my head in disbelief. 'Would you fucking credit it?'

Ten minutes later he returned, nodding his head as he glided silently past.

'He's found a way in,' Clive confided. 'Two of them, Tony and a stick man, can burst through some doors at the far end. They reckon if it's done as a DA with some sort of distraction to get his attention, then they can be on him before he can react.'

'Sounds good to me,' I said knowledgeably. Having never pointed a firearm at anyone in the past, let alone discharged one, I just wished I felt as confident as I sounded.

Tony and the stick man darted past, vanishing silently through the door opposite. How the fuck does he do that? I thought.

'*STANDBY, STANDBY!*' We had been at the scene for three

hours. Now I was suddenly jerked to life by the urgency of the voice in my earpiece. 'He's coming out. Repeat, he's surrendering. What do you want him to do?' After four hours holed up in that small room it must have suddenly dawned on the suspect that there was no place to run to, no place to hide. And after all, like most of them when all's said and done, he didn't really want to hurt himself.

I could physically taste the tension. This was when we were at our most alert – for one false move, one disobeyed command could end in disaster.

Clive slapped my shoulder. 'Steve will talk him out. Standby,' he called over the net.

This was for real! Tensing slightly, I slipped the safety to fire, resting my finger lightly on the trigger guard. The team stacked on the stairs as I joined Paul in the hall.

I cleared my throat. 'In the room,' I bellowed. 'We are armed police. Do you understand?'

'Yes,' came the muffled reply.

'Come to the door. Do as I say and you will not be harmed. Do you understand?'

Again, 'Yes.'

The handle turned slowly and the door opened with a slight creak. I was aware that Tony would be standing to, ready to react to the slightest deviation in plan. 'Let me see those hands,' I screamed, aware of the adrenalin rush I was experiencing. Two shaky white mitts appeared; I was in control.

'Walk slowly out of the door with your hands in the air. Do it *now!*'

I was confronted by my first real armed suspect. Six feet tall, square jawed and dressed all in black, he fixed me with his thousand-yard stare! Did he bollocks – whatever image I may have created in my own mind, I found myself confronted by a five foot seven pot-bellied northerner, wearing jeans and a T-shirt and reeking of petrol. I levelled the MP5 at his chest and called, 'Now walk slowly towards me with your hands in the air.' He nodded. '*LOOK AT ME!*' I screamed. It was imperative that he concentrated.

Paul covered the corridor. Although we believed this man was alone, the room had not been cleared and was therefore considered a danger area.

The suspect was ten feet away. 'Go down on your knees and keep your hands in the air,' I said. 'Lie down and place your hands behind your back.'

The team moved swiftly from the stairwell. *'LOOK AT ME!'* I screamed again as he averted his gaze.

CRASH! Further along the corridor I was aware of Tony's two-man entry team sweeping the boardroom. 'Room clear, room clear!' came over the net. 'It's a starting pistol,' Tony called as I led the suspect away.

I was elated. I had done what I had been trained for. I had stared at a man down the barrel of a gun for the first time – and it had ended peacefully.

'Two-thirty in the morning, lads,' Clive called, putting down the phone. 'We've got a job.'

'Blinding,' I said. 'What is it?'

'Not a lot, really,' he replied. 'Just another dig-out.'

I was happy – it would be my first. Dig-outs, or early morning spins as they are often referred to, were the bread and butter of the Level Two teams; indeed, it was for this type of lower-grade operation that they'd been conceived. Like everything, once practised, then the SOPs (Standard Operating Procedures) could be applied to virtually any job.

'What do you think?' asked Stevie later, putting down a well-deserved pint. Having been on the teams three months longer than me, Stevie was now considered to have earned his wings, whereas I was still very much a fledgling.

'About what?'

'About this job – PT17.'

I nodded. 'Yeah. I think I might like it.'

He laughed. 'Like it? I've never done anything like it. I love it. You know I was a shot on the TSG but never did anything? This is the dog's bollocks! Want another?'

I nodded. 'Is it always like this?' Since the initial boredom of the first week I had noticed that jobs were starting to come in thick and fast.

'Like what?' he said, ordering another beer.

'Well, this busy?'

He grinned. 'I've never earned as much overtime in my life. Looking forward to tomorrow?'

'Yeah, why not?' I said. 'First dig-out and all, should be a good laugh.'

Stevie smiled.

Next morning, I donned my coveralls for the first time. I looked in the mirror and nodded, happy with the overall appearance. I adjusted my beret to a jaunty angle before heading for the briefing room. After all, I was quite proud of myself; I knew I had a hell of a lot to learn but at least I looked the part, and this was the one bit of kit I'd been issued that actually fitted. I'd had it styled by a friend of mine, an ex-Marine, and although initially I felt a right twat sitting for two hours with a sopping wet beret on my head, I was pleased with the result. Worn for years as the standard head-dress of the British Army, ours came in a variety of shapes and sizes, resembling anything from a blue keema naan, to a helicopter landing pad.

Pausing outside, I adjusted my holster. Having point blank refused the left-handed one, I'd later heard that the storeman had tried to palm it off on some of the other new guys. I'd eventually been found one with broken stitching, but at least it was on the right side.

Pushing open the door, I strode in. The team were sprawled around on chairs drinking coffee. Clive choked. 'Where the fuck did you get that lot?' he screamed, pointing at my oversized coveralls.

'You should have seen them before,' I said, pointing at the hastily repaired knee.

He shook his head. 'See me later and I'll sort you some out.'

Clive outlined the plan. 'This is a one-bedroom flat.' He pointed at the neatly drawn plan displayed on a flip chart. 'From the FUP we'll feed in the rear, then the front containments. When we're happy, the team will move up on foot and breach the door. Stevie, you're MOE,' he said, nodding across the floor. 'Once we've got access, the shield man will come up on the door, and Steve can do the call out.' He looked at me. 'OK?'

I nodded, somewhat flustered. I had thought I'd be watching the first one; instead the team would be watching me! This was my debut.

Mounting the carrier, we moved off for the formal briefing. A suspect wanted in connection with an armed robbery was believed to be housed at his parents' address on the notorious

Tufnell Park council estate. He was considered to be armed and dangerous. A PT17 Level Two team had been called in to effect an arrest and search.

Stevie quietly positioned the arm of the hydraulic ram and nodded. A faint *whirrr* cut through the early-morning calm. *CRACK!* The thin door-frame yielded to the ten-thousand-pound-per-square-inch pressure exerted on its flimsy structure. *CRASH!* The door flew inwards, smashing with a loud thump against the internal wall, and Stevie followed up with the manual battering ram, nicknamed 'Baby'. The arm of the hydraulic dropped from the doorway with a metallic clatter. The whole entry had taken no more than five seconds.

Suddenly the shield was up, filling the doorway. I peered around the frame. Nothing. Just silence. 'In the house,' I called. 'We are armed police.'

Movement! I held my hand in the air, fist clenched, indicating contact. A metallic click from inside suddenly heightened my senses.

'In the house. We are armed police,' I repeated. 'Show yourself now or I'll send in the dog.' Heavy breathing from behind me announced the animal's arrival. The handler was waiting for my command; the dog, straining at the leash, ready to go to work, barked loudly.

I waited. *Click* – it came again. Concentrating on the hall, I was aware of the containments being advised of the situation on the radio.

Click.

'Standby,' I screamed as a long metal tube slid round the door at the far end of the hall. 'Don't move. Don't move!' I shouted. 'Let me see those fucking hands *now*.'

'Hold on, hold on,' came a voice from the hall. *Click*. The crutch came into sight.

God. Day of the bleeding Jackal, I thought as the old man appeared.

'Now listen to me,' I called. 'We are armed police. Do you understand?'

'Yes,' he replied.

'Right. I want you to drop those crutches and walk slowly towards me. You will not be harmed.'

'I can't do that,' he shouted aggressively.

'Yes you can. Now do it, and do it *now*!'

Take control, we'd once been told. *If a suspect thinks you're nervous, then he'll play on it. That won't happen because they play by our rules, and we don't negotiate.*

The crutches fell to the floor with a clank.

'Good. Now slowly walk towards me.' Not that fucking slowly, I thought after a couple of minutes. Any slower and he'll be in reverse.

'Steve,' Stevie whispered in my ear, 'there's something I think you should know.'

'Not now,' I hissed, concentrating on the suspect, who had finally reached my position. The reception team moved in and quickly hurried him away.

'In the house,' I called again. 'Come out, or I'll send in the dog!'

Silence.

'Dog up,' I whispered.

A blur shot past and through the hall as the furry Exocet was released. Checking the rooms of the small flat one by one, he indicated to his handler that the premises were clear. Although a magnificent working aid – that is in effect what dogs are, an aid – before we could hand over to unarmed officers I had to be certain in my own mind the place was totally clear. And that meant a slow, methodical and thorough search.

Stacking up behind the shield man for cover, we advanced through the open door. Five minutes later we emerged. 'Front and rear containments stand down. We're clear.' I announced happily into the radio.

'That didn't go too badly, did it?' I asked the unsmiling Clive.

'No,' he said. 'I think it was a fucking miracle!'

'Well,' I smiled, 'I wouldn't go that far.'

'I would,' he said. 'That poor bastard has been a raspberry for ten years; he simply can't walk without the aid of crutches. If we're lucky, he won't sue the job.'

The months seemed to fly past. With them I grew in experience and was eventually accepted by the team. Frequently bumping into the unsmiling Chris, I quickly came to realize that rivalry between the three Level Two teams was more than just 'friendly'. Grey Team (under Clive's command) were pretty much middle of the road, if not a little serious. Black were considered maverick, even in those days; while White were simply referred to as the 'Slow Methodicals'.

After four months, I found it hard to remember the specifics of any one particular job, there were so many – but there were changes afoot. It was planned that, if suitable, Level Two men would undergo a vigorous re-selection and would amalgamate with Level One. So, gone would be the days of the two-tier system of low-grade dig-outs and high-risk ambushes. And from this melting pot, new teams would be formed within one big unit of SFOs (Specialist Firearms Officers). I could hardly wait!

6

Trojan 27

'Fucking hell!' Pecky smiled broadly. 'I passed!'

'Well done, mate,' I said, patting him on the back. 'How was it?'

He thought carefully. 'I can't lie, mate – it was fucking hard. I was the only Level Two bloke on the course, so everybody else had a headstart. I was playing catch-up from day one.'

I grimaced. This didn't bode well. Pecky was the first Level Two man to pass the new SFO course, and if he found it difficult . . . I shook my head. 'What did you find hard, then?' I asked, digging a little deeper.

He looked down at the floor. 'Well, the physical side was not too bad, but they're at you constantly. I can't really put my finger on anything specific, it was just the pressure!'

'How'd the abseiling go?' I asked gingerly. Much as I hated to admit it, I didn't like heights – but I knew that if I wanted to be an assaulter I had to conquer my fear.

'Yeah, it was OK. In fact I really enjoyed it.' He smiled.

I looked down at his wiry frame. 'Yeah, but you're built for it. Look at me – I'll probably dangle around like a fucking conker.'

'Yeah, or one of them big demolition balls.'

'Oi!' I smiled, pointing at him. I was secretly pleased for Pecky. Over the months I'd come to enjoy his company and, although we'd been on different teams, we'd instantly hit it off. But now it was all behind him. Having passed the course he could afford to relax a little, assured of a place on an SFO team. I knew many would not be so lucky, and with a churning in my stomach I certainly didn't cherish my turn.

* * *

75

'This is a pass or fail course,' the inspector whined, surveying the twelve anxious faces. I'd heard other people nickname him 'the Cat', and studying him now I had to agree, for with his shock of curly ginger hair and his high-pitched voice he did indeed resemble a ginger Tom. 'Some of you will be unlucky. At the end of these three weeks, those that have passed will be awarded a certificate, and can be pretty much assured of a place on a team,' he purred.

Looking to his right, I made eye contact with the sergeant running the course. Russ, an instructor and Level One team leader, was certainly a larger than life character. Brash and somewhat eccentric, he revelled in practical jokes. I'd not really spoken to him since joining the department, but had certainly heard of his exploits and professionalism. Like Fifty Fucks he was also known not to suffer fools gladly. He stared back and sneered. Jerked back to reality, I was aware of the Cat running through the timetable. It would consist of a fitness test, various team tasks, the dreaded abseiling and 'fast rope', lots of room combat, recces, planning, respirator shoots, a final classification shoot (one that had caught a lot of hopefuls out), first aid, an aircraft assault, ladder work, and lastly, putting everything together, a final hostage rescue. As the only sergeant on the course the pressure was on from day one. And I felt sick!

Scooping up my kit, I made my way back to the billet to change into sports kit for the PE test. Deep in thought, I hadn't heard the footsteps behind me. I felt a tap on my shoulder. Spinning round I found myself staring at Russ.

'So, you're the one they call Edd the Duck?' he said seriously. I grinned.

'Well, Edd.' He smirked. 'I've heard a lot about you. You've managed to make some enemies already.' Tell me something I don't know, I thought.

'Well, I just want you to know that I'm running this course, and you're after my fucking job.' Smiling, he turned on his heel and headed for the canteen. I stood there, dumbstruck. It was day one, week one, and I'd already virtually been threatened with failure. Fucking great!

The only good thing about the whole three weeks was that I was not alone. Apart from Ollie, a tall, rather portly officer who comprised practically the entire firearms team for the island of

Guernsey, everybody else was Level Two. So, unlike Pecky's course, we were all starting off on level footing. It somehow made me feel a little more secure, having the support of Stevie and Mas, and some newer pals: Nigel (another ex-firefighter from Grey Team, already pushing forty and still one of the fittest men I knew), Jim (the well-spoken member of White Team, nicknamed 'Dandy') and Mario (from Black Team, a soldier who sported along with numerous others a 'Death Before Breakfast' tattoo).

'As you can see – ' Russ smiled evilly as he looked over the edge – 'provided you've got confidence in the rope to lean back, it's easy.'

I gulped as I stared across the aerial view of London at Battersea Power Station in the distance. It was a glorious day but slightly windy, and we found ourselves standing on the roof of Tintagel House, a Metropolitan Police office block overlooking the Thames. It was fourteen storeys high.

Mas looked cautiously over the edge. 'Fucking hell.'

Checking his abseil harness, the despatcher attached the line. 'You can try one of two methods,' he had said. 'The rollover [I'd already tried that; rolling from the parapet, the carabiner that held the line to the harness had snagged on the edge. I looked down before deciding I didn't like it, not one little bit!] or the step off.'

Mas chose the latter. Facing backwards, he slowly fed out the line and lowered himself until he was standing at almost ninety degrees to the side of the building, grinning. He stepped back. 'Walk in the park,' he shouted nervously as his head disappeared from view.

'Look down!' Russ screamed as I hurtled off the edge. My twisted logic was: *Get down as fast as you can; if you have to do it get it over and done with.*

Landing heavily on the ground, I winked at Stevie the brakeman. 'Another one over. I fucking hate this,' I said dejectedly, walking back to the lift that would return me to the top.

The day progressed in much the same vein, with the only moment of sheer terror being the 'rescue'. And I had Ollie as my 'victim'. Trapped half-way down the building, he had locked off and was dangling helplessly to simulate a casualty. Dropping my line alongside, I knew I had to time this to perfection; if I dropped just inches below his position I would have to abort, drop down the rope, go to the top and start again. Fuck that for a game of soldiers – get it right first time!

Locking off above him, I spread my legs wide, feet against the wall and started to 'crab', swinging the line from side to side until I resembled some sort of demented pendulum. Snaring Ollie's line, I wrapped my legs round his body and lowered myself slowly. 'Fuck this, mate!' I said. 'Do you think the line will hold our weight?'

'Course it will,' he said in his soft West Country twang. 'They reckon it will hold the weight of a Land Rover.'

'They said that?' I asked.

He nodded.

'Bollocks.'

Still attached to the line I worked feverishly; Ollie the 'casualty' was of course unable to help. Locking our carabiners together, it was the moment of truth. I had to disconnect him from his line while we were joined at the waist by a small piece of metal. Taking a deep breath, I uncoupled him. With the combined weight now on my line we dropped a couple of feet until the elasticity in the rope found its own level. 'Fuck that!' I screamed.

Ollie laughed, and all our anxiety suddenly vanished. We were still laughing when we hit the ground.

The abseiling was bad enough; I needed a 'fast rope' like I needed a second arsehole.

'We probably wouldn't do this over sixty feet,' Russ smiled inanely.

I looked at the thick woven rope hanging from a gantry on the roof of Old Street. 'How do you attach yourself?' I asked naively.

'Simple,' he said seriously. He threw me a pair of welder's gloves. 'With these. And seeing how you asked, Edd, you can demonstrate it!'

The technique with fast roping is easy: you treat it as you would a fireman's pole. For short distances it's easier than an abseil option where you'd have to disconnect your line. With this, you simply ditch the gloves.

'Don't forget,' Russ added wickedly, 'It's all too easy to grip so firmly that you won't move, you'll just hang there till you fall. The knack is not to hold on too tightly. Look down, spread your legs, and keep you feet clear of the rope.'

'Yeah, course,' I muttered, terrified. 'Fucking simple!'

CRASH! I hit the safety mat at terminal velocity, bounced, then flew down the small flight of stairs. 'Course it's easy,' I mumbled. 'You just have to take in to account the extra four fucking stone of kit you're wearing when you grab the rope!' By the end of the day, however, we were spiralling down the line four at a time.

That evening, weary and sore, we returned to the billet, showered and went to bed.

The majority of our time was taken up with room combat. As a hostage response team we full knew that if the shit really did hit the fan, then we would have to get it right first time – and you could only do that by training. There were no second chances in this game!

One of the ranges at Lippitts Hill had been converted into a series of rooms, each reached by an interconnecting door, each with a curtained window. 'Innocent' and 'hostile' targets were concealed in the rooms. Behind each one was a steel plate which would stop the 9 mm 'frangible' rounds we were using.

It was the first time any of us had experienced this type of training: using live ammunition, movement, and crossed arcs of fire. Safety was of the utmost importance. 'For fuck's sake, switch on,' Russ had warned us. 'Even in full kit and body armour, frangy will kill you. It shatters on impact and is just as lethal as our standard 9 mm soft-points. As it's a hostage rescue scenario you'll also be wearing respirators. These will cut down your peripheral vision by about fifty per cent, so be aware of your number two's position.'

We'd choreographed our movements for hours in dry runs; we knew our weapon drills back to front. The only way now was forward.

'First four,' Russ called.

I stepped forward with Nigel, Jim and Mas.

'Right,' Russ grinned. 'It's easy to get carried away and rush, so take it easy – we don't want any fucking casualties.'

We stacked up on the door as we'd been instructed. I was number one. I nodded.

'Standby, standby. *GO!*' Russ shouted.

The door burst inwards. With laboured breathing I stared through the respirator's eyeholes, desperately searching for a target.

CRACK, CRACK! Nigel, standing to my left, had engaged a hostile target. My senses were now heightened, even though we were shooting cardboard targets, and the only danger was in the form of a stray round from a team-mate.

I recalled what Tony had said months previously: 'If you don't imagine what it would be like to shoot somebody when the bullets are coming back at you, when real bodies are falling down – then when it does happen for real, you'll be the loser!'

Moving forward, we cleared the rooms one by one before heading back to the start.

'What the fuck was that?' Russ said, slapping his head.

'It was fucking dangerous, that's what it was.'

He glared at me. 'Slow it down. We can build it up later. You practically ran through that!'

I nodded.

Dressed alike, we'd chalked our names on the backs of our body armour. This made it easier for the staff to assess individuals. 'Turn around,' Russ said, producing a piece of chalk. Grinning, he stencilled 'BEWARE: MAD DUCK' on my back.

We sweated, and we worked. Russ was right; watching the others, it did seem as if live ammo made you want to charge through like some sort of avenging angel. It was also very dangerous. Time and time again we swept through different scenarios, gradually adding different techniques until we got it right. Russ heightened the confusion by throwing thunderflashes in an effort to distract us from our task. With the smoke and noise it made it doubly hard – but then again we'd volunteered, and nobody had said it would be easy!

As the weeks progressed, so did our combat skills. We were now proficient in casevac (casualty evacuation), and clearing a 'stoppage' during a full-blown assault. We did however have our moments. When one thing goes to rat shit, everything seems to goes wrong; but, in the words of Dennis Norden, we felt sure that it would 'be all right on the night'!

*　　*　　*

My nerve-endings tingled as I stacked up on the door.

This was training – of that I was aware – but training for the real thing. As the days of room combat training had passed I'd become more aware that the first (and for that matter the second) man was totally on offer when entering a room, and that if confronting a true professional the odds of taking a hit were dramatically increased. From somewhere deep in my memory I dug out the initials S.A.S.: Surprise, Aggression, Speed.

'Standby, Standby. *GO, GO, GO!*' Russ screamed into the radio. My muffled breathing became faster as the adrenalin started its rush. *BANG BANG!* The shotgunner blew off the door's hinges with the specially designed Hatton round. Constructed of powdered lead and wax, it dumps its energy on impact, blowing off the hinges without the risk of over-penetration. With a clenched fist I made a jabbing motion over my right shoulder, the signal for a grenade. In the periphery of my vision a black-gloved hand appeared, showing me the grenade, pin removed. (Earlier that day we'd seen one student struggling to remove a pin. In a real situation this could be potentially life threatening; I was determined not to make the same mistake.) As the door collapsed inwards, the small black projectile left his hand and sailed through the air. Striking a strategically placed target, it bounced straight back out and between our feet. *BOOM!* It exploded loudly, filling the room with smoke. Thank fuck we're not using a multi-burst, I thought momentarily. (Multi-burst, the standard multi-explosion ops grenades, were saved for the final exercise. Big Joe, a Level Two Black Team man, had made exactly the same mistake using one of these grenades. Perched on top of a ladder, he'd thrown it into the room with such force that it had hit the wall opposite and rebounded. He'd climbed in through the window when it exploded with an awesome concussion that ripped his scrotum to pieces. In true Black Team tradition Joe had carried on, only to display later his bloodied, battered and bruised bit of kit to the rest of the lads.)

'Shit! *GO, GO, GO!*' I screamed, oblivious to anything apart from maintaining the momentum of the assault. The door inside was locked. 'Window, window, window!' I yelled, dropping to my hands and knees. I groaned as the air was forced from my lungs. Nigel jumped on to my back and dived through the window, emerging the other side with a curtain wrapped round his head. *CRACK, CRACK!* He engaged a hostile target as the third man screamed, 'Stay down!' After three, I pulled myself through the frame and joined the stick.

CRACK!

'Stoppage!' I shouted, dropping to one knee. In a single movement I ditched the MP5 and drew my Glock.

CRACK, CRACK! Nigel came over my head, knee in my back, indicating that he was covering. We were working as a team.

Clearing the stoppage, we moved on. 'End-ex, end-ex,' Russ called, grinning broadly. 'A few mistakes, but you carried on regardless. Yes, it looked quite good.'

Fucking hell, praise indeed, I thought sarcastically.

It was the end of the second week. On the Monday Russ had again reminded me that if we couldn't crack room combat then we were off.

'OK. Stand down, fellas. Have a good weekend,' he called. 'A word outside, Edd,' he said to me, unsmiling.

Bollocks, I thought, trudging meekly along.

'Some people don't like you,' he said sternly. Then he beamed. 'But from what I can see, you're a fucking star. And as far as I'm concerned, you can have my job any day!'

I stood in stunned silence. It was with a spring in my step that I left for home that weekend, for a well-deserved rest.

The final week progressed relatively well. Now well rehearsed in room combat, we were beginning to gel as a team; from ground-floor entries we had progressed through abseil techniques and finally ladder work.

I passed the classification shoot with well over the ninety per cent required. I found that it was this last discipline that fazed people the most: Glock handgun at twenty-five metres, multi-positional, with a reload on a one-second exposure of the target. Sure it was tight, but as Tony had demonstrated, it was certainly that fast in reality, if not faster!

The old green bus laboured pathetically as the driver frantically sought a lower gear. With a crunch it engaged. Springing forward, we continued our laboured journey up the hill. I'm not surprised, I thought. The amount of gear we'd thrown on was enough to sink a battleship. We were loaded to the gunnels. Even the assault ladders, their ends wrapped and taped in

. Depicted on the front page of the *Evening Standard,* the author leaves the scene of a
iege in Harlesden that left one man shot dead and a police officer seriously injured.

2. The scene in Hammersmith outside the house where a terrorist suspect was killed in a dawn contact with armed police. Five other men were arrested as part of a nationwide operation which may have thwarted a massive IRA lorry bomb attack.

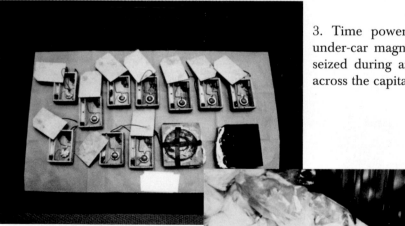

3. Time power units and two under-car magnetic booby traps seized during anti-terrorist raids across the capital.

4. Police issue picture of three Kalashnikov rifles, two handguns, ammunition and home-made explosives on a large wooden crate (believed to be part of a lorry bomb) seized during anti-terrorist raids across London.

5. The scene at the abattoir after the shooting. Chalk rings the spots where spent cases fell to the ground. The heavy police ballistic shield leans against the wing of the security vehicle whilst displayed in the foreground is the robbers' awesome arsenal of weapons.

6. The crashed getaway car moments after the bungled robbery attempt in Woolwich where three robbers were shot by armed police.

Daily Mail

TUESDAY, NOVEMBER 24, 1987   22p

For the second time in just 36 hours a gunman lies dead, shot by police bullets

AMBUSH

THIS was the scene of a deadly showdown in a London suburb yesterday.

On the left, a gunman lies dead, sprawled on his back in front of his BMW getaway car. He had been shot by a police marksman.

Beside the open passenger door is gunman No. 2, hit in the shoulder by a second police bullet.

And behind the car a third, uninjured

MAIL PICTURE EXCLUSIVE

man lies on his side with a detective standing over him — all under the muzzles of police guns.

The shoot-out came when the gang screeched into the yard of lock-up garages in Sunbury Street, Woolwich, SE, after a security van hold-up.

They spilled out of the BMW ready to switch to a gold-coloured Mercedes parked nearby — but found themselves cornered by six members of Scotland Yard's Tactical Firearms Unit, named PT17, backed by Flying Squad officers.

In the blazing gun battle that followed the head of the gun squad, Inspector Dwight Atkinson was hit in the leg and

in this exclusive picture — beyond the wall — he is being helped into an unmarked police car.

It was the second time in 36 hours that Britain's policemen had shot dead a gunman. Early on Sunday morning marksmen killed 'Wild Man' Glyn Davies, 29, as he walked towards officers after a chase in the West Country and raised a pump-action shotgun to his shoulder.

Yesterday's shootings took place opposite a children's playground and the yard is overlooked by flats.

Police representatives defended the tactic of deploying armed officers. 'It is regrettable and is an unfortunate situa-

tion but it is necessary,' said Police Federation chairman Leslie Curtis. 'Police must use like force when faced with armed people.'

Close to the dead man and his injured accomplice, police recovered two revolvers and say at least five bullets smashed into the wall on the right of the picture.

The marksmen fired at least six shots, some hitting the BMW.

Independent investigators were trying last night to establish who fired first. At least one witness has claimed the police did so after the man who died had dropped his gun and had pleaded 'don't fire.'

But other witnesses say the first bullet came from the BMW, hitting the inspector. Then the squad returned fire killing

Turn to Page 2, Col 3

7. AMBUSH! The aftermath of a shoot-out in Woolwich between a gang of armed robbers and Firearms Unit Officers. One robber lies dead, his two companions captured. One police officer was shot.

. In this posed shot 'Black Team' display some of the weapons at SO19's disposal. The
uthor is second left on the back row.

 & 10. Fully kitted for a hostage rescue - an SO19 MOE (Method of Entry) man with
quipment frame and armed with a Remington 870 pump-action shotgun.

11. Some of the staggering 4.5 stones of personal equipment carried by an SFO team member (see list p. 209).

12. Weapons available to SO19 specialist teams (see list p. 207).

13. Selection of MOE equipment (see list pp. 208-9).

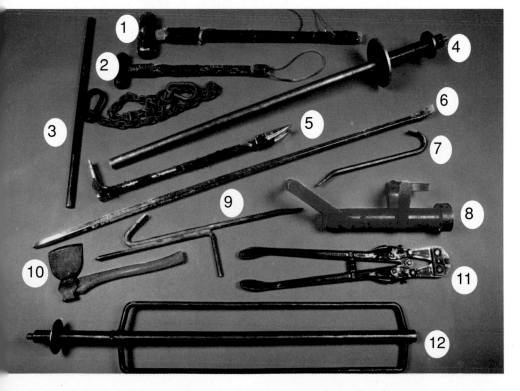

14. A team goes through a live firing practice on a simulated building assault at Lippitts Hill range.

15. Hooded and ready - an SO19 team 'sniper' locks on to his target.

16. 'Locked-off' - an SO19 'assaulter' armed with a Glock self-loading pistol abseils down to the 'stronghold' in this training scenario.

17 & 18. STAND BY, STAND BY! - moving stealthily forward a team 'stacks up' ready for the go in a simulated hostage rescue.

19. Lincoln's Inn Field's siege in which a solicitor was taken hostage. Balancing on a ladder, the author prepares to enter the stronghold.

20. 'Time on their hands' - in a moment of 'down time' on a protracted incident, SO19 dogs pose for the camera.

21-26. Published by the *Sun*, this unique security camera footage captures the Crouch Hill robbery on film:

21. Charalambous dressed in plastic police officer's helmet approaches the post office van, the pistol clearly visible in his right hand.

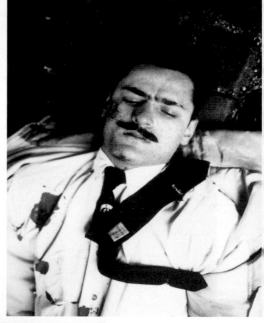

22. Moments later he lies bleeding, cut down from the rounds of an MP5. Clearly seen are his false moustache and the tie severed by one of the bullets.

23. Lying in shock the robber is covered by a blanket to preserve body heat. His weapon, now made safe, lies in the foreground.

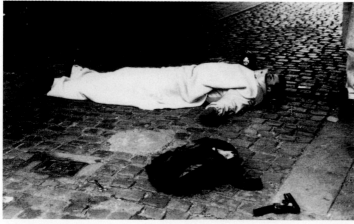

24. The air ambulance sets down in the hastily cordoned-off street.

25. The second robber lies face down and cuffed.

26. SO19 team members look on as the air ambulance crew quickly set about their life-saving tasks.

27. 'All in a day's work' - stun grenades were used in this hostage rescue in London. Unfortunately the hostage was already dead. The author stands behind the suspect in the foreground who took his own life with a shotgun.

28. Taken by a local resident this spectacular photograph shows SO19 and SBS Commandos storming the vessel *Foxtrot Five* as part of Operation Emerge.

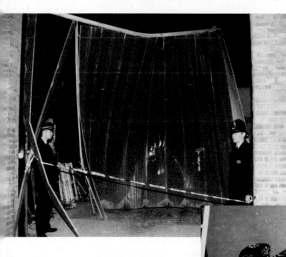

29. The doors of a drug baron's fortified 'slaughter' breached by SO19 using an armoured JCB.

30. Part of the £160 million cocaine haul recovered on Operation Emerge - each sack has a street value in excess of £4 million.

THE Sun

sday, July 15, 1993   **20p**   TV: Pages 36 and 37   Audited daily sale for June 4,017,062 (including Today)

BIG, BIG V-A-L-U-E FOR ONE SMALL COIN **20p**

ON YER KNEES

nowhere to run . . . marksmen train their gun-sights on the IRA bomber at the bus stop yesterday. In his bag was a 10lb Semtex bomb

Armed cops capture IRA suspect with bomb in bag

By MIKE SULLIVAN

ON his hands and knees, an IRA bomber crawls for his life. From every angle, police marksmen train their guns on him.

One barks commands to the 20-stone bomber from behind a wall. The others, fingers on triggers, watch for any sudden movement that will spell death for the terrorist.

The photographer who took the picture said: "One false move and I reckon they'd have let him have it."

This was the incredible scene in Oxgate Lane, Cricklewood, North London, at 9am yesterday.

By the bus stop lies a black bag containing a 10lb Semtex bomb — enough to demolish a four-storey building.

The man, described by security sources as a "major IRA player," had driven overnight from an IRA safe house in Scotland to plant the bomb in the City or the West End. Luckily his mission was foiled at the bus stop in Oxgate Lane.

Police tailed bomber on 750-mile trek — Page Seven

31. 'ON YER KNEES' - IRA bomber Rab Fryers taken out by SO19 at a bus stop in north London. The bomb in a bag lies on the footpath as the author takes cover behind a vehicle in the foreground.

hessian to prevent noise, were stacked up the centre aisle. The twelve-man team were crammed in where they could, sitting in uncomfortable silence among the heavy bergens and entry gear.

This was the final exercise. The instructors would be watching, taking notes, seeing how the guys performed during a full-blown assault, how they coped with the recces as information slowly leaked their way. More importantly they were watching me, the team leader. How would I handle the intelligence? How would I control the team? What would be my ER/DA and surrender options? No advice had been given; it was too late for that. There would be nobody to hold your hand outside – because next week it could be for real. I actually preferred that option, for during this exercise I was under the critical gaze of Fifty Fucks, who'd come to watch.

'Come on, Come on,' screamed the instructors, piling on the pressure as the coach juddered to a halt outside the deserted hospital. 'There's a fucking siege going on, people's lives are at risk. Get your fingers out of your arses and unload this kit.'

'Where's the control, Staff?' I asked.

'Control?' he screamed. 'Why do you want a fucking control? It's obvious what's going on – now fucking deal with it!'

Unimpressed, I played his game. 'I'm not deploying any of my men without a briefing. It's obvious that the ARVs have a containment, they know the geography of the building and what they're dealing with.' I paused. 'To come up with a half-decent ER I need to know what's going on! And I can only find that out from control.'

He nodded, apparently happy with what he'd heard. 'It's over there,' he grinned, pointing to a single-storeyed building opposite the coach.

Setting off swiftly, I looked over my shoulder. 'Mas,' I called. 'Six of you in full assault kit, ready to go. Leave the other five to unload the coach.'

'Right.' He nodded enthusiastically.

The control room smelt of freshly brewed coffee and was a hive of activity. It was apparent that the 'siege' had been going on for some considerable time. Reams of handwritten notes adorned the walls, detailing the day's events. I almost felt sorry for the controller who, scribbling frantically on a piece of paper, was trying to listen to the incessant babbling of the radios. Other operators were drawing up the plans as the TI was relayed from various points around the stronghold. It seemed like hell. But at the end of the day a well-run control can make or break a job.

Bending over the table, the controller looked up sharply. 'All right, Sarge?'

'Yeah,' I said, raising my eyebrows. 'Looks busy.'

'It is,' he grinned, breaking off from his tedious task.

'What you got?' I asked.

'Well, from what we can make out, up to four X-rays [hostage-takers] have taken over this part of the building.' He pointed to a hastily drawn map. 'They are on the first floor. We have a containment at the rear and on the stairs at the front. They seem to be coming out on to this flat roof.' He indicated with a pen.

'Yankees?' (hostages) I asked.

'Not known at this stage. About ten, we think – male and female. They seem to be some sort of animal rights group, and one machine-gun has been seen.'

'Cheers,' I said, scratching my head. 'What channel are you on?'

'Ninety-nine.'

'OK.' I nodded. 'My team is split, Trojan 201 – Alpha and Bravo. I'm Trojan 27.'

He scribbled on the log sheet.

'It'll take a short while to get the kit together, but at all times when something happens I'll have at least half a team standing to.' I sighed, weighing up the options. 'If they break out or surrender in the meantime, your boys can deal with it with us standing to. Happy?'

He nodded. 'I'll let the containments know.'

'Yes. And tell them to expect movement. We'll need some recces, but we'll clear it with you first.'

'Cheers,' he said, going back to the unintelligible cries of the radio.

'What's going on, Sarge?' The voice from behind made me jump. The Cat and Fifty Fucks had been listening to my conversation.

I outlined what I knew. 'I'll need to send some men out to have a look at possible entry points,' I added.

The Cat nodded.

'I'm the commander,' Fifty Fucks said. 'I authorized you. Are you putting a plan together for a hostage rescue?'

'Why, yes, sir,' I stammered. 'That's obviously why we're here.'

'Not to me it's not. I'm a commander, and I want to be treated like one,' he boomed, now well into role play.

I swallowed hard. Perhaps I was missing something here. 'Well, sir,' I said. 'How do you treat a commander?'

'Like a cunt,' he said.

'Well, sir,' I gulped. 'Far be it for me to treat you like a cunt . . .'

'Well, I want you to,' he growled, marching towards the controller.

The ER I'd come up with was to hit the first floor via two main entry points. Both could be approached on the blind aspect of the building, and both could be reached by ladder. Alpha would enter by a window on the right, with Bravo assaulting the building from the flat roof.

The Cat nodded. At least *he* seemed happy.

Things were coming together quite nicely. With the team split in two we had set up our own briefing room, and with the information gathered from the CTRs we started to build on our plan.

CRACK! A shot rang out.

'Trojan 27, Trojan 201 – standby, standby,' the controller screamed down the net.

I frowned. Perhaps they intended to go with the ER? 'Bravo, stand to,' I yelled.

Picking up their ladder, they sprinted towards their FAP.

'Alpha, stand to,' I called, pulling on my resi.

'Trojan 27.' The controller sounded frantic. 'A hostage has been shot in the leg and thrown on to the roof. The commander wants him rescued.'

'Yeah, he would,' I mumbled into the tight confines of the mask. Bravo were standing to, Mario (the team medic) and Jim stripped down to their coveralls. With a Double German and a carry sheet, they jogged to the scene. It had been negotiated with the suspects inside that the casualty could be removed.

This was a further test of our ingenuity. Placing the ladder silently against the building, Jim climbed to the roof and attended the victim, a male in his twenties. Placing a field dressing tightly against the badly wounded leg, he pondered the casevac. How would they get him down?

Mario appeared over the parapet and grinned. 'Easy,' he said confidently. 'Fireman's lift, over my right shoulder.'

Jim looked between him and the worried casualty. 'How much do you weigh?' he asked.

'Fifteen,' the victim gulped, desperately wanting to stay in character but dubious of the twenty-foot drop.

'Fuck me,' Mario muttered, shaking his head. 'Come on then!'

Easing the casualty headfirst over the edge, Mario took the weight with a groan. By the time they reached the bottom the casualty was white-faced, and not through loss of blood!

Two of the team had gained a useful insight of the building. Also, in a calculated move (which hadn't been noticed by the ever-watchful eyes of the instructors), they had left the ladder in position. Should the shit now hit the proverbial fan, we could be into the stronghold in seconds.

Having presented the commander and the Cat with the finalized plan (the DA consisted of three four-man teams, Alpha, Bravo and Charlie, with three seperate entry points, one at the front and two at the back; the ARV containment in the stairwell would initiate the assault by triggering a ten-shot rapid – a distraction device which simulates machine-gun fire), we waited. We were already six hours into the day. Now the plan was formulated the end was nigh.

'So,' boomed Fifty Fucks. 'What percentage on casualties can you give me, if I authorize your plan?'

'I'm afraid it's unethical for me to give you that sort of information, sir,' I said nervously. 'We can only do our best.'

'How long do you need?'

'For the DA?'

He nodded.

'Three minutes, just to get the ladders in position.'

'Oh, so you're using ladders, are you?'

'Well, yes, sir. Obviously . . .' I held up my hand. 'Sorry, sir,' I grinned. 'I forgot you were a cunt.'

He smiled. 'Good luck.'

'I have control,' hissed the Cat. 'Team Alpha, are you in position?'

Perched on top of the ladder, I could hear my own laboured breathing through the resi. (Fuck me, I'm surprised they can't hear it inside, I thought.) I pressed my PTT (Press to Talk) switch three times in response to the command.

'Three clicks received. Team Bravo, are you in position?'

Click, click, click.

'Three clicks received.'

It seemed like an age, waiting, cramped in the foetal position, ready to hurl myself through the window.

'Team Charlie,' the Cat co-ordinated, 'are you in position?'

Click, click, click.

'All teams are in position.'

I tensed.

'Standby, standby. *GO, GO, GO!*'

BANG, BANG, BANG . . . The ten-shot rapid exploded into life as the small black grenade arched through the window. I heard the clatter inside of machine-gun fire as one of the teams engaged. My hand rested on the door knob, waiting for that all-important tap. A hand on my shoulder. Nigel nodded as the door flew open.

Chaos. The blur as another small black projectile hit the landing. *BOOM!* It exploded with an ear-shattering din. Smoke filled the building. Torchlights cut through as Bravo and Charlie teams sought their limits of exploitation. Still there was the clatter of gunfire above the shouts.

I kicked the next door. 'Fuck. Locked. Hatton, Hatton!' I called as Ollie lumbered across the hall. A sharp tap indicated the presence of a number two.

With a fist over my shoulder I indicated the need for a grenade, and the object appeared. Nodding to Ollie, I waited.

BANG, BANG! The Hatton rounds from the Remington 870 sawn-off pump-action shotgun ripped through the hinges. The door collapsed and the concussion from the second grenade shook the building.

I entered, MP5 at arm's length, torch mount scanning the room, finger on the trigger. From my right came the sharp report of two rounds from my number two. They found their mark. The 'terrorist' collapsed, releasing his grasp on an old .38 revolver. Muffled shouts of 'room clear, room clear' echoed down the hall.

'Re-org, re-org,' I shouted, and it was finally over.

The whole assault had taken a minute and a half. Russ, the 'terrorist' leader, armed with a Kurtz machine-gun, had lain in wait in a cupboard on the landing, fully intent on taking out the whole team as they came up the stairs. The three entry points, along with the ten-shot rapid, had thrown him. But not as much as the grenade that had bounced into his hidey-hole, effectively taking him out of the game. ('I thought you were trying to fucking kill me,' he later said.)

With the hostages plasticuffed, they were led from the room. Played by police civilian staff, they looked shocked and bewildered. Lucky we didn't use gas, I thought as they passed. In a despicable act one 'terrorist' had taped a gun to the hands of a hostage. In the onslaught that followed he was killed; having been confronted with a gun an officer had fired. But then even monkeys fall out of trees!

Four X-rays, one Yankee dead; nine Yankees rescued; no police casualties.

As I came down from the adrenalin high I suddenly felt quite tired. It had been a long day – no, it had been a long three weeks.

'I came here today to watch how you handled the final exercise,' Fifty Fucks said, shocking me back to life. 'I like what I saw, and you haven't fucking let me down.' He grinned. Somehow I couldn't help thinking that there was some sort of hidden agenda. It was almost as if I was a guinea-pig on which he'd staked his money. Taking me under his wing, he confided, 'With the new reshuffle, you'll get your team. I like your fucking attitude!'

'Thank you, sir,' I said, a tremendous weight lifted from my shoulders.

The Cat nodded. 'Load up, back to base.'

'Well done, Steve,' Nigel said, struggling with the ladder.

'Yeah, well done, Edd,' said Mas, patting my back. 'Can I come on your team?'

I smiled. 'You little sod, you've been eavesdropping.'

'I'd just like to say,' Dandy piped up, 'I'll follow you anywhere.'

'Why, thanks, Jim,' I said, slightly embarrassed.

'Yeah,' he added. 'Mainly out of idle curiosity.'

7

When Black Team Calls

'I'm definitely going to give up the booze, I thought as I made my way swiftly to the kitchen and a strong cup of coffee. My intake had about doubled in recent months, and it certainly hadn't been that healthy in the beginning!

Shaking my head, I put it down to the hours of work and the extra strain of the job, but at the back of my mind I realized I may have a problem. 'Right, that's it. I'm not going to have any drink tonight,' I lied to myself with a nod.

Slouching into the crew room, I noticed the soft hum of whispered chatter. 'They out yet?' I asked, plonking myself down next to Nigel.

'No,' he replied, smiling.

'Yeah,' I said, 'I guess they've only had a couple of months to sort it out. That lot couldn't organize a piss up in a brewery. Oh!' I groaned, holding my head.

'Talking of breweries!' he said.

I held my hand up. 'Never again!'

At eleven o'clock they eventually arrived. The room fell silent as the admin sergeant shuffled in, carrying a sheath of papers. 'Steve,' he said, holding out a copy. I shakily took it and studied the typed script.

'Well?' said Nigel, eagerly trying to catch a glimpse of the new SFO Team List.

I smiled. 'Black Team, with you!'

'Oh, nice one!' He grinned, slapping my shoulder. 'Who else we got?'

I scanned the sheet. 'Oh, that's not too bad,' I said conspiratorially. 'Just one bloke I don't know. We've got quite a few of the old Black Team with us, And John's been made acting guvnor.' I thought back to the days at Croydon, and the little sergeant I'd met there. 'We've got Mario.' And his Death Before Breakfast tattoo, I thought. 'Big Joe (his scrotum now intact), Brad –' a balding ex-Para whose pipe never left his mouth; while on Level Two he had been the first man in the department to shoot a blagger with an MP5; Brad was also extremely fit (despite his smoking) and was one of the teams Physical Training instructors – 'Ninja Nick – ' a short, strong, black-belt karate instructor from the old White Team, who despite his abilities was as quiet as they came – and Chris.' I groaned at the mention of his name, knowing we were bound to have words. I pointed at a name on the list. 'He's the one I don't know.'

'Yeah,' said Nigel. 'You must have seen him about. He's a Level One instructor – tall, dark-haired bloke.'

I thought carefully. 'Does he instruct at Croydon?'

'Yeah, that's the one,' he replied.

'What's he like?'

'He's sound. Been on quite a few of the big jobs. He was with Tony at the abattoir. Very experienced. The blokes nicknamed him "Sinex".'

'Why?' I asked.

Nigel grinned. 'Because when he gets up your nose he lasts for eight hours.'

Secretly I was quite pleased. It was evident that the cliques on Level One had pulled some strokes, with their teams remaining practically unchanged. Apart from Sinex, and a recently pro- moted Brad, we were all ex-Level Two.

So it was that a young and virtually inexperienced Black Team was born. But I wouldn't have had it any other way, for over the years we would certainly stamp our mark!

The rag-tag army eyed each other cautiously as I shuffled the team list.

'OK, fellas,' I announced. 'As it's the first day, we'll have a team meeting, get to know each other and sort out some responsibilities.'

'But we already know each other,' Chris barked. He was right. In essence, apart from Sinex, Nigel, Ninja and me, it was the same old Black Team. Even John with his new role had been the team leader. He now sat, watching how I would handle the situation. As a liaison between the department and any outside agencies, the day-to-day planning and running of the team was strictly down to the sergeant.

Well aware that Chris had enjoyed his place in the pecking order, I smiled pleasantly. It was imperative that I gain the confidence and respect of all of them. 'Look, lads, I'll make no bones about it. Yes, I'm new to this job, but I earned a place here the same way as you!' they nodded in response. 'I know a lot of you have been on jobs where it's all come on top, and it's that experience I'll be relying on. I don't profess to know everything, and rank certainly doesn't assume knowledge. Anyone who thinks they have the monopoly on tactics is a fucking liar. If I don't know something, I'll ask. All I promise you is that I won't ask you to do something I wouldn't do myself, OK?'

They nodded. Speech over, we got down to business and the day-to-day management of our lives. I'd never experienced anything remotely like this, and now that I found myself in the exalted position of team leader, it struck me that it was no simple task. I'd always assumed it would be quite easy – turn up at a job, bish bash bosh, do the business, write some notes and ride off into the sunset leaving the locals to clear up the mess. I was wrong!

Apart from the individual responsibilities – such as loading the ladders, first-aid kits, MOE equipment, guns, distraction and pyrotechnic devices, abseil kit, ballistic shield and anything else we may need in the course of our work – there were other roles to fulfil, such as the appointing of a team medic (Mario volunteered happily after Sinex informed us he had once been threatened not to help a wounded team member), a sniper (this job did fall to Sinex, as the only one qualified to use a Heckler & Koch 93 .223 rifle), MOE (this originally went to Brad and Chris), and a stick man (Big Joe was the obvious choice, having already broken the arm of a maniac who had foolishly attacked the team with a Samurai sword).

The other question was what to do with a team of men when we hit a slack period and had no role to fulfil. A training programme was devised. As a Physical Training instructor, the responsibility for PE and classification shoots went to Nigel. Tactical training was to be undertaken by Sinex and Brad. By the end of the day we were sorted. We were an SFO team, and we were standing by, vehicles loaded and ready to go. Now all we had to do was wait . . . and wait . . . and wait!

'Dave, Dave. It's Don,' called the negotiator, ringing the bell of the first-floor flat in Feltham.

'Go away. Go away, back off, *now*!' came the muffled maniacal scream from within. 'You hear me? *now*!'

Don rang again. 'Dave, who you shouting at?'

A demented cry: 'Your officers out the front. Back them off and get them out. I know what's going to happen – you're going to nick me because of what I've got in my hand.'

'What you got, Dave? Whatever it is, just put it down,' Don said calmly.

'*Nooo*!' A high-pitched wail. 'I've got a forty-five Magnum, and I'm going to fucking use it on myself.'

'Dave, please don't do that. That's not going to solve any-thing.'

At the RVP I ran through my options. Sure, John was present, and I guessed it was to lend a guiding hand, should one be required, But by now we both knew the score. It was my ball game, and I was holding the ball.

Dave, a middle-aged man deserted by his wife and child, had turned to drink. He lived in a small first-floor flat in a thriving council estate surrounded by tower blocks. In a moment of des-pair, he had foolishly pointed a handgun at other residents from his balcony. Police were called in an attempt to make contact, and in the hour that followed a siege had quickly developed. Arriv-ing swiftly on the scene, the ARVs had set up a control point and established a containment. In consultation with the local senior management, they had requested the presence of a team. In the meantime, however, the dreaded negotiators had arrived.

I scanned the estate and the large grassed area. 'Fucking hell, John,' I muttered, 'look at all that open ground. From where he is he has a commanding view of the whole estate across the open ground!'

He pointed to a balcony in the tower block opposite. 'Yeah, that's his balcony up there. What do you think?'

I squinted. 'Well, on the surface, it looks like we can operate a forward control [a control point purely for the team within the 'sterile' cordon] from above. That way, if the shit hits the fan, we can fast rope down on to his balcony.' I groaned inwardly. Why had I said that?

John shook his head. 'While you were at the RV, I've studied it.' He passed me his binoculars. 'Take a closer look!'

I concentrated. 'Bollocks. Chicken wire.' In an effort to deny pigeons access to his balcony, Dave had erected a makeshift barricade. In doing so he had unwittingly fucked up our options. But by the same token we were known for our ingenuity, and it really mattered little.

'Steve, some of Orange Team have turned up. What the fuck do they want?' snarled Chris, clearly pissed off. 'We can handle this on our own. It's only one fucking bloke.'

I nodded. He was right. But as a team leader I had a duty to maintain the fragile peace between the teams, and that meant diplomacy – something that didn't really figure that high in my vocabulary.

I nodded at them as they strolled over. 'All right fellas?'

'Yeah,' said Paul, an old Level One sweat. 'What you got?'

I ran through the story.

'Anything we can do?' he asked.

'Possibly. I reckon we'll probably hit the door, providing it's not fortified. Balcony could be a secondary option, but I'll know more when I've had a good look.' I pointed to the open expanse. 'The thing that bothers me is the open ground. It's impossible to evacuate everybody. And if he starts shooting from the balcony his rounds could end up anywhere, especially since it's a forty-five.'

Paul thought about this. 'We're in an armoured Land Rover. How about putting that out back? With a ladder inside we could drive across, put it on the roof giving us extra height, and make the balcony easily.'

I thought it through. 'Yeah, good idea – but containment only. Black Team will hit the building as and when.'

He smiled, slightly dejected. 'Sure. It's your ball game.'

'You got a ninety-three?' I asked.

'Yes – why?'

I pointed up at the tower block across the grass. 'See if you can get a sniper option from up there. If he does come out shooting we can slot him before he knows it.'

'Right,' he said, breaking towards the van.

Once Paul was in a position to cover our approach, I made certain that contact was made with Dave at the front door. Sprinting across the open ground, we darted into the dimly lit stairwell of the target block. Inside, the ground floor was a hive of activity. Uniformed officers with shields mingled with the negotiators and control. In one corner stood a huddle of senior officers, deep in conversation. Stopping, they looked up sharply as the team swept in, bristling with weapons. John strode purposefully over. He was their liaison, their tactical advisor and their saviour. The look of relief on their faces was something I would witness hundreds of times in the years that followed.

Grabbing Chris and Joe I made my way swiftly up the stairs. Touching the containment (inner armed cordon) man lightly on the shoulder, I stared down the hall at the two negotiators outside the flat.

'For fuck's sake,' I hissed, 'he's supposed to have a forty-five, and they're not even wearing body armour.' I shook my head. 'When will they ever learn?'

'I'm sorry, Sarge, we don't carry any spare.' The containment man seemed to take the slur personally.

'I'm not blaming you,' I said calmly, 'but this is a firearms situation, and it's our duty to protect these blokes whether they like it or not!' I glanced across the landing. 'What's that door directly opposite his flat?'

'It's a neighbour's flat, Sarge,' he stammered. 'The woman inside is just putting on a brew.'

I sighed in despair. 'You mean we've even got members of the public in a sterile area, and they're making the fucking tea?'

He nodded glumly.

'Joe,' I snapped, 'get downstairs, pick up the long shield. And see if you can't get some body armour for those two fucking heroes.'

Tapping my shoulder he sprinted off, his long legs taking the stairs three at a time.

Evacuating the charlady was easy. We made our way to her flat, covered the door with the large, heavy shield, and took hold of her. Sinex swept her down the corridor to the safety of the cordon.

With the negotiators in body armour and behind the relative

safety of the shield and a team standing to, I felt slightly more comfortable. Utilizing the empty flat to its full potential as a forward holding area, I posted a three-man stick in the hall and, reclining on the sofa with a cup of coffee, mentally ran through the options again. Initially, all we had to do was wait – and that was certainly something we were good at!

'Back them off. Tell them to go away,' Dave snivelled from behind the security of his door. 'Or all you're gonna hear is one loud bang.'

'Please don't do that, Dave,' the negotiator said pleasantly.

I smiled. It was funny in a way – here we were, both in the same job, trained to the highest standards, but with totally different ways of tackling a task. The negotiators were chatting quietly away with an armed and clearly totally deranged suspect. Their ideal solution was a peaceful surrender. I, on the other hand, was like a Rottweiler straining at the leash. All I wanted to do was storm in there and rip the little shit's head off!

Click. It was a sound I'd heard hundreds of times in the past. Leaping from the settee, I drew my Glock in one single movement. Grabbing the body armour of the man in front, I tagged on the end of the team, who were poised to react.

'You want to hear it?' Dave screamed. 'The gun's cocked. Back 'em off.'

'Standby, standby,' I whispered into the net.

'Dave, Dave,' the negotiator said, 'I have no control over what's going on outside.' He was referring to the sound of movement downstairs.

'*GO AWAY AND FUCKING DO IT!*' he screamed insanely. 'I know you're going to nick me for what I've got in my hand.'

'We don't want to nick you, Dave. We're here to help. I've even put out a message for your wife to come here. Would you like that, Dave?'

Click. 'I'm warning you! I just want my son to remember me as he always knew me. *NOW I AM GOING TO BLOW MY FUCKING BRAINS OUT!*'

Tensing, I saw Joe raise the ram. This could well be it. Things had certainly reached a crescendo. Then, as suddenly as the situation had peaked, it hit a trough.

'My son knew I had a drink problem,' Dave wailed. Then, calmly: 'Who you got out there now?'

'Nobody,' the negotiator said, winking at Joe. 'Just one of my men. Now come on, Dave. We both have children . . .'

'Just *ONE*!' He screamed the 'one'. 'I've even tried to save my marriage by dropping the charges against her brother. He hit me over the head.' He was totally confused. 'I've got twenty fucking stitches.'

'Come on, Dave.' The negotiator tried a new tack. 'That could be why you're acting like this. Why not come out and talk to me – face to face?'

Click, click.

The negotiators had certainly defused the situation for the moment, but how long would the fragile peace last? And with the ominous cocking of the hammer, I was far from happy. Dropping back slightly, I raised John on the net. He agreed that, due to the unpredictable behaviour of the man, half the team should stand to at all times, swapping over at hourly intervals.

And it was like this that the day dragged on.

'Who's with you now?' he called for the umpteenth time.

'Joe. Joe is with me.'

'Yeah. With a gun.'

'No. Joe isn't holding a gun.' The negotiator eyed the protective shield.

'Well, if you promise me that there's nobody out there with a gun, I'll let you in to talk.'

From the safety of our room I looked towards Chris and nodded, and picking up our kit we glided silently into the hall.

'Look, Dave – the negotiator sounded thoughtful – 'you're telling me you've got a Magnum in there with you. If it's a real one – '

'I don't know if it's a fucking real one!' Dave interrupted. 'All I know is it fires and it goes bang and everything else . . .'

'Well, whose gun is it?'

'My mate's. He does rodeos and all that sort of thing.'

I raised my eyebrows. It was obvious to me that he was definitely a fucking fruit bat. But they are often the most unpredictable.

'You can come in. I'm not going to shoot you,' he sobbed. 'My word of honour. But just you – nobody else!'

I shook my head.

'I'm sorry, Dave, I can't do that,' the negotiator apologized. 'Not while you have that gun in there with you!'

'I've taken some tablets I found,' he sighed. He was breathing heavily.

'Why, Dave? Is it for the pain – the one in your head? If you want I can get you a doctor – '

'*NOOO!*' he shrieked like an animal in pain, then calmed a little. 'If I throw the gun out, will you come in?' he pleaded.

'Yes, Dave. I will.' The negotiator spoke softly. 'Now, poke it out through the letterbox.'

I shook my head sharply, tapping him on the shoulder. All we needed now was a nutter poking a Magnum through the letterbox.

'*NO!*' he called sharply, changing his mind. 'I'm gonna open the door. At the moment I don't give a shit if they do open up on me.'

It was a classic scenario, common in the States and one we'd all come across in training: 'Death by Cop'. Many situations had developed in the past where so-called 'suicidal' suspects, unable to do the deed themselves, came running out brandishing a firearm. The rest is history. Now I was becoming deeply concerned by Dave's attitude.

'Please don't do that, Dave!'

'*WHY?*'

'Because if you come out of that door with a gun in your hand you'll frighten the shit out of me. That's why!' He mopped his brow.

The minutes turned into hours, punctuated by constant toing and froing as the team changed over. Only Joe chose to stand his ground and remain in situ for most of the afternoon, as the negotiators went about their unenviable task.

Click click.

'I'm warning you. I'm out of it. Out of my head on drugs,' Dave slurred.

After three and a half hours the situation had worsened.

Calling John on the net I needed a decision from the powers that be – if the moment was right, could we go?

'I know you're going to slap me in irons,' Dave continued, almost comically.

I smiled.

'No Dave,' the negotiator called, 'we won't slap you in irons. The first person you'll see is a doctor.'

'No, I thought to myself, the first person he'll *need* is a doctor.

'They'll section me!' he screamed. 'Because I hung myself in hospital. *UURRGGGH!*'

I'm no doctor, but it was now apparent that his mental state was rapidly declining. Like a cornered and wounded animal he was now at his most dangerous. I whispered to Chris, 'If I give the go, hit him and hit him hard. Cut down his reaction time.'

Dave screamed: 'I want to talk to one person and one person only. Anyone comes through that door and I'll fucking blow them away!'

'Calm down, Dave. We're here to help you.'

'*NAARRGGH!* I can't cope with any treatment without my wife.'

Click, click, click.

'You know what I've got in my hand? *NAARRGGH!* A forty-five. Now all I want is my wife – *BACK HERE NOW!*'

'You don't sound too well to me, you know, Dave. Have you been taking any more pills?' the negotiator asked anxiously.

'I've taken loads. But don't worry about it. *Forget it!* Now, I want my wife, and I want her here – *NOW!*'

'Sorry it's taken so long, Dave, but we're still trying to trace her.'

I certainly had to admire this man's endurance in keeping up the dialogue. Because sitting there on the settee sipping coffee I was getting extremely pissed off.

Click.

'Now come on, Dave. Please stop playing with that thing. You're making me very nervous.'

'But I love my wife,' he whined. 'I love my son!' He paused. 'The mood I'm in I'm gonna come out of here blazing.'

'Now, please, please don't do that, Dave.' The negotiator's hitherto calm exterior was beginning to crack He looked down at our weapons, knowing full well that any conflict would be a one-sided story.

'I'm going to do it! I couldn't give a monkey's who's out there!'

'Calm down, Dave, please! You don't mean me any harm – or Joe – do you?'

Joe grinned maniacally as the negotiator looked down at the ram by his feet.

'Now we're not going to start smashing down doors, or anything you see on television,' he added seriously.

I sniffed and looked at my watch. 'Bloody hell. Four hours, and I already smell like a Turkish wrestler's jockstrap,' I muttered, pulling at my sodden coveralls. 'How much longer?'

'Don't worry,' Chris drawled, 'we've been on overs for two hours.'

Nodding, I relaxed; overtime was certainly one consolation. 'I heard a rumour the other day,' I said, breaking the ice.

'Oh yeah?'

'Yeah. One of the old Black Team guys said you and John don't get on.'

He grinned. 'John's fine,' he said. 'But I upset him once – and that was it'.

'Oh,' I said, intrigued but not wanting to pry; they both seemed to have a good working relationship and that was enough for me. John was the acting guvnor and that was it.

'It's nothing really,' Chris said, opening up in his southern drawl. 'You remember we met at Croydon?'

I nodded.

'Well, John's into hunting and shooting, all that sort of shit. He's got a couple of gun dogs that never leave his side, travel everywhere with him.'

I cocked my ear as Dave screamed something unintelligible from behind the door. Then Chris continued: 'John used to instruct at Croydon range, bring his dogs to work and leave them in the car in the nick's multi-storey.' I nodded, remembering the layout exactly.

'Well, one day he comes to work and can only find a spot on the roof.' Chris smiled as he picked up the threads. 'Come lunchtime he goes up and lets them out, throwing a ball for them to fetch.

Anyway, on this occasion he threw it too hard. The ball went straight over the parapet with the dog in tow!'

'Fuck's sake,' I hissed. 'That's terrible. But why does he blame you?'

A smile cracked his features. 'He don't blame me for that – but when he came in the next day he was well upset. I'd heard the story, and I tried to cheer him up.' I grinned. 'What did you say?'

'I asked him if the dog bounced back up. "How could it bounce back up? It was fucking dead," he scowled. "Oh, sorry," I replied. "I thought it was a Springer!"'

I laughed. 'I hope you never try to cheer me up.'

'I'll talk to you, but only with this in my hand,' Dave now sobbed. 'I've lost my wife – everything – so what the *fuck* have I got to live for?'

'Dave, I can see that you're getting upset in there.'

'No, I'm not getting upset. I'm getting fucking *FURIOUS*! Now where is my wife? I don't even know if this fucking thing in my hand will do it!'

I frowned. For the first time that day it dawned on me that perhaps the gun may not be real. I quickly pushed that dangerous thought to the back of my mind. Too many American officers had died through hesitation; we'd learnt that in the States and Canada villains had taken to painting their weapons in fluorescent pinks, greens and yellows, in order to get the cops to hesitate, thinking they were plastic toys. That hesitation could often prove fatal.

As the drama continued to unfold I became increasingly bored with Dave's incessant babbling.

'They'll section me,' he wailed again.

'Why should they do that?'

'I hung myself in a fucking hospital! *Do you want it in fucking writing?*'

I sniggered, hardly able to contain myself. I desperately wanted to shout, 'Well, you could have made a better job of it!'

Dave continued to ramble, holding conversation with himself. 'I don't want anybody interfering,' he said. 'I thought you was fucking proud of me . . .'

BOOOM! The negotiator dived for cover. 'Fucking hell!' My

heart missed a beat as the loud report echoed along the corridor. I dived off the settee, spilling coffee.

As calm as ever, Big Joe nodded. He was ready. Punching my PTT, I whispered into the radio: 'One shot. One shot from inside the premises. No casualties. Over!'

'I thought you was proud of me when I kicked open the door of that burning building,' Dave moaned. 'Then she goes and has a fit when I threw a burnt curry in the sink!' He was obviously losing it – if he ever had it in the first place. Now he was making little sense at all.

'Dave, was that your gun?'

Sobs. 'Why?'

'Because you're scaring me, that's why.' He sounded convincing.

'My head hurts,' Dave sobbed uncontrollably. 'My head hurts.'

'Dave' – urgently – 'Dave, I'm here to help you.'

'But I can't stand the pain!'

'Dave, there's a doctor out here. He wants to help. He's not a mental one either!'

Thank God, I thought. There's enough mental people up here at the minute!

'I will talk to my wife, and only my wife!' he screamed.

'All right, Dave. Bear with me please, and I'll see what's going on.'

'Fuck this,' Joe whispered, propping the shield against Dave's door. 'I've been standing here for four fucking hours.'

I looked at my watch. 'More like five – but you volunteered.'

'Yeah, well bollocks to him,' he said defiantly. 'I'm having a cup of tea.'

From the comfort of the settee I sat and watched.

KNOCK, KNOCK, KNOCK!

I froze as Dave tapped on the door. Placing a finger to my lips I motioned for silence as the mumblings from within were replaced by heavy breathing. With no movement in the hall it sounded as if he had pressed his ear to the door in an attempt to listen.

'Hello?' Whispered.

I suppressed a chuckle.

'Hello?' In his deranged state it now appeared that he thought we'd all gone home and left him. *One, two,* I motioned with my fingers. Chris and Joe nodded and made quietly for the door. I could hear faint sobs.

'He's at the balcony at the back,' the radio crackled.

'Oi! Get out of that vehicle *now!*' Dave screamed at the armoured Land Rover parked on the wasteground at the rear.

'Don't shoot him,' said the negotiator from the comfort of his chair.

'*NOW, NOW, NOW!*' Dave was frantic.

'I have visual.' This was the detached voice of the sniper in the tower block opposite. 'He's on the balcony and he's very agitated.'

'Fuck,' I sighed. The last thing we needed now was for him to open up from the balcony.

'Ring the bell, ring the bell,' Joe hissed to the negotiator, conscious of the need to get him back into the flat.

Ding dong, ding dong.

'*WHAT?*' Now he was back at the door. 'You've got a vehicle out there. I told you to clear off!' *Click.* 'Ohh,' he wailed. 'I don't want all of this. I know you're going to do me!'

'Nobody's going to do anything, Dave.'

'*OOWWW!*'

'Dave, Dave,' more urgently. 'Are you all right?'

'*NOO!* I am not fucking all right. I'm bleeding like a stuck pig!'

Once again I stifled the urge to laugh as I looked at the grinning face of Joe.

'This is your fault! There's a law vehicle out back, and I've just ripped my fucking stitches open,' he groaned.

'How, Dave? How did you do that?'

'The window. The window came open straight down on me fucking head. It's split all me stitches open!'

Cupping my face in my hands, I slowly shook my head. In his haste to shout at the Land Rover outside, Dave had pulled at the window. Opening fiercely, it had crashed down on his head.

'Blood's pouring out! Now I want that vehicle moved. I've hurt my head!'

'Look, Dave, why not let me get you that doctor?'

'*NOO!*' He laughed hysterically. 'I want my wife!'

Click, click.

'Standby.'

'I'm going to the window again. *GET OUT! MOVE, MOVE!*'

'Get him away from that window,' I hissed, knowing that was where he was at his most dangerous.

'Dave, Dave,' the negotiator said frantically. 'Dave, please!'

'BACK OFF, BACK OFF! NOW!'

Darkness was falling. If things didn't start happening soon we'd have to think about calling in another team. Looking round I saw the lads were in high spirits, probably because the mercenary bastards were earning. But we could only keep it up for so long without some proper rest. 'Look, we really have to do something to end this,' I called to John. 'What's going on your end?'

'Standby. Just waiting for a decision, but the pressure's on. He could be in there for ever!'

'He *has* fucking been in there for ever,' I muttered.

SMASH! The sound of breaking glass from within. *'Now.* You've only got seconds.'

'Dave, please don't threaten those men outside,' the negotiator called, clearly conscious that somewhere out there was a sniper. We had never actually told the negotiators of our plan or our tactics, but they knew basically how we would operate. Because they had built up such a close rapport with the suspect, if they knew an attack was imminent they could inadvertently let him know. That's why our controls were kept totally separate.

I jumped as the letterbox suddenly snapped open and the small dark barrel of a gun appeared. Using the shield, Joe closed it down in an instant.

'Dave, please don't wave that thing through the letterbox,' the negotiator called from down the hall.

'My head,' he groaned. *'AARRRGGGHHH!* My head!'

'Look, Dave, my throat's a bit sore. I could really do with a cup of tea.'

'Oh, yeah, you could probably make me one too. No! No, *go away!*'

The frustration in us all was clearly evident. Over the past five or six hours I had witnessed Dave going rapidly downhill. Now, not knowing how badly he was injured, we had to act. He was clearly deranged and bordering on incoherency. 'John, we

103

need that motor out back moved, I called down the net. Three minutes later it was gone.

'OK, Dave. As a token of goodwill I've had the vehicle moved,' the negotiator called. 'Look out of the window, but don't wave the gun. Has it gone?'

'*YESSS!*' A victorious shout.

Click, click, click.

'Dave, please don't click that gun.'

'Why not? There's only two rounds in it!'

Five minutes later the negotiator tried a different tack. 'Dave, I've got some good news for you,' he said, raising his eyebrows. 'Your wife's here, she wants to talk to you. If I go and get her will you speak to her?'

'Course I will.'

'OK, Dave, but she may be a little frightened. Just hang on and I'll go and speak to her!' He retreated down the corridor.

'I'm fucking fed up with this arsehole,' Joe stormed. 'Where's the fucking tea?'

'No milk.' Sinex grinned at Joe's bulky frame. For the duration, Joe had stood by the door looking after the negotiator. And it was now apparent that Dave was not top of his Christmas present list.

'Hello?' Dave whispered. 'Hello?'

We waited silently. Then we heard a metallic scrape as the security chain was drawn back.

'Fucking hell,' I whispered. 'He thinks we've all pissed off.' Chris and Joe were ready.

Clunk: The handle turned and the door opened a fraction. The gun barrel was clearly visible from our vantage point across the hall.

CRAAASSH! Joe's sixteen stone, bolstered by an additional four stone of assault kit, hit the door at terminal velocity.

'*AARRGGHHH!*' The bewildered suspect, already in pain, collected it in the gob as he flew backwards through the air into a glass display cabinet of crystal ornaments. *SMAASSH!* The cabinet toppled and shards of glass cascaded across the floor, settling in heaps on the carpet. Chris and I followed the momentum. *SMASH! WHACK! WHACK!*

'*ARRGGH!*'

Joe jammed his thumb behind the gun's hammer as Chris

grasped the cylinder. All four of us were rolling around the room. Grabbing the barrel I swung it wildly in an attempt to break Dave's grip.

'Pressure points, pressure points,' Brad screamed from the door.

'Drop the fucking gun,' Joe screamed at the hapless suspect.

Dave stared into Joe's fearsome eyes.

'Drop that fucking gun or I'll break your fucking head!'

'Standby, standby,' called John's familiar voice from the hall. Dusting myself down I looked at the pathetic form spreadeagled on the floor. It had been over in seconds. Picking up the gun, I examined it warily. 'Fucking replica,' I moaned, tossing it on the settee. Joe and Chris grinned. 'Dunno what you're so fucking happy about,' I smiled. 'You're doing the statements!'

'Listen in lads,' came a quiet, authoritative voice with a mild Scottish accent. Looking up, I studied the man, taking in his long, fair, matted hair and beard. Wearing a donkey jacket and tattered jeans, he far from resembled the archetypal image of a detective sergeant on the Regional Crime Squad. In fact, stick a tin of Tennents in his hand and he would more than resemble the type of down-and-out you'd expect to find in this part of Deptford.

In the couple of weeks that had followed the Feltham siege we were inundated with work. So the phone call we received at the end of that period had sounded more than promising. Now the buzz of conversation dimmed as the lads seemed to sense a good job in the offing.

'Before the boss comes in,' the DS continued, 'I'll give you a run-down on what's happening. At the moment we are running a long-term operation codenamed Emerge. Now we don't have a problem with you guys, but because of the total need for security I must ask you not to discuss this outside these walls.' He was right. Although we worked most of the time in plain clothes we were still considered by many of the squads as Woodies (Woodentops). But because we were never involved in any investigative role we were sound and we knew it. Unlike many of the squads that court the press and leak information like sieves, we always closed ranks, never discussing one squad's jobs with another. To put it mildly, I didn't altogether trust them!

'You may have a bit of a problem there, Mike,' I piped up. 'You know the way our department likes to work. If this job runs long-term I can't guarantee you'll always have the same team. In fact, that's highly unlikely – and as they like to share the workload around it's inevitable more people will hear of it.'

He smiled. 'Don't worry, it'll be squared at the highest level, believe me.' The tone in his voice convinced me. He continued. 'At the moment we're expecting a very large consignment of drugs to be delivered to one, possibly two slaughters. Could you handle that?'

'Slaughters' were villains' secure premises, where drugs, bonded loads or hijacked lorries could be safely divided up and moved on. They were often fortified. I took a sharp intake of breath. 'Depends on the plot.'

'Yeah. I know you guys always like to see the ground, but I'm afraid this time, fellas, it's not on. Both plots are extremely Zulu. But we do have aerial photos, drawings and plans in the highest detail. We'll deliver you right on to the plot. All we ask then is that you do what you do best!'

From the little information we'd received it was evident they were playing their cards close to their chests. That was more than OK by me, because it certainly wouldn't change the way we dealt with things, and if I was to be asked at a later date in court any specifics, I could honestly put my hand on my heart and say 'I don't know'. After all, we were nothing more than a support service, brought in at the last minute to activate the plan.

Mike continued. 'We know that this particular gang is involved in the importation of drugs from South America. Some members are also believed to be involved in contract killings.' My ears pricked up. 'We think that two of these guys went to the continent to carry out a hit on a rival dealer in Amsterdam. The shooter confronted him on the street and whacked him with a twenty-two. Unfortunately for him the guy was wearing body armour. He got up from the ground and blew him away with a forty-five. The driver left him in a car at Calais and got the ferry back.' We laughed. 'Lads, these are good South London villains. Make no bones about that!'

He was right. Over the years the teams had crossed paths with numerous robbery gangs from this part of London. Always well tooled up, they never seemed to hesitate when it came to having a go, and if that meant shooting at the police, then so be it. Eventually it got to the stage where so many of them had been dealt with on the plot that they were dubbed 'The Bermondsey School of Armed Robbers'!

When Mike had left we studied the plans. 'They might be good,' Sinex said. 'But I hate going in without at least one of the team seeing the plot.'

I nodded. 'Perhaps we can have a late-night CTR. Trouble is we don't know what facilities the lads here have got. And if we showed up on a video poking our nose around, it might just blow the whole job – and wouldn't do our reputation a lot of good either. No, the best we can hope for is a quick look-see before the hit.'

Mario picked a photo out of the file, depicting some heavy steel doors. 'Fucking hell. How do we get through these?'

'How about the angle grinder?' asked Ninja.

'No good.' Sinex shook his head. 'Take too long, and we'll be well on offer.' I had to agree. Using the angle grinder was quick enough but it took a lot of setting up, with the user being assigned a cover man. That would deplete our small force even further. The other drawback was it was heavy and unwieldy.

For the next five minutes we huddled down and held a Chinese Parliament, with everybody chucking in their ten pennorth. Eventually we decided that if it did come off today we'd have no option but to drive a Range Rover through the shutters and worry about the consequences later (fully armoured with upgraded brakes and re-bored engines, they cost the firm about a hundred grand each; and the commissioner didn't take kindly to anyone wrecking his vehicles).

The DI entered, cellphone in one hand, pager in the other. 'Sorry, guys,' he said apologetically. 'The gear's still at the other end. It's a stand down for today, I'm afraid.'

After the initial euphoria of the briefing we felt suddenly quite deflated. 'Will you need us tomorrow, guv?' I asked hopefully. 'Dunno, Steve – but I've got your pager number. Black Team, isn't it?'

I nodded.

'Sorted!' he said.

*   *   *

'You're getting the new guvnor,' John moaned.

'When?'

'He's here already.'

'Well, what's going to happen to you?'

'Don't worry, I'll be with you for a while yet. He's shadowing me for six months.'

Beep, beep, beep.

I rolled over in bed.

Beep, beep, beep.

'Shit.' Turning on the bedside lamp, I shielded my eyes against the intense white light. I shut the pager off and stared at the small fluorescent screen. 'U101.' An innocuous enough message, but one that meant a great deal to me. This was the code to get to the base – yesterday! Running a toothbrush round my mouth I stared at the dishevelled face in the mirror. There was no doubt about it, the drinking and the hours were certainly taking their toll. Dipping my head in the sink I damped down my hair, then looked at the clock. Two-fifteen. Even though we were on call it must be serious if the ARVs couldn't handle it. I pulled on my jeans. Better check in first.

Dialling the number from memory, I was immediately met with the engaged tone. 'Shit!' Only on the third attempt was I greeted with a harassed reply.

'SO19.'

'Yeah, Steve Collins.'

'Sarge, there's a big siege going down in Harlesden. PC shot. One dead. Squaddie with automatic weapons. Black Team's been called in!'

I shook the wooliness from my head and remembered I'd given Brad and Nigel the night off. 'I'm down to five men.'

'No worries, Sarge. You've got Big Len and Phil from Blue.'

'Cheers.'

'Do you need a fast run?'

'Nah, by the time they get here I'll be well on my way. Nothing about this time of the morning. See you in twenty-five, thirty max.'

I dived into my car and roared off into the night, knowing that from the time I'd received the message I was effectively on duty. This seige sounded serious, and it was only a month since the fiasco with Dave!

The countryside rolled past. (I'd chosen to live in Surrey rather than London itself.) Dropping down a gear, I accelerated through the amber light and towards town.

WAHHH! Glancing in my rear-view mirror, I saw a cluster of blue lights. 'Balls.' Pulling over, I quickly dug out my warrant card as I stepped from the car.

'Where's the fire, Stirling?' said the young Surrey plod standing in my way.

I eyed him thoughtfully and bit my tongue. 'I'm Sergeant Collins, Met Firearms Unit, on an urgent call-out,' I said, showing my warrant card. 'If you don't believe it, phone the Yard or check the motor, it's blocked. But I'm on my way.'

Taken aback, he said, 'Oh. Oh, sorry, sir.'

'You don't have to call me 'sir', son. I'm only a sergeant.'

He regained his composure. 'In that case, can I give you an escort to the border?'

I nodded towards his clapped-out old Astra. 'Sorry, mate, don't think you'd keep up!'

The yard resembled a battlefield. Bits of kit littered the tarmac as the team worked furiously, checking off the gear we would need for a full-blown assault.

'You all right up there?' I called to Joe as I climbed out of the car.

'No, I fucking ain't,' he shouted, teetering on top of the van and strapping down the ladders. 'Where the fuck's Brad? This is his job!'

'He's off tonight.' I smiled as Joe muttered to himself. Team nicknames were fast becoming the fashion. Apart from Sinex and Ninja, I was now called 'Dolph', a name which I'd awarded myself, due to my uncanny resemblance to the tall, blond, good-looking movie star Dolph Lundgren. And, besides, I was the sergeant!

We moved off. Andy, the new guvnor, rode up front with John, who by now had ditched his sergeant's stripes and taken to wearing pips and calling himself 'Inspector'. We followed behind. By this time Chris had become my unofficial driver. I now found I enjoyed his company, and that he, I and Joe had formed a firm bond of friendship. Over the preceding few months I'd come to realize that my first impressions of him as a brash, humourless Bastard were totally unfounded. In reality it was nothing more than a façade behind which he hid his true identity. A devoted father of two children, he was also a professional in every sense of the word and, as he confided in me one day, a veteran of a number of shooting incidents.

Including Brad's.

Chris told me the story of what had happened. The crew room had buzzed with conversation that cold morning. Chris, Brad and Mario formed the nucleus of the old Level Two Black Team. Even in those days they had a reputation for getting the job done whatever the cost. On this occasion they were joined by Bob, a smart, good-looking guy with a droopy moustache who, whenever he passed a mirror, never let the opportunity slide to check out his reflection or groom his hair. Bob's good friend and drinking companion was Big Steve, who, with his large and powerful frame and broken nose, looked every inch the ex-Tank Regiment boxing champion. Lastly there was 'Mad Dog', so called because of his deeply penetrating, wildly staring eyes.

The previous day the team had been allocated a robbery plot. The information had apparently been so good that the job was a dead cert to come off. So much so, in fact, that when the duty Level One team learned of its existence, it was quickly reallocated, leaving Black Team out in the cold. As luck would have it, though, another job was later put up by the Flying Squad at Barnes.

Moving off to the initial briefing, the team were told that a gang of three villains with previous convictions spanning years planned to rob a sub-post office but the plot was unknown.

Deploying in pairs, the team had quickly made their way to their designated 'gunships' and left with the squad.

After about forty-five minutes, Chris had become aware of growing radio traffic from the squad's surveillance team. He sat forward and listened.

India One, Two and Three had met up as predicted and swiftly walked to a lock-up garage in the back streets of north Acton. With eyes about, they had removed the padlock from the old paint-blistered door. Inside was a stolen black Ford Escort XR3i and, much to the team's delight, they were carrying a rather heavy looking 'happy bag'. Things were beginning to shape up nicely.

Oblivious to the unseen eyes that followed, the would-be blaggers drove around looking for a plot. By now Chris knew they were game on, and that all the gunships were hurtling around, looking for a place to hide in case of a 'third eye'. The last thing they wanted now was to blow it!

In an open display of bravado, the stolen car cruised slowly around the side streets of Brentford, coming to a halt ten yards past a small corner post office. Hastily pulling on their balaclavas, the two passengers snatched up their sawn-off shot-guns, got out of the vehicle, and, along with the driver, strode purposefully towards the shop housing the post office. It was the point of no return.

'I'll never forget the big man, Alexander,' Chris told me. 'He was the main player. Nasty looking, a huge basketball type. He had a sawn-off double-barrelled shotgun. His mate was a lot smaller. His weapon, although only single-barrelled, turned out to be all the more deadly.'

With an urgency borne of despiration, the gunships quickly moved the team on to the plot.

Crashing through the door, the two gunmen made directly for the counter.

'As they went in, the attack command was given,' Chris recounted. 'Only, something out of the ordinary happened.'

Seeing the men burst in, a female shop assistant made for the telephone and quickly dialled 999. Back at New Scotland Yard's information room the entire incident was captured on tape.

'There was a small kiddie in the shop,' Chris continued. 'Outside, the three gunships fought desperately to deliver us on to the blind side of the building. On the telephone they could hear screams from inside, but no shots. With the child inside we knew it was best to get them on the way out. It was happening too fast!'

Inside, panicked by the display of aggression, the proprietor complied with the robbers' demands and was in the process of handing over a bag of cash. Chris, Bob and Mario ran towards the building wall. Brad, armed with an MP5, took up position at the corner of the shop, while Steve and Mad Dog ran and crouched behind a nearby post box.

'The screaming seemed to stop momentarily,' Chris said. 'Then all hell broke loose . . .'

In the action that immediately followed, a number of significant things were to happen. The tall man, Alexander, was first out, hitting the street fast, a sawn-off in his right hand.

'ARMED POLICE! STAND STILL!' Steve and Mad Dog yelled in unison. Moving out from behind the post box, they levelled their Smith & Wesson revolvers at Alexander's broad back. Making for the getaway car, the robber reacted to the calls, looking over his shoulder as Brad levelled his sights. In one practised action Alexander swept the sawn-off round at hip level. It was his last conscious act.

The sound of gunfire reverberated along the street, and smoke and cordite permeated the cold morning air as Steve and Mad Dog fired, their revolvers accompanied by the high-pitched *crack* of Brad's MP5.

'He was wearing a grey top,' Chris recalled. 'One minute it was clean, the next a neat red hole appeared.'

Brad's 9 mm round slammed into Alexander's back, then the slower .38 rounds also found their mark. One round hit him in the elbow, while Mad Dog's bullet shattered the back of his skull, pitching him forward into the street.

'I'll never forget that moment,' Chris recalled quietly. 'One minute he's up and running. The next he resembled a puppet with the strings cut.'

Taking in the macabre scene, the second man threw his hands up in surrender as Chris screamed out a challenge. Throwing his weapon to the pavement, he quickly dropped on top of it. Chris covered as Bob rolled him over.

'He was still in a state of shock,' Chris remembered. 'Bobby asked him if the gun was loaded, and he said it was.' (It was only during subsequent forensic examination that the weapon was found to have a hair trigger. The slightest pressure or movement could well have caused it to discharge. Amazingly, it hadn't gone off during the robbery.)

Now the scene was chaos, as squad men rushed towards the post office from all directions and the streets were blocked with their vehicles. Realizing escape was fruitless, the getaway driver had dived over a fence and was now hiding in a nearby garden. He was captured and arrested with the cash.

'By now Mario and Bob were attempting first aid,' Chris said. 'Alexander was lying face-down where he fell. Steam was rising from his head in a strange circular motion.'

Mario immediately checked his vital signs and looked for visible injuries.

'Mario pulled up his balaclava,' Chris said. 'Alexander looked really weird. He had blood running out of his eyes and was making a strange gurgling sound. Mario pulled the balaclava further over his head, and – *URGGHHH!*'

Brain, skull and tissue oozed from a gaping wound in the back of his head. A six-foot stream of blood gushed into the gutter. Replacing the hood, Mario looked around at the team and shook his head.

Once the scene was secure, the team were moved out to Brentford nick where they were met by a commander.

'What really gripped my shit,' Chris told me, 'was that he only shook hands with the guys that had slotted him. That's always been my trouble. Always the bridesmaid, never the fucking bride.'

Whacking down the A40, we arrived at the RVP in twenty-five minutes. I checked my watch – just over an hour since the initial call out. Not bad. Not bad at all.

Nicoll Road, Harlesden NW10: a grey street of Victorian semis, slap bang in the middle of the North Circular. With Wembley way off to the north-west, Acton to the south and desirable Kensington to the east, it harboured a healthy mix of nationalities, professions and religions. With their many large and airy rooms, many of the houses made ideal bedsits. This was a quiet residential area, not normally given to violence. That was about to change.

During the early hours of the morning, two uniformed police officers – twenty-six-year-old PC Royston Daniels and his partner, WPC Kim Galloway – were on routine patrol, working out of Harlesden. As a result of raised voices and sounds of a disturbance from the third-floor bedsit of number twenty-five, worried neighbours had telephoned the police. Arriving quickly on the scene, the two officers made their way swiftly upstairs. Inside was a thirty-year-old Coldsteam Guardsman, holding his girlfriend hostage. Unlike the Feltham siege, this suspect wasn't armed with a replica, but a state-of-the-art high-powered SA80 rifle, standard infantry weapon of the British Army, that he had stolen from his base.

On hearing a scream from behind the partially open door, PC Daniels had attempted entry. It was probably the last thing he remembered before waking up in the nearby Central Middlesex Hospital. *CRACK!* The loud report had echoed through the confines of the hall as the high-velocity 5.56 NATO round left the muzzle. Striking the heavy wooden door at such short range it had failed to stabilize, making it all the more deadly. As it exited the door, still tumbling, it struck PC Daniels in the arm, rocketing him back across the landing. What came next was pandemonium – screams and shouts as anxious neighbours peered from their doors cautiously, seeking the source of the commotion. WPC Galloway worked furiously on her colleague in a desperate attempt to stem the bleeding, at the same time calling for urgent assistance. With the smell of cordite hanging heavily in the air, the smoke had barely cleared when a neighbour ran to help. *CRACK!* The second round followed the first, striking the hapless victim squarely in the chest. He fell to the ground, mortally wounded.

By now reinforcements had started to arrive, and quickly set about removing both casualties to safety. Ambulance paramedics worked feverishly outside, but to no avail.

Inside, the soldier closed the door again, sat, and waited.

ARVs were swift to arrive, quickly clearing the area, establishing a cordon, and sealing off the building. For the next hour, all was quiet.

'We need to try and make contact,' Andy said.

I nodded. Over the last few weeks I'd come to like the new guvnor; he spoke a lot of sense and, like Tony and Chris, came from an SPG background. Tall and with a shock of dark hair, he had a natural air of authority about him.

'OK, guv. Negotiators are on their way, Joe is at the front – I'll give him a shout.'

Calling on the net, I was greeted by Joe's familiar voice. 'We need someone up high,' he called. 'I'm at ground level and he's upstairs.'

'OK. I'll see what I can do. Guvnor wants you to try and make contact.'

'Yeah, I'll have a go. Oh! By the way, do you know there's still seven people left in the address? They couldn't get them out in time. Apparently they're locked in their rooms.'

'Fuck,' I muttered, mentally crossing gas off as an option.

'Steve.'

I spun round, startled by the voice, and looked into the face of Sinex.

'I heard what Joe said, I've got a ninety-three in the van; I zeroed it this week. Do you want me to work through the back gardens opposite and get a sniper position?'

'Yeah. Cheers, mate,' I said, slightly flustered. There was a lot to do. With Joe and Phil – the other guy from Blue Team who'd turned up in place of Nigel – at the front, and Sinex as a sniper, I was getting thin on the ground. Andy and John were liaison, which left only myself, Chris, Ninja and Len as a four-man assault team.

Somebody passed me a cup of tea. 'Ta,' I said. From a hundred yards up the street I could quite plainly hear shouting. Inclining my head a little, I soon realized that it was Joe, holding a conversation with the suspect. He'd obviously learnt something quite significant from Dave's negotiator, because he was certainly not known for his small talk, to say the least. But in so doing he had drawn the suspect to the window where, behind the obscurity of the net curtain, he believed he was safe.

The radio crackled. 'In position directly opposite,' whispered Sinex with no hint of emotion. An ex-rifleman, this is what he'd trained for. 'I have visual into the flat. Male suspect, one female. Standby, he's coming to the window.' Inside his OP Sinex tensed, easing off the safety catch and squinting into the telescopic sights. 'I have cross hairs dead centre of his forehead if you need to end it!'

I knew that the slightest pressure on the trigger would send the deadly .223 round smashing through the man's skull in a fraction of a second, and I was all for it – but the decision wasn't mine, and the hierarchy wanted to negotiate a peaceful conclusion. If you could call one dead and one wounded 'peaceful'.

'Hold, hold,' I called softly, knowing he was professional enough to accept the decision.

From down the street Joe had worked marvels. He had struck a chord with the suspect and quickly established a good rapport, talking about everything from the armed forces to football. At the mention of this, the squaddie had confided that he was a rugby union fan. Joe realized the internationals were due to start that week, and so it was that they found common ground. Having now refined our plans for an ER and DA, we stood to at the end of the road. If the suspect now surrendered, Joe and Phil (supported by the ARVs) could deal. It was a tense moment, and I mentally checked my kit: MP5 (I tapped the mag for the hundredth time, making sure it was seated), Glock, spare mags, grenades, helmet, respirator, plate. This last item I also tapped for reassurance. Made of ceramic, the large, heavy panel was designed to fit in the front (or back, if you were running away) of your body armour, thus upgrading it even further to protect your vital organs against high-velocity rounds. Satisfied, I turned to Ninja and Len. 'Listen,' I said, beckoning them with my finger, 'this could go one of two ways, fellas.' They huddled down close. 'Firstly, Joe will bore the poor fucking bastard out, or secondly he'll top himself.'

It was five o'clock.

John came on the radio. 'I need Chris to drive the armoured Rangey. We have to get the negotiators to Joe's position, and it's the only way they can get there. Over.'

'Fucking hell, John. That'll put me down to three men,' I protested. In reality three was the ideal number for an assault on one room, but nevertheless the stakes were high on this one, and we knew full well what he and the weapon were capable of.

'Joe,' John called.

'Go, go.'

'There'll be movement in thirty seconds. Chris will be bringing negotiators to your position, Standby.'

It was at times of unexpected movement that suspects tend to get startled, and as a result they may react in an unconventional manner. So it was, that as Chris prepared to move, we resi'd up and slipped off to our FAP.

Passing without incident, twenty minutes later they had established a dialogue. (Joe later told me with pride that when a woman negotiator had butted in, the squaddie had told her to fuck off. 'I want to talk to Joe,' he'd said. 'He's the only fucker that does,' Chris quipped.

'They want a telephone,' John mumbled.

'What sort of telephone?'

'A land line. You know – a field telephone. They're fed up with shouting at him.'

'How are they going to get it?' I asked, knowing the answer.

'Don't worry. I've sorted it all out, one end can stay with their control. Chris can drive up the road feeding out the wire, and drop the other end off.' He turned. 'Chris, mount up ready to drive to the address.'

Chris nodded. Five minutes later, after shouted negotiations, the suspect finally agreed for a phone to be used.

'This has to be timed perfectly,' John said nodding a wink. 'Everybody stand by. OK, Chris, move up to the address now.'

Giving the thumbs up from behind his armoured window, Chris gunned the accelerator and pulled off into the street. Twenty seconds later his gruff voice penetrated the net. 'OK, John, I'm outside the address now. What do you want me to do?'

John looked around, bewildered. 'Put the phone outside the door. Over.'

'What phone?'

'The phone you're delivering. The one they just spent five minutes negotiating over.'

'You told me to drive to the address. Nobody mentioned a fucking phone!'

I slapped my forehead. In his haste to sort it all out, John had told everybody the plan except the driver. Three minutes later, after a return journey, the matter was resolved. But Chris was clearly pissed off.

'Too many people treat this joke like a job!' I quipped.

Negotiations continued for the next thirty minutes or so. Then, 'Standby, standby,' Joe called into the radio. 'Hostage coming out. Hostage coming out.'

Walking unsteadily on her feet, the woman emerged, dazed and shaken. Calling her towards his location, Joe pulled her to safety. It was five forty-five, and once again we were down to a 'Dave' type scenario: one man, one gun, no hostage. Over the next ninety minutes, cigarettes and chocolate bars were traded in an effort to gain his trust. The woman had by now been debriefed, and confirmed the presence of more ammunition. The whole sad incident, it transpired, had been over her leaving him!

117

By seven-thirty I was drained. The constant 'standbys', the pulling on and off of the resis, and the wearing of full kit was begining to take its toll. Rubbing my eyes, I slumped against the wall. What a way to make a living!

'Standby, standby.' That all-familiar phrase shocked me back to the situation and I found myself automatically tightening the straps on the rubber seal of the resi. 'Everybody stand to.' Now I was instantly awake, the adrenalin coursing through my veins. This was no ordinary standby; this was something different.

The radio blared loud in the confines of the resi. 'He's coming out, he's coming out. Stand to.'

Slipping the safety from my MP5, I quickly adopted a kneeling position behind the cover of an old brick wall as others around me darted to safety. I was joined by Ninja. 'Fuck off, this is my wall,' I joked.

'Bollocks,' came the muffled response.

All eyes were now on the door. I instinctively knew that Sinex would be peering through the scope and could take him with ease, should the need arise. Now it was down to Joe, who having made him place the weapon outside the door, quickly retrieved it. 'Stand still,' he screamed. 'Now, keep your hands in the air and walk slowly towards me. *NOW!*'

Suddenly he appeared, tall and upright, with a military bearing but looking dishevelled and distraught after the six-hour ordeal. With hands held high above his head, he walked slowly from the flat. Butterflies danced in the pit of my stomach as I experienced the age-old fight-or-flight syndrome. If anything were to go wrong, now would be the time.

'Now, with your hands in the air walk slowly towards me. *Slowly.*'

The squaddie complied. Making him lie spreadeagled on the ground, Joe and Phil covered as ARV men rushed to help. Once plasticuffed, he was unceremoniously bundled from the scene. Thinking it was all over, the locals started to emerge. 'Keep back!' called Andy. Yes, we had the gunman. Yes, we had the gun. But it would be totally unprofessional of us to allow unarmed officers into a building which we still considered insecure. After all, he had a firearm; he could also have had explosives. No, we wouldn't hand it over until we were satisfied it was secure, and we couldn't do that until we'd searched all the rooms. One by one.

'John,' I whispered urgently into the mike.

'Go, go.'

'Inform the containments we're moving up now. I'll link up with Joe and the dogs at the front door blind side.'

'Received. Move up now!'

The four of us darted swiftly forward, stacking up on the wall to the right of the door. I peered inside. The sight that greeted me was one of total carnage. Torn clothing, bandages, clotted blood and pieces of bone from a shattered ribcage littered the carpet.

I turned to the team. 'One man cover up the stairs, the rest of us will do a slow methodical using the dogs, and clear the ground floor.' Joe nodded. *Sluurrrp*. I felt something brush against my leg. *Sluurrrp*. The noise again. Looking down, I saw the dog. To me the whole scene resembled a butcher's shop. The dog didn't make that distinction. To him, meat was meat, and he was getting as much of it down his neck as he could. 'You dirty bastard,' I shouted, kicking the animal sharply in the ribs. Yelping, he retreated to the relative safety of his handler's legs from where he eyed me warily.

Working our way slowly through the house took a further thirty minutes, until finally we reached the target floor. More blood, more bone, more tissue. The dog skulked back as I eyed him evilly.

I examined the holes in the door, so tiny you could barely see through them. Kicking it open, it banged loudly against the wall. We entered fast, weapons high, covering each other. It was empty. Pressing down the hall, we evacuated residents as they appeared. It was hot, it was sweaty and it was unpleasant.

Finally we reached the last door. I tried the handle – locked. 'Shit,' I cursed, bracing myself. I was about to kick it open when I saw the hinges. 'It's a fucking outward opener,' I hissed. 'Who's got the hooley?'

'It's downstairs,' Joe moaned, 'I'll get it.'

'Forget it,' Len called intensely. 'I've had enough.' His huge frame tensed as he pulled back his large gloved fist. Then, like something out of a movie, he punched straight through the door. His arm disappeared up to the elbow. Grabbing it by the centre panel, he then ripped it right off its hinges before tossing it up the hall in a cloud of dust. The room was bare. 'Clear,' he announced. 'Can we go home now?'

As we packed up our gear the barriers came down and the press circus poured through. Mounting up, we drove slowly back to base, knackered. I for one couldn't wait to get back home and straight into bed. It's been a long night, I thought as I slowly drifted off.

My eyes snapped open as Chris braked heavily outside the base. 'Bastard,' I muttered, fishing in my coveralls for the keys. I pulled open the heavy metal gates. It was nine o'clock. Shit, I thought, dragging out my bergen. I'm really going to catch the traffic now.

'Get into civvies and grab some grub, fellas' John called. 'Squad job. Leave here at twelve.'

I studied his serious face. 'You're not joking, are you?'

He shook his head. 'All the other teams are out.'

'*Urrghh*.' I moaned, examining the sole of my boot. 'What's that?' I pointed to the gleaming white object trapped in the sole.

Joe looked over my shoulder, 'Looks like a lump of bone,' he said thoughtfully. 'Ribcage, I'd guess.'

'Get it out for us?' I said distastefully.

'Bollocks, I'm not touching that!'

Even though I wore those boots almost every day, the disgusting object remained stuck there for the next three weeks before I eventually lost it.

The squad job was a joke. After sitting around all day in gunships, it was eventually stood down, but not until eight o'clock. By then we'd been on duty for eighteen hours. Shooting across the road for a quick beer I decided the car could stay, besides I was too tired to drive.

My head bounced off my chest with a rhythmic rolling movement as the train rattled its way southwards. I quickly fell asleep. As the carriage slowed I looked up sharply, only to be confronted by a face I knew well. Rubbing my eyes, I tried to focus. Yep, I knew that face all right. I ought to, I'd been wearing it for thirty-five years. The businessman opposite jumped with fright as I leaned forward and pushed his paper up for a better look. There, plastered in full living colour across the front page of the *Evening Standard*, was yours truly. I cringed, and had good reason to, for next day it appeared in every national newspaper in the land.

It was four months later that Chris and Joe were suddenly pulled from a job and whisked to Isleworth Crown Court. Standing bemused in jeans and T-shirts, they were addressed by his honour Judge Colgan, who was presiding over the case of Dave and the siege at Feltham. In his summing up he concluded: 'In my view, your acts were that of bravery. The public should be grateful to have in the police force men of your calibre, and I commend you both to your superiors for the courageous way in which you performed your duties in this case. Thank you.'

Eighteen months later, in a ceremony at the Yard, both would be awarded Commissioner's Commendations for Bravery.

8

A Propensity for Violence

As things turned out, Andy was so good at the job that John was pulled off the team well before the six-month deadline. He'd always played his cards pretty close to his chest and we'd had some good times, but it came as a shock when he announced one day that he'd applied for a transfer to North Wales police. Whether the fact that he was now taking a back-seat role out of the spotlight prompted his decision, nobody asked. But Andy was now in sole charge.

We'd been over the pub one afternoon when Andy gave me a tug and quietly confessed that with his ARV commitments he'd still be relying on me to run the team with few changes. He liked the way we worked. Showing me a typewritten list, he confided that they would soon be upping the strength of the teams by one. Who did I fancy?

I glanced quickly down the list of names. 'Bill,' I said. 'No contest.'

'Good,' he smiled. 'I've already picked him'.

Bill had been with the department four years. Short and stocky with a droopy moustache, he originally came from Liverpool. An ex-Marine, he always had a story to tell, and like many extroverts on the department was a larger than life character. Like most Liverpudlians, Bill was blessed with a quick wit which constantly had you on your guard. The lads would be happy, for like Brad, Chris, Joe and Mario, Bill was ex-Level Two Black Team, and a good choice. He started the following week.

'What you got there, Bill?' I asked, peering over my copy of the *Sun* at the face of the friendly scouser.

'Oh, nothing really. Just some new lenses,' he replied matter-of-factly, plonking himself down beside me. Pulling a ballistic helmet from his bergen, he removed the protective goggles and offered up the amber replacements. 'Fucking hell, they fit,' he announced.

Putting down my coffee, I watched intently as he swapped them over.

'Have a look through these,' he said, offering me the new-look piece of kit.

Holding them up to my eyes, I quickly adjusted to the amber tint as I scanned the crew room. 'Bloody hell, they really seem to filter the light. I'll bet they're good for shooting.'

'Yeah,' said Bill, holding up his new trophy.

'Where did you get them?'

'Oh, I don't like to talk about it. From an Argie in the Falklands.'

Don't like to talk about it! I thought. We never heard anything else. I knew Bill's war from the moment he landed. Throwing stones at lifeless Argentinians to make sure they were dead before advancing. Bill had been the company armourer – or, more correctly, as he often admonished people: an engineer of death. 'What, a dead one?' I asked seriously.

'Well you don't think I'd fight a fucking live one, do you?'

The shrill ring of the phone cut through the laughter. 'Tone it down a bit, fellas,' I called, picking it up.

'Steve.' Andy's disjointed voice on the line. 'Head towards south London ASAP. Full hostage rescue kit. Sit rep to follow. This one's for real. I'll meet you there!'

Three minutes later we were mobile. *Brrpp, brrpp.* The cellular phone interrupted the shrill scream of the siren. 'Hello?' I called above the din.

'Steve. It's Andy,' he shouted from the other end. 'Orange Team are already there and kitted. But it's all coming on top. I need you there urgently!'

'Go, Chris,' I shouted, as we sped towards the nominated location.

Jamaican 'Yardies' – the notorious 'black Mafia' that infest the heavily populated ethnic areas of every major city – are cold, callous and extremely violent. When we hit them we hit them hard, leaving no avenue for escape. Living their almost nocturnal life to the full, they regularly partake in all forms of criminal activity, be it drug dealing, prostitution, torture, guns or even murder. Their strange philosophy of life is: 'If I live past thirty, it's a bonus' – such is their violent culture. Hated and feared by those around them, they demand 'respec'.

Over the past few years, more and more of these so-called posses (or gangs) have managed to secure a foothold, particularly in Brixton and the south-west of London. As such, confrontation with the police is an everyday occurrence. Knowing full well that local officers never carry guns, they have the upper hand from the start. It was only when Armed Response Vehicles started to patrol their so-called 'turf' and SFO Teams began to hit their 'flops' (safe addresses) that they began to realize we're not all the same. They respect aggression. And with us they got it. In the words of one Yardie who, when confronted by a team, surprisingly threw down his weapon. 'We don't mess with the men in Black.'

Officers from the Regional Crime Squad, backed up by SO11 surveillance, had received intelligence that a white gangster had been kidnapped on London Bridge after an ill-fated 'meet' (meeting). He owed the Yardies money, and in so doing had failed to show them 'respec'. Bundling him into a car, they had speeded off to a sprawling council estate.

An OP had hastily been established on a twelfth-floor flat. And so they watched and waited. By Monday there was still no movement inside. The powers that be decided to hit the address. It was a job for SO19!

'We'd better fucking get there before Orange Team deploy,' scowled Chris, who as always wanted to be at the forefront of any action. He kicked down the accelerator as we picked up speed.

Brrpp, Brrpp. 'Hello!' I shouted. 'Steve, it's Andy. *Get here now!* It's all gone tits up. Orange Team's out of the game!'

'Fucking hell,' Joe called from the back seat. 'They slotted someone?'

'Dunno,' I said. 'But we'll find out soon enough. It's just round the corner.'

We screeched to a halt, Chris slewing the Rangey at an angle to block the road, as I struggled to fathom what had happened. The scene before my eyes was one of total carnage.

Early-evening shoppers gathered, craning their necks in an effort to gawk. A black Granada was sitting in the offside lane, its front end smashed and 'welded' to the bonnet of our covert van. Paramedics from two ambulances anxiously worked on the still forms of bodies strewn across the road. Water pissed from the ruptured radiators, running in rusty brown streams across the tarmac. Uniformed officers held back the crowd that tried to surge forward for a better view, as sirens battled in the distance through the heavily built-up traffic.

Still dressed in full kit with MP5s across their knees, some of Orange Team sat half in, half out of the van. Another sat on the kerb cradling his head in his hands. Andy stood in the centre, with the team skipper directing operations in an attempt to preserve the scene. Striding his way, I bumped into 'Mad' Jack McMad, madder than a mad thing! An ex-Marine and member of Orange Team, he seemed one of the only ones that was *compos mentis*.

'What the fuck happened here, Jack?'

He grinned. 'Do you know the score?'

I shook my head. 'No. Only up to the point where the kidnapped guy had been taken to a flat, and they wanted it hit!'

'Yeah,' he said, nodding to a figure in the back of the Granada surrounded by medics. 'That's him over there, poor bastard. Half his guts are hanging out!'

I peered over for a better view as the medics set up a drip. 'Look's about fifty-fifty,' Jack said seriously. 'We were standing to, waiting for you. Two teams were going to hit the flat, because we didn't know how many were inside. We were kitted for an ER when the surveillance gives the standby. Apparently the reason there'd been no movement is because they spent the weekend torturing him. Looks like they took turns in sticking knives in his guts and groin and twisting them. He's in a right state!' He shrugged matter-of-factly. As our day-to-day life was spent dealing with people designated too dangerous to be dealt with by any other means, nothing surprised us any more. I'd even heard of one job where the guys found a Colombian drug dealer in the throes of sawing off a man's leg. Not with a chainsaw, mind you – no, that would be too quick. He was doing it with a wood saw! 'While they were waiting for us to get our shit together,' Jack continued, 'they spotted three of them dragging him into the car. They think they were taking him away to finish him off and dump him somewhere, so they moved us up.'

The surveillance team had in fact tailed the car off the estate and into the side streets. At the same time, Orange Team were 'running' towards the scene with Mad Jack at the wheel. Spotting a follow, the driver of the Granada took off at Mach ten.

Jack smiled, savouring the moment. 'I got a call on the radio – Black Granada. The High Street. Well, that's where we were, but going the other way. He was coming straight towards us. It all happened so fucking quickly. The two Rangies further up the hill tried a 'block' but missed. We were the last resort. I saw a black Granada take off over the top of the hill. I knew the guy's life was in danger, but on the other hand it could also have been a minicab or something. Next thing I know, he's lost control and he hits us.'

I looked at the position of the vehicles and knew immediately what had happened. Taking the bull by the horns, I guess, Jack had rammed him head on. The only trouble was he had no time to warn the guys in the back. One minute they're doing fifty, the next they come to a dead stop. Only the momentum would have carried them forward, cracking their heads and covering them with equipment. However, judging by the three bleeding suspects handcuffed on the floor, they came off better.

'Nice one, Jack. You know, you really are fuckin' McMad.'

Beaming at the compliment, he turned towards the unsmiling face of the Accident Investigation Officer.

'Steve!' Andy called, beckoning me to his position. 'Get kitted. There's still the address to hit, we need to preserve the evidence. He doesn't look too good.' he added, motioning towards the stretcher being placed in the ambulance.

'Sure. Where is it? I'll need a quick recce.'

'No time,' said the young detective at his shoulder. 'I've been plotting this address all weekend. The door's nothing. I'll point you in, but we have to go now!'

I shook my head. 'No, mate. We don't go in anywhere cold.'

Andy agreed. 'I do know that, Steve, but he can take you in. At the end of the day it could be a murder inquiry.'

I nodded. 'OK, boss, but I don't like it.'

'I know,' he replied.

I quickly briefed the team. 'This will be a no-nonsense rapid. Straight in – and be careful, you know what they're capable of.'

The rest of the team, having expressed their reservations at going in unrehearsed, mounted up. Moving silently away, the scene of devastation quickly disappeared in the rear-view mirror.

'We're going to have to move quick, Sarge,' said our guide. 'The whole estate's well eyes about.'

'Don't worry about that,' I said curtly. 'Just show us the door!'

We entered the estate through a short winding road. Typical of most late-sixties council estates, it was a mixture of low-level and high-rise pre-cast concrete dwellings. Explaining to the surveillance officer that we needed an FUP out of sight of the address, we found ourselves flanked by tower blocks. Gliding quietly into a residents' parking bay, I quickly took in the geography before sliding out and silently closing the door. Beckoning to the crew of the second Rangey, we quickly regrouped.

'OK,' I hissed to our guide. 'Let's go. Once you indicate the door, back off. Understand?'

He nodded in consent and moved off at a trot.

Luck was on our side. As in most major estates the lock to the communal door had been ripped off and not replaced. Darting inside, I made for the stairs. 'Lift's this way!' our guide called. I shook my head. 'But it's the twelfth floor,' he protested at my back as I moved off. We never used the lifts in tower blocks – or anywhere else, for that matter. The reasons were twofold and tactical: first, noise travels, particularly at night – on a dig-out at three in the morning, merely calling the lift could alert the suspect; second, one of the old Level Two teams had tried it once, piling in with so much kit that the weight caused them to get stuck between floors. Now we all know that Trumpton (the fire brigade) love the sound of their sirens, even in the early hours. Blaring on to the estate, they quickly gained an audience – including the suspect! If the embarrassment of being dug-out themselves wasn't enough, they'd blown the job. And so it came to pass that we walked everywhere. With CID puffing along behind.

Pausing for a breather on the eleventh floor, I peered through the wire glass window at the two front doors either side of the lift. There were four flats on each landing. Directly opposite was another swing door leading to another stairwell. One floor up, our guide pointed to a roughly painted door, then backed off as instructed. I drew my Glock, and we were ready.

Leading off, Chris raised the Enforcer and headed towards our objective. With MP5s raised in support, the team quickly followed. I don't know why, call it a sixth sense or something just as intangible, but on this occasion (and totally out of character) I hung back and covered the stairs.

Chris looked up. I nodded sharply.

CRASH! The flimsy door, taken totally by surprise, imploded from its hinges and disappeared up the hall. The team filed in. 'Armed Police, Armed Police!' came the muffled cries from within.

Joe emerged, stifling a laugh. I watched as he escorted a little old lady firmly from the premises, complete with hairnet and curlers. She seemed unfazed by the whole sorry mess. 'I think you want the flat downstairs,' she announced. 'They've been torturing some poor soul all weekend. Terrible screams they were.' She gave a toothless grin. 'I had to turn the telly up.'

'Fuck,' I cursed, and went to find the detective.

'I don't understand it,' he mumbled apologetically. 'This is the flat I've been watching.'

'Well it's the wrong fucking one,' I screamed.

Darting quickly back through the door, I took the stairs four at a time, well ahead of the team. Hitting the landing on the eleventh floor, I kicked the glass reinforced door open. With a loud crash it hit the wall. With the Glock held tightly in two hands I punched it swiftly out in front and followed the door. Standing in front of me, mouth open, was a large black male with a rolled-up and bloodstained carpet draped across his shoulder. He froze momentarily.

'Armed police!' I shouted. 'Don't fucking move!' Already I could hear heavy footfalls as the team, realizing I was alone, leapt the stairs. Dropping the carpet, the man turned about to bolt back through the open door. He may just as well have put his head down and run full pelt into the wall. Because in that split second of reaction time he met the team from the opposite stairwell. *WHACK!* He flew back, stunned. Leaping over his inert body, I kicked the front door, going left into the bathroom. The team headed right. 'Armed police! Down, down, down!'

Thirty seconds later, a calm peacefulness hung in the air. Trussed up and staring silently at the floor lay the suspects. The bathroom was a mess. Smeared blood decorated the walls and floor; the carpet was missing. It seemed the victim had been handcuffed and left in the bath – ideal for the blood to drain away. Quickly handing over the scene, we mounted up and drove angrily back to base.

Some months later I found myself called to the local Complaints Unit (set up to investigate complaints made about police officers). Apparently, after making a full recovery, the victim came to his senses. Fearing the inevitable consequences of reprisals against himself or his family, he withdrew his allegation. With the star witness gone, the authorities had no option but to release the suspects without charge.

The piss-takers, presumably in an effort to seek compensation, had actually made allegations against *us* of excessive force. It was bollocks, and I told them so.

Over the next couple of weeks the team seemed to be decimated, either through illness, courses, or annual leave. As a result, morale seemed at an all-time low, with the department going through an unusually slack period. It was at times like this – bored, and with the inevitable banter – that people began to get on each other's nerves. What we really needed was a good job!

It was during these prolonged periods of down time that different teams liked to occupy their time in different ways. Some liked to train or work on their personal fitness. Others honed their shooting skills, or, as in the case of Green Team (under the almost hypnotic influence of Tony), they invented projects to work on. Black Team, however, in their own indomitable style, liked to sit down and relax. And take the piss.

The day had started out much like any other. Early team, first response, and no job to be getting on with. Bill, Ninja, Brad and Sinex had been bolstered by Tony and Billy, who were strapping from Green Team. After breakfast we checked then loaded the kit on to the van. Although there was nothing going on, we would at least be ready for the off in the event of an emergency. With that done, the team set about their various tasks. Ninja and Bill went to the gym. Sinex went for a run. Brad lit his pipe, while I watched breakfast TV. Tony and Billy, on the other hand, had a project on their mind. Green Team had found an old premises stacked with tailor's dummies. Tony, who as always was bursting with new ideas, had negotiated their release, and wanted to use them on one of our specially adapted ranges at Lippitts Hill. Dressed accordingly, they could be decked out as either hostages or terrorists. Rather than the usual monotony of shooting pop-up cardboard targets, this would greatly add to the realism of the shoot, causing the team to switch on and visually scan the figure for any sign of a threat. In doing so they would benefit from the authenticity of shooting at a human form. And if the dummies got shot to pieces – so what?

'Any chance of nicking the old call-out wagon for a while?' asked Tony, 'I need to collect these dummies.'

I nodded, looking up from the screen. 'Who's going with you?'

'Billy. If that's OK. Our personal kit's on the van. But we'll take weapons and body armour with us in case of a shout.' He raised his eyebrows. 'We can link up with you at the RVP.'

I looked at my watch. 'Yeah, no sweat. There's fuck all happening anyway. Be back by two. You can buy me a pint.'

He laughed and headed for the yard.

'Fuck this, I'm bored,' I moaned.

Brad tapped his pipe out, stood up and stretched. 'Coming for a run, Dolphenburg?' (For some reason he'd come to the conclusion that I was of Germanic extraction.)

'Bollocks. I'm not that bored,' I replied, flicking the controls.

Greenford, Middlesex. Hardly a stone's throw from Harlesden. Bounded by the Grand Union Canal, with Wembley to the east, and north of Southall, its small, leafy tree-lined streets made the ideal location for the large, mainly Asian community to set down their roots and prosper. Yet it was in this close-knit community that the peace was to be dramatically shattered for a young Asian couple.

Living in a smart semi in a quiet street surrounded by their family and friends, life in this one particular house apparently couldn't be better. But nothing was further from the truth. Dogged by constant rows, things had finally reached boiling point.

The neighbours' curtains twitched as raised voices screamed abuse from behind closed doors.

BOOOMM! Suddenly all was still as the blast from twelve-bore shotgun echoed around the walls.

Inside the house the young wife ran to freedom. Reaching up for the door catch, the blast had caught her unawares. Confusion played across her once pretty features as her addled brain attempted to decipher what her eyes were seeing. Her right arm, almost severed by the impact of hundreds of tiny pellets, hung limply at her side, held only by a small flap of skin. The white of bone shone through the mangled tissue. And then – the pain!

BOOOMM! The second round from down the hall ripped squarely into her back, penetrating vital organs as she dropped silently to the floor and the fast-spreading dark red pool.

A few doors down, her mother had heard the commotion. Fearing the worst, she slipped into her coat and dashed quickly to the scene. Overcome with emotion, she peered intently through the letterbox, and was met with the sight of her daughter's prostrate form, her blood seeping into the carpet. Switching her gaze to the window, she was aware of the scream of distant sirens. Sitting in the front room, shotgun across his knees, was her son-in-law. Her daughter's husband. And would-be executioner.

Beep, beep, beep. In one movement I grabbed for my belt, turned the TV down and reached for the phone. 'Steve Collins.'

'Yeah, Sarge.' The baseman's urgent voice. 'Guvnor's at a siege. Looks bad. He wants a team ASAP.'

'Where?' I asked, studying the wall map.

'Greenford.'

I ran my finger west. 'OK. Page everybody with the location.'

Ninja and Bill sat in the van, sweat running from their bodies. In the gym they'd received the message, dashed outside, and were now gunning the engine. Sinex and Brad appeared, pulling themselves into the Rangey. With two-tones screaming we headed for the RVP.

'What's going on then, leader?' asked Brad from the back seat. He pulled on his pipe and Sinex winced.

'Dunno. Some sort of siege. Sounds like the shit's really hit the fan this time. Andy wants a team.'

'What about Tony and Billy?'

'They're making their own way. I hope!'

The heavy traffic was a nightmare as we blatted down the A40. Hurtling through a red light I saw the cordon dead ahead. A young PC snapped the blue and white incident tape. As we cut the noise and glided silently into the side street, pandemonium greeted us. The small crowd was held back by a handful of officers. Ambulances and police vehicles littered the narrow road. Further down, ARV officers took cover, MP5s trained on a house.

Opening the door I looked for Andy. 'Full kit, fellas,' I called. 'I'll see what's going on.'

'Steve! Over here,' Andy called, beckoning with his hand above the small throng of senior officers. Heads turned in my direction. I took in the scrambled egg and braid. This was certainly serious. 'This is Steve Collins,' Andy announced. 'Team leader.' They nodded in unison as I acknowledged.

'What you got, Andy?'

Viewing the destruction and her daughter's limp form propped against the door, the mother had become hysterical. Alerted by the commotion, neighbours had flooded into the street as the first officers had begun to arrive on the scene. But they were powerless. Knowing an armed and dangerous man was holed up in the house with a woman who could be bleeding to death, they were still unable to approach, for fear of getting shot. Within ten minutes the first ARV had arrived and quickly went about establishing a control and armed containment. To them it was undoubtedly a hostage rescue. As Andy had arrived it was evident what he had to do. Without delay and the relevant authority he'd dispatched a team. And across London we had started our run.

Using vehicles for cover, Andy had gone down and recced the building. It consisted simply of a front door to the right and a bay window to the left. It was through this window the gunman had been seen. But by now all was quiet.

'Steve, he's under a lot of pressure to end this,' Andy said, nodding to the Deputy Assistant Commissioner. 'We've got to go in fast. We don't know if the girl's dead or alive.'

I nodded. 'No probs. Tony and Billy should be here soon. But if not, with you there's six of us.'

He nodded.

'It'll have to do. Here's the plan'.

Sprinting back to the Rangey, I dragged my bergen from the boot and began to strip off in the street. Throwing on my coveralls, I called, 'Brad. Get the Hatton. Ninja, smash and cover. Bill, dig out some stunnies. We're going in two!' Seating the mag on the MP5, I let the action forward with a loud metallic snap.

'Gather round, fellas. This is what we'll do.' Brad, Hatton gun over his shoulder, puffed peacefully on his pipe. 'Andy will take us a safe route in. We don't know the condition of the woman, but she's behind the front door. The FUP is behind a tall hedge to the right of the drive.' As luck would have it the family car was parked in the driveway to the house, covering our approach. 'Take a second to get your shit together then we'll start our move up.' I looked up as they stared intently. 'ARVs have a containment in position. Brad, move to the door ready to Hatton the hinges.' He nodded. 'Ninja, you're Bill's cover man. On the attack, smash the bay window and engage the suspect. Bill, hit the room with a stunnie. It will give us some breathing space. The rest of us will stack on the door as the main assault. Any questions?' I scanned their faces. There were none. We all knew time was of the essence and we had to move fast!

With sirens blaring, Tony and a cursing Billy were two minutes away as we started our approach. Pausing momentarily at the hedge, I peered round the corner at the address. Nothing! The silence was strange, almost eerie. Like the man inside was a predator awaiting his prey. I nodded. MP5 raised, Ninja started down the drive using the vehicle as cover. Jabbing the stock in my shoulder, I stared down the sights trained on the window. Sweat ran in rivulets down my spine. In a split second we were at the door. Brad kicked the bottom lightly, and it gave a little. It was held only on the Yale lock. Pushing the PTT, I nodded. Changing tack, Brad levelled the sawn-off 870 squarely at the lock. Bill pulled the pin, showing Ninja the grenade. He raised his axe.

'Standby, standby!'

Tony screamed into the RVP like a bat out of hell. Screeching to a halt, his grisly cargo of twisted plastic arms, legs and heads flew forward, landing in a heap. Grabbing his Five, he threw his body armour over his head and hit the pavement, moving fast.

'*GO, GO, GO!*'

BOOOMM!

'Fuck it,' Tony cursed as he and Billy sprinted down the street.

SMAASHH!

'What the fuck's going on?'

BOOM BOOM BOOM BOOM, BANG!

The uniformed officers dived for cover.

Brad's round had shattered the flimsy lock, blowing it across the hall and implanting it in the plaster of the wall. The front window imploded under Ninja's axe. Raising his arm, Bill threw the small black egg-shaped grenade through the makeshift opening. It danced around the floor in a spectacular, disorientating display of sound and vision, shattering the screen of the TV and igniting the curtains. Brad kicked the door. It yielded slightly. Shouldering it, he charged into the hall, Hatton raised, Sinex at his shoulder.

I entered fast, momentarily looking down at the slaughter. Shredded arm twisted at a grotesque angle, the woman lay still. I instinctively knew she was dead. Skidding on the sweet-smelling, sticky red puddle, I followed, Tony at my heel. Going left, I hit the front room door.

It was over. With the suspect lying on the floor, Brad stood over him, cradling the Hatton. Sinex kicked the shotgun aside. A large mass of crimson tissue had piled high around a cavity in his chest as blood and organs had exploded from his body.

Sinex knelt down. Removing his glove, he felt for a pulse. He looked up sharply. 'I think he's alive.'

Grabbing at the radio, I called for the paramedics. The air ambulance had arrived.

'Steve,' Brad called.

I looked up.

He nodded at the suspect.

'What?'

He pointed to the Hatton. I thought of the paperwork as I looked at his injuries, my brain working overtime. 'Oh, fuck. You didn't whack him with the Hatton?'

'Nah. Topped himself. Probably as we came in.'

I relaxed, thinking back to the multiburst. With so much going on I hadn't counted, but was the last *boom* actually a *bang*? I shook my head. It was academic really. He was fucking brown bread. Didn't really matter how.

Mounting up, we drove happily back to the base. The girl was dead. Probably before she hit the floor. Her husband also. And I was pleased with the boys. We had gone in cold but performed like a team, with each man knowing his role. It had gone like clockwork. But there was still that niggling doubt. Was he waiting, shotgun poised, for the first man through the door? Changing his mind and taking his own life at the last moment? The simple answer was: we'll never know!

So it was that I was on quite a high as I entered the base the next morning. Not only had the job gone well, but I'd just received information that Operation Emerge seemed likely to shape up in the next couple of weeks. True to his word, Mike had secured our involvement. And Andy and I had been summoned to the Yard for a top-level meeting on tactics. Although they were still playing their cards close to their chests, I got the impression that this was more than merely the importation of a little bit of dope. This was to be something extremely big!

9

Operation Emerge

Following the initial meeting at the Yard, Andy and I left later that day feeling somewhat exhilarated. Having sworn us both to secrecy, the Detective Superintendent had taken us into his confidence and brought us up to speed. Finishing, he'd arched his eyebrows in our direction. 'Bearing in mind this could go off as early as the end of next week, we need a plan that is both feasible and flexible.' We left, promising to get back to him by tomorrow – and I resigned myself to the fact that it would be a long night!

Three weeks prior to the meeting, the 115 foot, 300-ton Panamanian registered oil-rig support vessel *Foxtrot Five* had sailed from its berth at Greenwich for the Gulf of Mexico. Customs had received information that it was to pick up a staggering 1.1 tons of pure cocaine, with a street value well over £160,000,000. With the cargo safely stowed on board, the crew then proposed to sail back across the Atlantic and offload it somewhere in the vicinity of Greenwich, where, once loaded on to vans, it could be taken to the slaughters. At a time designated by the senior investigating officer, SO19 would hit the cargo and arrest the players. Simple! Not quite.

Ringing back early the next day, we arranged another meet to discuss our options. Our proposals were bordering on the controversial, as we hoped to enlist the aid of the SBS (the Royal Marines' equivalent of the SAS). We also decided that, due to the potential number of players involved, and the possibility of hitting one or maybe two slaughters, plus an ambush and possibly a waterborne assault, we needed more men. Orange Team and their skipper Clive seemed the logical choice. With his contacts at Hereford and the Marines' base at Poole, Clive was considered to be the natural 'unofficial' negotiator who could test the water to see if they could provide the assistance we required.

By now things at our end were certainly starting to shape up. With a skeletal plan in our pockets, we went for the meet. As it turned out it was to be one of many over the next week or so – for just as we honed our scheme to perfection, just as we thought it was right, they'd throw a spanner in the works, causing us to go away, sit down, and rehash it. Which we did probably half a dozen times. Finally it was approved, and we were given the go-ahead to start training.

Over the week that followed we were to experience a number of highs and lows. Approaches had been made both unofficially by Clive and officially through the recognized channels. Employing the aid of Special Forces was not as easy as we had expected. Strict LOEs (Limits of Exploitation) had to be carefully drawn up, specifying the exact extent of their involvement.

It was considered unlikely that *Foxtrot Five* would be hit while at sea. Although the investigators had gained a vast amount of intelligence, they still believed that only the crew would be on board. Thus it was deemed far better to hit the cargo at the slaughter(s) when the money men had come to inspect their investment. That said, if it should be unloaded on the water, then we needed to be ready to act. Fail to plan, plan to fail!

After countless telephone calls, Clive and a couple of his team were invited to Poole, where he filled them in on the operation. At the time the Metropolitan Police Thames Division possessed nothing like the 'rapid' inflatables used by the Marines, and so it was with cap in hand Clive asked, 'Can we borrow some of your boats, please?' only to be met with a resounding 'No'. Not to be dissuaded easily, he explained that we would need to keep a respectable distance from the target ship, but at the same time have the capability to move up fast and board it as necessary. They explained: firstly, their 'ribs' came with a highly qualified coxswain, capable of manoeuvring the craft in any situation; secondly, they asked whether we had any experience of boarding a moving vessel. And did we have the relevant equipment and life jackets? Clive reluctantly admitted that, apart from 'barge hopping' on the Thames, we really had little or no experience of an amphibious assault.

'OK,' they said. 'Suppose we let you have our ribs piloted by a coxswain, and give you the relative training and equipment. What do you propose to do when you board the vessel?'

The answer to that was easy. In time-honoured tradition, we'd put everybody down at gunpoint and plasticuff them. 'Great,' was the reply. 'But who steers the ship?' Three hundred tons floating out of control on a relatively narrow and busy stretch of the river? Clive took their point and reported back.

While Clive was away, I'd got the plans and photographs from Mike and had a scrum down with the team. If the gear was unloaded and went to either (or both) of the slaughters, we'd need a forward holding area. Studying the map, we'd picked the section house (single officers' quarters) at Greenwich. It was equal running time to both plots and also sported a canteen. Mike informed us that although they were unsure of which slaughter the drugs would end up in, he favoured the lock-up under a railway arch in Surrey Canal Road, Deptford, the metal doors of which had recently been highly fortified. For the purposes of this operation, this warehouse was codenamed 'Flannigan's'. The other site, an industrial unit on a nearby trading estate, was designated 'Terminus'.

I shook my head as I looked at the photos. 'Fucking hell, look at that door at Flannigan's! I doubt we'd be able to do it with a Rangey. Besides, it would smash it to fuck!'

'I know what would do it,' Mario smiled.

'What?'

'A JCB.'

I laughed. 'Leave it out.'

'No, honestly,' he insisted, 'the job have got a couple at driving school, fully armoured. They're for clearing burning barricades during riots.'

I turned to Chris. 'You're the new MOE man. What do you think?'

He pondered this. 'They'll be a bastard to get through.'

I turned to Mario. 'How do we get hold of one, and whose authority do we need?'

'Yours, I guess. I'll phone Hendon.'

I nodded and went back to the plans. 'This other door is an

outward opener. It's also made of metal, but has a letterbox.
How about giving my new bit of kit a try?'

'Sure, why not?' Chris said suspiciously.

This was a heavy metal bar with an eye welded to the middle.
Through the eye was attached a heavy-duty chain. The idea was
to run up to the door under cover and post the bar through the
letterbox. We would then take up the slack and attach the chain
to the tow bar of a hastily reversed armoured Land Rover. The
driver would pull sharply away, literally ripping the door from
its hinges. I was so proud of my invention that I had Technical
Services make me one up. This particular piece of kit was now
gathering dust in the MOE store, but I was desperate to try it!

Clive's enthusiasm for the role won the day. Having negotiated a compromise, he quickly set about a training package
for his team down at Poole. The SBS would provide the ribs
and coxswains, the life jackets, and a small contingent of men
to secure the bridge and maintain control of the ship. For our
part, SO19 would provide the main assault team for the rest of
the ship.

Par for the course, we hit another hitch. All incidents involving armed police officers travelling through another force's area
require the authority and approval of the Chief Officer of Police
for that county. As we envisaged picking up the ship in the
mouth of the Thames estuary, we found we would in fact be
encroaching on two separate force areas – Kent to the south
and Essex to the north. Kent were extremely accommodating
and, apart from a liaison officer, would leave us pretty much to
our own devices. Essex on the other hand were not so obliging
and decided that their Tactical Firearms Unit should also be
involved. Not open to discussion (even at the highest level), we
had to capitulate and somehow write them a role. Eventually we
cracked it and the plan was finally rubber stamped. Now all we
had to do was wait.

The next week or so passed with the monotony of early morning dig-outs and 'no show' robbery plots, which we carried out
with an almost robotic efficiency. What we really needed was a
big job to clear the air, and Emerge was on everybody's mind.

It was while going home on the tube one day that I suddenly
looked down at my increasing waistline. It was by no means
an addiction, but at the end of the day I always seemed to find

myself in the pub. It seemed a good way to chill out, and after a few pints I would wind my way home strangely released from the tension of the day. Policemen, by the very macho nature of their job, will never admit to anybody (including themselves) that maybe, just maybe, they might occasionally suffer from stress. And as a result they have a laugh over a drink as a form of release. I think that by this stage the hierarchy had started to notice that I may have been on ops a little too long, and as a result they were pushing me to take time out and do the instructor's course. I, on the other hand, was having none of it, and fought vehemently and with a dogged determination to keep the team. (From a purely selfish angle, I was earning good money.) And besides, I kidded myself, they were short of sergeants.

I sipped my coffee and looked absentmindedly at the clock. Two-thirty. I was really begining to hate these early-morning jobs. Staring blankly at the 'Home Sweet Home' sign Pecky from Green Team had put on the wall, I took another bite of toast. I'd been so wrapped up in work that only now did I realize that Christmas was only six weeks away and I hadn't done a thing. I'd also been told that in a couple of weeks' time I'd be strapping as the skipper on Green Team. Much as I hated to leave the boys with a 'caretaker', it was only for a few days. And the change might do me good. Besides, Green Team were as professional as they came.

Closing the curtains against the glare of the watery afternoon sun, I pulled back the duvet, climbed into bed and closed my eyes. It was three o'clock, and the twelve-hour stake-out had been a complete waste of time. Shivering against the cold, I had spent the best part of the early hours sitting cramped and uncomfortable in the back of a 'Trojan horse'. On this occasion it was nothing more than a hired van, and the thin metallic walls and bare floor seemed an ideal conductor for the cold. We didn't even have a pot to piss in, and so when I eventually got out I was bursting.

(West London had recently been been plagued with a series of armed robberies on security vehicle custodians delivering sealed units of currency to cashpoint machines. At around forty grand a time, a gang of enterprising opportunists had taken time out to rob them. In the operations that followed, all deliveries were now being monitored by the Flying Squad, with SO19 static on the most likely plots.)

Back at the local nick, I had relieved myself with pleasure.

'This job's shite,' Chris had said, two traps away.

I had to agree. 'Yeah, too soon after the last one. They're probably still out clubbing it on the proceeds while soppy bollocks here is freezing his nuts off.'

No sooner had my head hit the pillow when the incessant screeching of my pager shattered all thoughts of sleep. I fumbled on the bedside table until I located the annoying little object. Eyes still heavy from lack of sleep, I peered at the screen, lips moving slowly as I silently read the script: 'EMERGE LIVE. PARADE OLD STREET 6PM TONIGHT.' Diving in the shower, I just had time to change my clothes before heading back to base. It was sure to be a long night.

Having been put on standby that afternoon, Andy had a lot to do. Dragging the bulky file from the 'Ongoing ops' drawer, he carefully thumbed through the typewritten script until he located a handwritten flysheet of things to do. Not only were the teams to be warned, he needed to contact the liaison officer at Poole, who in turn would put their own wheels into motion. There was the organization of vehicles and paramedics, and the outside forces would need to know. The FHA would also have to be alerted. Driving school at Hendon would have to organize a low loader to deliver the JCB, and nominate a driver. The list was endless, the task thankless, but none the less important for the overall success of the operation.

'Listen in, fellas. This will take a little while to get through,' Andy called, surveying the sea of twenty odd faces in the cramped briefing room. Many of them were on chairs, others slouched; the majority sat cross-legged on the floor. But all listened intently as he outlined the plan. 'This operation will be in three phases. I'll outline the information to date. Clive will fill you in on phase one, and Steve phases two and three.' The room was silent.

'Emerge is a continuing operation involving the smuggling of large quantities of drugs into this country. It is also investigating supposed links being forged between British gangs and certain notorious South American drug barons, notably the Colombian cartels. About four weeks ago a 300-ton ocean-going barge left Greenwich for South America, and a major pick-up of drugs, estimated to be in the region of one ton of pure cocaine.' A low whistle echoed through the small room. 'Exactly. These are major-league players. For a while the vessel was lost, but we now know that they have the consignment on board and are heading home.'

(In fact the drugs had been loaded on to the ship off the coast of the small island of Aruba, situated at the northern tip of Venezuela.)

'Are they under surveillance?' a voice asked.

Andy looked to me.

'Yes. We know the American DEA are involved, probably by AWAC [Airborne Warning and Control System], certainly Customs cutters.'

Andy continued. 'It's anticipated that the drugs will be off-loaded somewhere up the Thames, probably Woolwich or Greenwich – somewhere near the slaughters. Once on the vans the load will be taken to Terminus or Flannigan's, possibly both.'

I interrupted: 'The hits have to be co-ordinated, but it's hoped that with all that gear the main players will want to turn up for a look-see.'

'Clive?' Andy motioned.

Clive nodded. 'As you all know, we've had to change the initial plan to write Essex in. Andy will be mobile in the control vehicle with the other heads of shed'. Customs reckon they'll pick the boat up visually somewhere off the Scilly Isles. Once it enters the Thames Estuary we'll start to shadow it at a discreet distance. Behind us will be two inflatables carrying the Essex contingent. The plan is quite simple. Once the vessel docks and the cargo is unloaded and away, we'll come hurtling in and secure the ship and crew. Essex will purely be in support.' He surveyed the quiet room for a moment before continuing. 'You may be wondering why we're coming up the river and not simply hitting it from an OP near the dock.'

'Yeah, cos you wanted a fucking jolly,' someone muttered beneath their breath.

Clive grinned. 'Firstly, we're not sure where it will land, and

142

secondly, it's possible that they might anchor up during darkness and load the gear into inflatables.' I nodded. Clive certainly had it well covered. 'Should that be the case, our two ribs will take the ship as per the plan, with the two Essex units taking off any smaller craft. Now we've not done any training with them, but we're told they're capable . . .' I smiled as a chuckle coursed through the room. 'Should one of these craft actually make the shore, the land-based units will deal. Steve?'

I nodded. 'Thanks, Clive. Right, Black Team will be responsible for the non-amphibious side of the operation. Chris . . .' He stood and uncovered a montage of photographs, maps and drawings. 'Have a good look later, fellas,' I said, pointing to the wall. 'When the op goes properly live our plan will be in two phases. Phase two, the strappers will man the OPs. Rick will be opposite Flannigan's and Billy opposite the Terminus. They will be our eyes and ears and will remain for the duration.' I looked up as the two new guys identified themselves. 'The rest of us in two Rangies will head for Dartford nick and a further briefing with surveillance.' Chris sighed loudly. 'I know. But it's important we get it right. Essex officers will mirror us on their side of the bank. Once the boat passes under Dartford Bridge we'll be told, and from there on we'll move out and await an update.' (Surveillance was actually to have a man suspended in a cradle beneath the bridge.) 'Our primary role will be to take out any players on the bank if Clive has to hit the ship at anchor. So apart from everything else, take dragon lights. Should this be the scenario, watch out for Essex in the water; that's their LOE. I don't want a Blue on Blue at any cost.' I looked down at my notes. 'Once the ship docks, and that's the general consensus, it's over to Clive. We head straight back to the FHA and await instructions as to which slaughter it'll be.'

'How will we know?' Joe asked. 'Is there surveillance?'

I nodded. 'Yeah, you better believe it. Imagine if we lost those trucks somewhere else.'

'Are the lookouts carrying?' he asked.

I grimaced. 'Yeah, some. But only for their own protection; they won't take part in the hit.'

'Great!' He shook his head. As a team that constantly worked and trained together and consisted solely of marksmen with a proven track record, we knew our capabilities. As a result I hated working with other armed units, who I reckoned quite frankly often couldn't hit a cow's arse with a banjo.

'Now comes phase three. Have a look at your individual briefing packs. Inside you'll find maps with highlighted routes from the FHA to Terminus and Flannigan's.' I pulled out a copy and held it up. 'Chris has driven both routes to make sure there are no roadworks to hold us up, and – more importantly – no width restrictions. Remember the JCB will be following.'

'I'll be in the cab with the driver,' Mario added.

'Great,' Joe mumbled. 'He won't get fucking lost then.' I laughed. Mario was famous for his short-cuts; trouble was you had to go to the A40 and start there. And that was way across town!

I continued. 'OK. Once we get the word we'll move off from the FHA and regroup at either FUP indicated on the map. Once our spotter in the OP lets us know it's quiet with no third eyes we'll move up and hit it. As previously discussed, we know who's been detailed to take out the third eyes, and the MOE to be used on each address. SOPs remain the same: everybody down and plasticuffed in situ. Any questions?'

'Hospitals?' Mario asked.

'Under "Admin" in your folder, but also at the paramedics' discretion. As always, police casualties will not go to the same hospital as the villians and will always be accompanied by a member of the team.' I paused. 'Comms will be seventy-five, but once again we'll communicate by pager until the hit.' The room was still. 'OK. Get some grub, sort the kit, and drivers make sure the motors are gassed up.'

Sitting drinking coffee after the briefing, I re-read the notes. Among the hustle and bustle of the lads checking kit, a movement caught my eye – something out of the ordinary. Looking up, I saw a short, thin, dapper-looking man in his early fifties. He wore a blazer, trousers, brogues, and a neat club tie, and had neatly clipped greying hair. Standing behind him (and totally out of contrast) was a young, slim, muscular guy dressed in a T-shirt and jeans. His blond hair was cropped close to his head.

Clive wandered over. 'Meet the Major,' he announced.

I eyed him cautiously; obviously this was a man from the ministry sent down to keep an eye on things. The younger man clutching a thick wad of operational orders was an SBS sergeant, sent to liaise.

At about ten o'clock that evening we got the message we'd all been anxiously waiting to hear – the ship had been picked up. We were game on.

Gunning their vehicles, the drivers took off through the late-evening traffic towards Dartford, only to find that the nick that was to be our base was closed. Sighing, I picked up the outside telephone and dialled. It was one hour into the operation, and already things were starting to go horribly wrong.

Twenty minutes later a panda arrived with the keys.

Making our way to the bar at Dartford (which incidentally was closed), we quickly spread out and found our own bit of floor space. By now I was totally cream crackered. Laying my head on a makeshift pillow of body armour, I quickly drifted off to sleep – only to be violently interrupted half an hour later with the noisy invasion of the surveillance team, and a uniformed superintendent who bore an uncanny resemblance to Barry Manilow. It struck me immediately that he was suffering from a serious sense of humour failure.

'Who's in charge?' he snapped.

'Dolph, over there,' groaned a half-asleep Brad, motioning with his thumb.

'All right, guv?' I said cheerily, giving him the benefit. 'Steve Collins, skipper Black Team.'

Looking down his nose (a magnificent feat in itself), he eyed my crumpled coveralls and muddy boots with disdain. 'Well, who's going to do the briefing?' he asked scornfully.

'I am.'

He stared in abject horror as I yawned and dragged myself to my feet only to have my space immediately nicked by some thieving surveillance bastard. 'Right!' he shouted. And for the next few minutes he tried desperately to get the attention of everyone in the room.

I smirked. It would have been easier to circumcise the Pope! Banging my hand on the table, I shouted, 'Listen in, fellas.'

Silence.

I had taken an immediate dislike to this man. He was the

typical 'rank assumes knowledge' type I had fought against for years. Once again, I found myself relating the entire plan, only this time from memory. 'Is that it?' he asked when I finished.

Is that it? I thought. It's just taken me half a fucking hour. Yes, that's *it*!

I nodded.

'What about Section 3?' he asked incredulously.

I sighed. That old chestnut – Section 3 of the Criminal Law Act, 1967. Stamped indelibly on the back of your pink card (authority to draw firearms), it reads: 'A person may use such force as is reasonable in the circumstances in the prevention of crime, or in the effecting or assisting in the lawful arrest of offenders or suspected offenders or of persons unlawfully at large.' I certainly didn't need reminding of it – I carried a firearm or two every working day – and the rest of the team knew full well their powers in relation to the use of force. This senior officer, however, hadn't managed to grasp that, and totally dismissed the entire contents of my briefing. He obviously thought he was Top Knob Jockey Banana, a real geezer.

I nodded. 'Oh, yes,' I turned to the team. 'And let me remind you of your powers under Section 3 – as I did, according to the manual, when I issued your weapons.'

Joe started to laugh, others joined in.

Barry Manilow took exception to this and glared. 'This is no laughing matter,' he stuttered. 'I don't think any of you fully understand the implications of carrying a firearm.' He then related *verbatim* Section 3. Pleased with himself, his bit done, he nodded, turned on his heel and left the room followed by muffled cries of *'wanker!'*.

As things turned out, it was to be a long and uneventful evening. Lying uncomfortably on the beer-stained, smoky carpet, I tossed and turned until finally I fell into fitful slumber.

Out on the river, Clive and the boys were huddled together for warmth, and were beginning to wish they hadn't pushed the amphibious side of the plan with such gusto. Even with the facial balaclavas, wet weather gear, body armour and life jackets, they were experiencing a piercing cold like never before.

For some unknown reason, the ship had anchored just off the coast, holding everything up.

*   *   *

146

At about two in the morning I was woken by the noisy movement of the surveillance team as they gathered up their kit and ran to the cars. 'It's on!' shouted a gaunt detective constable we'd affectionately nicknamed 'Belsen Eddie'. At the same moment, my pager beeped into life. 'IT'S LIVE! 70 CY 44 MOVE OUT.'

Snatching up the Greater London atlas, I quickly thumbed through the pages until I came to the right one. Using my finger, I traced down and across to identify the grid.

'Just under Dartford Bridge,' Chris growled from over my shoulder.

I nodded, thinking of the guy high above in the cradle. 'It's on! *Point One*,' I called to the team, who were already frantically packing up their grots.

Sitting in Colyers Lane at the junction with the A206 Northend Road, I reached across and turned the blower down. (Being armoured, we were unable to open the windows.) 'Fuck me, it's like a Turkish bath in here,' I scowled at Chris.

He turned it back up. 'It's fucking cold,' he moaned.

I smirked. 'I bet you were a right sickly child.' Then, switching to my best Coronation Street Mavis O'Reilly accent, I added, 'I'm sorry, Chris can't come to school today. He's got another cold in his chest!'

'Fuck off,' he snarled.

Spread out in the back, Joe laughed.

'I bet they used to call you Captain Kidd,' I said.

'Why?' Chris asked.

'Because you had a sunken chest. Do you know you're the only person I know below fifty who still wears a vest!'

'Just because Billy's not here to take the piss it's have-a-fucking-go-at-Chris week.'

The ship was fast approaching Erith. I studied the map under the harsh white glare of the torch, then held it aloft and turned to Chris. Behind me, Joe leaned forward and stuck his head between the seats for a better view. I pointed to where the map showed a large number of small jetties and piers on our side of the river. 'This would seem a good place to offload. If that's what they have in mind.'

They nodded. But it was not to be – the ship passed the point. And so it continued for the rest of the night. The pager would spring into life with, for example: '59 CR 40'. Looking it up on the map, we would find what appeared to be a suitable location within striking distance of the river, head towards it, and 'self plot'. But each time the ship continued its journey.

Finally, after a game of cat and mouse lasting nearly five hours, I received a message that made the hair on the nape of my neck stand to attention. It simply read: 'DOCKING 68 CH 41'.

6.55 a.m. Out on the river at a location not too far east of the Thames Barrier, Clive was staring at the message on his pager. 'CARGO IS CLEAR, I HAVE CONTROL, GO GO GO.' Silently mouthing the words, he picked up his radio and selected the National Firearms frequency. Swallowing hard, he pressed the transmit button. 'All units, Trojan Alpha. Attack, attack, attack.' Then, nodding to the coxswain, he tightly gripped the rail as, with an intense roar of the powerful marine engines, the bow of the rib left the water.

Hurtling at speed through the Thames Barrier, they headed a course for Anchor & Hope Lane. Witnesses to this dramatic event would later say tell the press that they believed it was a film stunt.

Meanwhile, the cargo of forty black plastic-wrapped parcels was loaded into a waiting van. As he quickly slipped away from the quayside, the driver was totally unaware of the surveillance team hot on his tail.

The dark green water of the Thames was whipped skywards in a flurry of slightly salty spray, soaking the occupants on board, as the sleek black ribs reached and berthed alongside the port and bow of *Foxtrot Five*. Like an army of ants, the black-clad heavily-armed assaulters swarmed over the ship, each pair heading for their allotted objective. It was all but over as the small Essex contingent finally caught up.

The ship was deserted.

'Steve!' Andy's voice crackled over the radio from the high-tech computer-decked van, designated control.

'Go, Go,' I called, sipping coffee from a paper cup at the FHA.

The single clipped word he then uttered placed weeks of training instantly into perspective: 'Flannigan's'.

'Yesss!' Mario raised his fist in triumph. 'I'll get the JCB offloaded,' he called, racing off.

'Boys and their toys,' whistled Joe.

Having moored the ship and unloaded the cargo, all the crew wanted to do after their five-thousand-mile journey was to go home, meet up with their families, and celebrate the jackpot. Payday had arrived. They split up and went off in different directions.

It had never been anticipated that once docked Clive would retrieve any of the haul, but he expected to capture the crew, seal off the ship and preserve it evidentially for the SOCO boys to do their bit. So the surveillance team were called upon to take out the crew. In the débâcle that followed, one surveillance officer drew his Smith & Wesson revolver and fell out of his car. *CRACK!* The .38 round left the muzzle heading nowhere in particular. *SMASH!* In a split second it had torn into the headlight of a waiting taxi, and with the popping sound of broken glass it fell noisily to the ground. Although totally unplanned (and for that matter extremely unprofessional), this had the desired effect: everybody (including police officers) hit the deck. The crew were arrested.

At the Forward Holding area, Joe, Ninja, Chris, Nigel and I sat with the RCS and waited, doors open, slouched half in and half out of the Rangies.

BRRPP, BRRPP. Snatching the cellphone from the dash, I punched the green send button. 'Hello.' 'Steve? Andy. Standby for Flannigan's. When you get the off you'll have to move fast.'

'I'll need to push the JCB up to an FUP nearer the site,' I said, 'or it'll never keep up.'

At the other end Andy paused, thinking. 'Yeah, you're right. Do it, I'll be in touch!'

Calling the lads together, we quickly had a scrum down in the yard. It was decided that Mario would move with the JCB, to an FUP we'd plotted on the map. The rest of us would hold at the section house. When we got the off we would move out, linking up at Flannigan's, and do the business. If while we moved the gear was transported to the secondary slaughter (Terminus), we could divert and hit that with our alternative method of entry.

Happy, I nodded. 'OK, Mario. Move out.'

Mounting the huge yellow machine and standing behind the driver, he grinned. With a huge ball of black smoke from its large exhaust, the JCB burst into life and leapt forward into the moderate early morning traffic.

The next twenty minutes that passed seemed like twenty hours. 'I can't fucking believe this,' I whined to a snoring Chris, glancing at my watch. 'They've not only had time to unload it, they could have snorted half of it by now.'

Chris grunted.

'OK, OK. Mount up.' This from a short, verbally hyperactive DI from the Regional. 'Let's go. Let's go, we're hitting it.'

'At fucking last,' Joe cried, diving into the back seat of the Rangey and slamming the door.

I approached the DI. 'Guv, I've got to call up the JCB, and bearing in mind we've not seen the actual plot, you'll have to lead us in.'

He sighed non-commitally. 'Don't worry, just follow us. And hurry up,' he added in a superior tone.

The lead vehicle pushed out of the T-junction and into the by-now-heavy rush-hour traffic. With the stick-on blue light flashing, the driver threw a block across both carriageways to allow the snaking column of five vehicles access on to Deptford Bridge. Then, tagging on to the end of the convoy, we started to blat our way towards our objective. Cutting the Blues and Twos a couple of miles from the plot, we inched and cursed our way through the solid wall of traffic. Unable to reach Mario over the net, I could only assume he was somewhere near Flannigan's, waiting for the call. I hadn't however reckoned on his famous short-cuts! Bouncing along the ancient cobblestoned backstreets of Deptford, we finally neared our target and stopped a hundred and fifty yards short.

Still trying the radio, I finally received Mario's faint reply; 'Five minutes from the plot.' Ten minutes later we were joined by two marked Essex Police Rangies, each containing half of the immaculately groomed team in dark coveralls and body armour, each man's head adorned with a perfectly styled beret.

Joe looked down at his crumpled, sweat-stained, sopping wet coveralls and winced.

'Where the fuck has Mario got to?' I demanded, strumming my fingers on the dash. 'Parked up here we stand out like a bulldog's bollocks.'

A face appeared at the window. Opening the door, I cheerfully greeted the DI with a large, cheesy grin. 'Won't be a tick, guv!' I lied with conviction.

'Well it's no good. You'll have to hit it now, they're all inside,' he replied curtly.

I nodded thoughtfully. 'And how do you expect us to get through the door? Knock?'

His terse reply was cut short by Mario. 'Two minutes to the FAP,' he called.

'Thank fuck for that. Dismount lads, we'll put in a containment,' I called eagerly.

With the Essex contingent as observers, we stacked up and slipped silently up the alley.

'One minute, one minute,' called Mario.

I looked up, confused now, for along the entire length of the alley were similar sets of innocuous-looking red metal concertina doors!

'Is this the one?' I hissed to the DI.

'I think so,' came the reply.

'*Think so*. I didn't expect it to have a fucking great sign saying "This Way to Flannigan's",' I moaned to Joe, 'But give us a fucking clue . . .'

'Yes, Yes! That is the door,' came an unfamiliar voice in my earpiece.

'What, this one?' I asked, pointing to the door to which Brad now held his ear.

'Yes. That one. They're inside.'

I looked behind me, seeking the source of the voice. 'OK. Everybody quiet,' I called into the radio. 'This is Trojan. Who is telling me this is the door? Over.'

'It's me – Rick. In the OP. Hit that door, they are inside.'

I held my thumb aloft in acknowledgement. Fuck knows where the OP was, but they were good.

Now where was Mario? Chris looked up and pointed. The cavalry had arrived. At the far end of the road stood the huge yellow dinosaur. Slammed into gear, the JCB suddenly lurched into life, charging headlong towards our position, It was something so spectacular I almost expected a Wagnerian chorus. Gathering speed it grew larger, filling the entire width of the alley.

'Back up, back up.' Mario screamed urgently. Diving for cover, the team watched in awe. The machine approached the door at such speed I thought it would charge straight past; then, suddenly and dramatically, it turned on the spot and threw itself to the left. *KERRAASSHH!* The doors folded inwards in a spectacular display of crumpled metal.

'*GO,GO,GO!*' I yelled, leaping from cover, a noise like church bells still ringing in my ears.

With an almighty roar, Brad charged through the opening, MP5 raised. I saw the van, side door open, black plastic-wrapped bundles partially offloaded on to a sack barrow. Standing white-faced, still holding one package and frozen with fear, stood the driver. He had every right to be terrified; if he'd been standing at the rear of the van he'd have been crushed in a frightening mass of twisted and tortured metal as the doors imploded. Hitting him head-on, Joe continued moving while he was left flat on the floor for the rear party to deal with. Reaching the office at the far end, Joe worked feverishly at the door, Nigel on his shoulder. With the muzzle of my MP5 I punched through the window to the office's interior. It was clear!

Twenty seconds later it was over. Dust still hung lazily in the rays of the early morning sun as the Customs arrest and search teams entered. Standing wearily outside, I surveyed our handi-work with a wry smile and nodded. 'Fucking nice one!'

Thumbing through the *Sun* the next day, I came across a head-line. Smiling, I put down my coffee and called, 'You seen this?'

'Yeah,' Joe shouted, disgruntled. 'Fucking Pongos!'

I read it out loud for the rest of the lads. 'LET'S GO! NAVY SAS IN £200M DRUG BUST.' It was nothing new. Special Forces. The Flying Squad or Special Branch were often credited by the media for ambushes on the mainland undertaken by us. In the eyes of the public SO19 was relatively unknown, and it suited us. Besides, *we* knew the truth! But I often felt the lads should somehow be credited with a job well done; we never even got a pat on the back from our own management, who would simply comment, 'That's what you're paid for!'

Later we laughed out loud as we were told that one of the Essex dinghies had broken down early in the game. Drifting out towards the sea, they had alerted the coastguard, who, seeing half a dozen heavily armed men dressed in black, with a 'pony' explanation, refused to rescue them until they surrendered their weapons.

Operation Emerge was hailed a huge success. An immense blow to organized crime; firm bonds forged between Customs and the police, SO19 and the SBS; Britain's largest ever cocaine haul – 1.1 tons, bringing the total seizure for that year to more than two and a half tons. Apart from a few small hiccups (which you would expect on an operation of this scale), it had gone extremely well – and I for one was elated.

10

Seventeenth Baddest Man in the World

Specialist Firearms Teams can execute on average well in excess of two hundred 'live' operations a year. Thus an officer's mind is usually on several jobs at once. One freezing December afternoon I was sipping coffee and gazing out of the window, pondering the week's activity – three dig-outs, a robbery plot that was a non-starter from the beginning, and a kidnapper ambushed outside Wembley Stadium; a good week's work by anybody's standards, and today was only Thursday – when the DI broke my train of thought.

'Look, I'm sorry about this waiting around. The DC will be back soon.'

I nodded. 'Well, as soon as my lads get back I'll give you a plan – although I certainly don't envisage any problems.'

Three of the team were currently out on the ground to recce the address we were to hit early the next morning. Once they'd seen what they wanted I would be able to assess what we would require from the locals in the form of uniform and CID support.

Three hours earlier we had been at the base, sitting on the floor in a huddle and checking and re-checking our personal kit. The din of the small room had been interrupted by the shrill ring of the telephone. Answering, I was informed that CID officers at a small station in south-west London had received information that a sawn-off shotgun was concealed in the bedroom of a flat on the Clapham Park Estate. A search warrant had been obtained under the Firearms Act, and advice was needed on the way forward.

It is the role of SO19 to provide not only support but good,

154

sound tactical advice on any operation where firearms are suspected. I listened intently. This was obviously an operation on which a team should be deployed. We were first response this week; it would be our responsibility to plan and carry it through. I promised the caller a meeting later that day to see the ground and discuss tactics.

Now a dishevelled and rather apologetic DC entered the office. 'Sorry I'm late. You must be Steve from SO19?' He offered his outstretched hand. 'I've just been out doing some background. Let me fill you in . . .'

It transpired that, to add to the original information, new intelligence had come to light. This particular part of the estate was recently subject to some racial tension, and was currently designated politically sensitive. To add to the dilemma, the occupant of the flat – a violent man with previous convictions for attacking the police – was black. Firearms and public order are not a good mix, there could be no mistakes; local senior management could not risk further unrest. However, a sawn-off shotgun is a devastating weapon in the hands of a criminal, and needed to be taken off the streets as quickly and clinically as possible.

To the locals, this was to be a major operation. With a firearms team deployed in their area the ramifications were endless. To us, however, it was just another dig-out – the fourth that week. Bread and butter, no big deal.

'Of course,' muttered the DI, 'the DCI will want to see you. She's with the superintendent at the moment.'

'She?' I asked. A female DCI was pretty much an anomaly to me. Although more and more women were taking up senior posts within the service, they normally remained within the uniform branch. A woman career detective was unusual to say the least, and I was surprised we had never met before.

'Yes, she's a character all-right,' Said the DI. 'Ex-Flying Squad, you know.'

Once more I looked at my watch. 'Look, guv, it's five o'clock. My boys will parade at two-thirty for a four-thirty hit – let's see her now and have the main briefing in the morning.' I rubbed my head. By the time I got home, showered, and grabbed a bite it would be eight-thirty. I would be up at one to start the new day. The only consolation was that it would be Friday, the end of our ops week. If we got the job over with quickly I could be back in bed by eight, then a few hours' sleep would give me two and a half days off and a well deserved rest. And If I believed that I would believe anything.

'Please sit down, Sergeant,' said the DCI, indicating a chair opposite her desk. She was a tall woman with short mousy hair, well dressed in a brown trouser suit with matching loafers. On the ring finger of her left hand she wore a thin gold wedding band. I immediately put her in her mid-forties

I sat.

'I'm DCI Burton,' she said without further ado. 'I believe you know the others.' She nodded towards the DI and the two DCs present.

I smiled in acknowledgement.

'Right,' she said, 'what do you need from us?'

I cleared my throat. 'My lads are having a look at the moment. That however won't affect the overall plan. We supply everything, you need nothing more than your arrest and search teams.'

'Well, of course you'll need Ghostbusters,' the DI piped in, trying to be helpful. 'The doors on that estate are solid.'

'Ghostbusters' was the name given to the Property Services Department, a team of civilian employees working out of a base nearby. Their primary role was to effect entry into buildings for police officers on drug raids or when executing search warrants. They used the latest breaking equipment and methods of entry.

But then so did we. I shot the DI a glance. 'We don't use Ghostbusters. We do all our own entries. I don't take unarmed personnel, particularly civilians, into a potential firearms situation.'

The DCI nodded.

'I'd like to keep this as low-key as possible,' I added, 'a quick in and out, and handover.'

'I agree,' said the DCI to nobody in particular.

'Well I'm wearing a bulletproof vest and one of those baseball caps,' said the DI.

I don't think you'll be getting that close, mate, I thought, looking around.

'Why?' the DCI asked, suddenly sitting bolt upright and studying him intently.

'Well, they look quite good . . . and I've never worn one before,' he stammered.

'Don't be a fucking prat, you'll look *ridiculous*,' she said, going up an octave. 'You'll leave it to the professionals, and don't get in the way!' She shot me a glance. 'I'm a hostage negotiator, you know. I've worked with your boys before.' Gazing around, she addressed her assembled entourage. 'Let me tell you, these men are the fucking dog's bollocks. I remember an exercise at an old hospital in Surrey . . .' She lowered her voice to a whisper. 'Hostages and everything. These boys and – you know – the SAS.' She looked around at her co-conspirators. 'They took me in through the undergrowth, had me crawling in all sorts of shit.' She looked at me. 'Steve, let me tell you, your boys have my admiration. They are brilliant, real fucking professionals.'

'Thank you, ma'am,' I croaked, feeling all eyes in the room on me, the heat spreading rapidly through my ears. After such a testimonial, nothing could be allowed to go wrong.

'No sweat,' John said as we pushed our way through the throng of Christmas shoppers. 'Stevie will lead us in.' 'Yeah,' Stevie said as we fought our way to the tube. 'No probs.'

Returning from the recce, the boys had decided to draw up the plans at home, and that suited me. We all lived south, so we didn't have to make the journey back to base first.

By now I was aware that we were drawing more than just the odd glance. John, a fitness fanatic, was wearing a huge Russian fur hat with earflaps secured at the crown. A large Russian Police badge adorned the front. He resembled something out of the Arnie film *Red Heat*.

Finding three empty seats in the carriage, we sat in a conspiratorial huddle. 'No problems with the door,' John said. 'Should pop first time.'

The train gathered speed, and as we moved further into the suburbs the carriage emptied. I looked around. Women sat hunched over huge bags of Christmas shopping while men sat with collars turned up against the bitter cold. What a drag, I thought. I hated Christmas, and this year I planned a holiday abroad. It would be good to get away.

The train stopped, then once again it picked up its rhythmical beat. I sat staring into space. Suddenly the beat was accompanied by pre-recorded pipe music, and an acoustic guitar sprang into life. Looking round, I saw a short swarthy individual attempting to play what I assumed to be South American native tunes. To me it sounded more like an animal in pain.

John broke the spell. 'He's having a fucking laugh,' he said, looking a round. A woman shopper sitting opposite looked in his direction and stifled a laugh (he was still wearing his hat). The commuter beside her suppressed a grin and pretended to concentrate on her newspaper.

'Well, he is,' said John, louder this time. 'That's bloody awful.'

Steve, sitting quietly beside me, started to giggle uncontrollably.

John had his audience. Lifting his hand, he untied the securing knot on the top of his hat, allowing the earflaps to fall. They came to rest at right angles to his head, resembling large wings. He looked every inch the cartoon character Deputy Dawg. I bit my tongue as laughter welled up inside.

The musician, oblivious to his surroundings, continued to torture his instrument. Looking across at Steve, I could see he was now unable to speak. Tears ran in huge rivulets down his cheeks; he had totally lost it.

A huge grin on his face, John looked about the carriage like some deranged bear. The woman opposite had by now dropped her paper and sat with her face in her hands, her body shuddering with pent-up laughter.

John began to stamp his left foot in time with the music. Looking skyward, he started to howl like a wolf.

Unable to contain myself any longer, I felt my bladder contract and seriously thought I was going to piss myself. I could hardly breathe. Looking around the captive audience, I could clearly see I was not the only one. John was putting on a better show for the travel-weary shoppers than the unfortunate busker. As the train pulled into another station, the hard-done-by guitarist produced a plastic saucer and began to dance his way among the bemused travellers.

'That's confirmed it,' John said seriously, 'ears' still horizontal. 'He is fucking mad.' Looking at him through tear-blurred vision, I began to realize I'd quickly developed an affinity for Green Team!

0200 hours. Swiping my security card through the machine, I heard the heavy clunk as the lock disengaged, and pushing the door I entered into the basement briefing room, met only by the inferno from the subterranean heating pipes. 'Look at this place,' I thought. 'It's like a fucking sauna down here.'

SO19 are considered by many to be the premier firearms team in the country. As a result, many people think we operate out of a plush suite of offices in Central London. In reality, 'home' to us is the basement of an old Victorian police station on the outskirts of Dalston. I passed between the metal racks housing our personal equipment, all stacked high to the ceiling, until finally reaching my shelf. Pulling my ops bag and body armour from the rack for the fourth time that week, I made my way to the main briefing room and headed straight for the kettle. I'm one of those people that can't function at that time in the morning until I've had at least three cups of coffee.

Pushing in the plug, I looked around the dingy room. I was half an hour early. Newspaper clippings adorned the peeling walls between the briefing boards. 'LAWGIRL FOILS GUNMAN', screamed a headline from the *Daily Mail*, depicting a suspect being led away. 'POLICEMAN SHOT IN LONDON SIEGE' said another, while a third, depicting Operation Emerge, read 'THE COKEBUSTERS'. It was nice to pick out those jobs which I had planned or been involved in; it gave me the satisfaction of a 'job well done'.

'You're only as good as your last job,' said Pecky, breaking the silence and a coffee cup as he struggled in under the weight of his huge bergan.

'Yeah, well, my last job was the bollocks.' I laughed, thinking back to Wembley and the kidnappers lying prone in the rain earlier that week.

It was standard operating procedure for a team to pre-brief on tactics prior to the main briefing for the agency concerned (in this case the local CID). This way we could iron out any problems 'in house', and it would also keep the main briefing short, having already worked out the ground, and our own particular tasks within the operation. In this case, this was a relatively simple job as far as we were concerned. A convoy of vehicles would go to the forming-up point (predetermined to be far enough from the target premises to avert a compromise). We would continue on foot, feeding in a front and rear armed containment as we went. Safe in the knowledge that the suspect was unable to escape if alerted, the team could covertly approach the front door and effect an entry. Once successful, they would call on all occupants inside to 'make themselves known'; they in turn would be plasticuffed (under certain circumstances) and handed to the local Arrest and Search teams, while the firearms team would systematically clear the building using specially trained SO19 search dogs. Only when the team leader was happy there was no further threat would the premises be handed to unarmed officers and the team withdrawn.

The briefing room became a hive of activity and chatter as the team assembled. CID officers handed out briefing sheets and yet more coffee, and I sat and read the information sheets (should the case later come to trial it was important that the original information was correct for reasons of legal disclosure).

Formal introductions over, I stood and lectured on the tactical and safety aspects of the day. 'CID will remain at the FUP and will only be brought forward under control. We have a paramedic ambulance here today, and I've asked them to nominate two separate and distinct hospitals; in the event of casualties it is important we know who is going where.' The DCI looked up sharply. Catching her eye, I explained this was standard operating procedure. Although we planned our jobs to the last detail it was still a firearms operation, and I couldn't categorically state that nothing would go wrong. In view of this, it was far better to have trained professionals on the scene than wait a crucial ten minutes or more for an ambulance. (We have always worked closely with the London Ambulance Service on such occasions, and the service provided is second to none.)

Fifteen minutes later I concluded: 'Now that everybody knows their particular role I'd like you in the yard at four-thirty sharp. That's ten minutes before we move to the FUP.'

'How's it going, Neil?' I asked an SO19 dog handler in the corridor. 'Haven't seen you for a while.'

'No,' he replied, 'I've got a new dog. I've been out of it for a couple of years.'

'Bloody hell, is it that long?' I asked incredulously. 'How's Jay?' His old dog, a real trooper.

'He's OK,' Neil said, following me into the toilet. 'Hates it when I go to work with the new one, though. Trouble is they retired him too soon – fucker escaped yesterday. I'm seriously thinking about giving him the needle.'

I looked at him, shocked. 'You're joking,' I said. 'My missus would fucking kill you if I told her that. You know what she's like!'

He laughed. 'Yeah, I do.'

'This is our firearms frequency radio,' I said, passing the DCI a set in the yard. 'You can monitor what's going on and I'll call your people forward when it's safe to do so.'

'Right,' she said excitedly. 'I'd better have a callsign. How about DCI? No – you can call me Janet, I don't mind.' With that she took the radio and disappeared in a flourish.

Walking to the vehicles I could see the team were barely able to cover their grins. Pulling on a ballistic helmet, I checked comms and climbed in the back of the Range Rover.

'She reminds me of a favourite aunt,' I said.

'That's just what I was thinking,' said Steve. 'Just like my aunt Joan. She's fucking mad too.'

The convoy slowed as the black Range Rovers snaked their way through the dimly lit South London side-streets. 'Thirty seconds to FUP. That's thirty seconds, kill the lights,' I said, looking back as darkness enveloped the seven-vehicle convoy. Killing the engines, we glided silently behind a row of communal garages and began to debus. It had been stressed at the briefing that absolute quiet was necessary at this point. Noise travels well at night, and a slammed car door or noisy radio could compromise the entire plan before the containments were in.

Twenty seconds later my earpiece crackled: 'Steve. In position at the back.' This was immediately followed by, 'Front containment in position. Move up, move up.'

'Let's go,' I whispered.

Dave was to lead, covering the team's approach with the heavy ballistic shield; behind followed the MOE men with the heavy rams slung across their shoulders. Entering by the communal door, we made our way swiftly to the second floor and stacked up on the flat's front door. Placing the arm of the hydraulic ram against the wood, John looked at me. I nodded.

As Steve pressed the control button the early morning quiet was broken by the electronic hum of the ram. The arm slowly extended, then suddenly we heard wood splintering as the teeth bit deeper into the framework. John took hold of the small red Enforcer battering ram, ready to back up the hydraulic if required. The hum became laboured as the hydraulic bit and strained, then there was a resounding *crack* as the front door flew inward. The whole episode had taken no more than ten seconds; inside the flat they would have heard nothing.

'Off, off, off!' John shouted as the ram's arm retracted and it fell with a heavy metallic clunk into the doorway. Dave had already filled the gap with his shield.

'In the address. We are armed police. Come to the door now!' Dave screamed.

Silence.

Again, 'In the address – we are armed police. Make yourself known.'

'OK, OK,' came the muffled reply from within.

'Let me see those hands first. We are armed police, we have a warrant,' Dave repeated.

'I'm coming,' said a nervous voice from the darkness. A young black male came into view wearing nothing but boxer shorts.

'OK. Put your hands on your head and walk towards me slowly,' I shouted from the doorway.

'OK, OK,' he said again, his speech heavy with sleep.

'This way, this way. Keep walking and listen to the officer on my right,' I instructed as he emerged cautiously from the door.

'To me, to me. Now face the wall and make a fist,' Steve said, applying a plasticuff to secure his hands and walking him past the growling dog.

'Who else is in the address?' I called to his back.

'No one, man. Just my old lady and baby.'

After years in the department, it never ceased to amaze me that normality to some people was to have armed police officers smashing down the door and arresting them in the early hours of the morning. It must add to their kudos or street credibility. I know for a fact that if it happened to me I'd have trouble keeping the 'tortoise' from sticking his head out of my arse.

'Listen to me,' Dave shouted. 'Get dressed and put a blanket round the baby – it's cold out here. The quicker you're out, the quicker you'll be back in.'

At this point we really had all the time in the world; unlike drugs (which can be easily disposed of) it would be very difficult to flush the component parts of a sawn-off down the toilet. It was with this in mind that we had decided at the planning phase to deal with the situation in this manner. I didn't really like doing dig-outs at a family address. Dragging women and children out of bed at all hours left a bad taste in my mouth. That said, I could never bring myself to believe that a wife would be totally unaware of her husband's wrongdoing. In my book that made them as guilty as their partner. Children, however, were another matter, being party to a mess that was not of their making and over which they had no control.

Handing the woman and baby to the waiting CID, I returned at a trot to tag on the end of the searching team. Neil's new dog proved its worth. Head down, searching in and out of the open rooms for hidden suspects, he swept through the building pausing only momentarily to indicate 'all clear'. Closely behind followed the team, physically checking cupboards and beds. I would not hand over until I was absolutely sure the premises were totally clear.

'What do you think, Steve?' Janet asked as I pulled my helmet off.

'Couldn't see anything. You'll have to pull the place apart,' I replied. 'I can only assure you that the place is clear.'

'Fucking blinding,' she said. 'See you back at the nick. I want to thank your boys personally.'

'Where the hell is she?' John stretched out on the floor of the CID office. 'I'm knackered, I want to go home.'

The effects of adrenalin on the human body are incredible. You can be totally shagged, but during an operation your alertness is second to none; afterwards, when your adrenalin goes down, you seem to be doubly tired. And in my experience we lived on adrenalin.

'Well done, boys,' boomed the DCI, charging into the room. 'Fucking brilliant, as ever. Now tell me, when are you getting women on the teams?'

'When they can pass the fucking course,' came an answer from the back.

'We do have women instructors,' I said weakly. I thought seriously: the truth of the matter was, yes, we had women instructors, and we were now being pushed to have women on the teams, but in my experience and I'm certainly not sexist – many of them really couldn't hit a barn from the inside.

'Well, I think you and the dog section are the last bastions of male chauvinism,' she snarled, glaring at the two handlers.

'I object to that,' said Dick. 'We do have women dog handlers, just none on SO19 yet.'

'Yes, but why?' Janet said.

'Because we won't work with fucking poodles,' said one of the team. The ice broken. We laughed, and Janet had taken it in the context it was meant. It would be only a matter of time before women filled our ranks. Personally, I had no objection to working with one that had passed the course fairly. So long as, in this age of *positive* discrimination, we didn't have to lower our standards to suit.

Crawling into bed at eight that morning, I fell straight to sleep.

Beep, beep, beep. The all too familiar sound of my pager. As I struggled with conciousness, I realized I had left it on my trouser belt next door.

Through blurry vision I looked at the clock. 10 a.m. I rubbed my eyes.

Beep, beep, beep.

'All right, all right, I'm coming,' I shouted, pulling off the quilt and stumbling next door to retrieve the annoying device. What's going on? I said to myself. I wasn't even on call.

Beep . . . I pushed the button, cancelling the high-pitched alarm, and looked at the faint glow of the display. Focusing my eyes with some effort, I read: 'CONTACT DUTY OFFICER, URGENT.'

Picking up the phone, I instinctively dialled the number of the base reserve.

'Hello, Steve,' said a voice at the far end. 'Guvnor's been looking for you. McLeod's been housed again.'

'Right,' I said, thinking back. 'Book me a fast run. Fifteen minutes.'

I cleaned my teeth and looked in the mirror. My gaze was met by a pale face and two bloodshot eyes. 'Great,' I said, pulling on my jeans. Two hours' sleep.

The name Nicol 'Razor' McLeod (which has been changed for the purposes of this account) was one to conjure with – and one that would dog me for the rest of my service. For the past eight weeks he had been a thorn in the side of the department, always one step ahead. McLeod had been described to me as an extremely violent, extremely large, psychopath. Currently on the run from a mental institution – on admission for beating up his girlfriend, the sister of a well-known sports personality – having learnt that he would shortly be transferred to Broadmoor, with no hope of early release. Armed with this knowledge, McLeod had effected his escape and made his way back to his old manor in South London. Here he had, to date, successfully eluded recapture. And on his own turf he ruled the area by fear. I can't honestly remember any one person of whom people were so terrified.

Fifteen minutes later, the car was speeding through the Friday afternoon traffic, blue lights flashing, on course for Old Street some twenty miles across London. As I sat in the back, listening to the shrill noise of the sirens and the occasional mutter of 'wanker' from the driver, I thought how McLeod had secured a vice-like grip on those around him.

Three weeks earlier (while on Black Team), I had been called to South London for a briefing with senior officers. McLeod had been considered so dangerous that an incident room had been set up in an effort to locate him. At this early stage there had been no mention of firearms, but as McLeod favoured the knife and machete, and as such had been placed in the category of 'cannot safely be dealt with without the use of firearms', our involvement became necessary. 'This week alone,' the SIO had said, 'he has caused grievous bodily harm to two members of the public he thought looked at him funny. He must be apprehended before a civilian or a police officer is killed.'

Apart from the obvious danger to the public, the incident room was also concerned that a lone police officer on routine patrol may inadvertently stop him only to get stabbed for his trouble. In a service that had recently lost good men to nutters with knives, this thought was obviously in everybody's minds.

The local officers had quite rightly dubbed him the 'Baddest Man in the World'. It was a label that stuck.

Later that evening my team had effected rapid entries on five addresses where the man was believed to be housed. On each occasion he had left prior to our arrival. It was very frustrating, and we wanted him badly. Since that time, contingency plans had been drawn up – and ARVs had attended numerous false alarms and bogus sightings.

The car screeched to a halt outside the base, jolting me back to the present. I looked at my watch. The journey had taken just over thirty minutes in heavy traffic. Thanking the crew, I got out to the smell of burnt brake linings, and pushing open the heavy door I made my way to the kit room for the second time that day.

'He's got a gun.' the Detective Sergeant shouted. 'Who in their right mind would give that nutter a fucking gun? He threatened a guy with it last Saturday.'

The incident room was quiet.

'We've done a lot of work and now know one hundred per cent that he's frequenting an address on this estate.' The DCI indicated a large map on the wall behind. 'We've got two OPs – one front, one back.'

The DS interrupted: 'The only problem is, he has his own OP in a tower block opposite. Not only do they watch the address for him, they also watch our OP. Christ knows how you'll get in.'

I looked up at the map. 'We'll find a way,' I said confidently.

For the past two days the OPs had monitored McLeod's movements without 'showing out.' He was without doubt a shrewd and cunning operator. Once in the address, he would remain for no more than twenty minutes at any one time. On his way out he had been observed ducking down between parked cars at any sign of headlights in the distance. He would certainly be hard to take.

'Hold, hold,' I whispered to Pecky, my Green Team number two. We were on the top floor of a tower block that gave a commanding view of the target premises far below. If we moved any further we would be within sight of the tower block opposite, and McLeod's own OP.

The target itself was a two-storey terraced house set amidst the sprawling South London estate, close to the river. The small rear garden was contained by a six-foot wooden fence. I had a good feeling about this aspect – it would certainly serve to cover our approach. The back door was fully glazed, with large windows either side giving access to the kitchen area. I made a mental note of the rabbit hutch below the window. A good step up, I thought.

At the moment the premises were in total darkness. I had seen enough.

'Who's this bird he's supposed to be shagging, then?' said Big Len. Len was now the MOE man on Blue Team. I had earlier decided I would probably need two teams for this operation. Get in fast, swamp the ground, and gain control. Len had just returned from a recce on the front of the building which was to be his team's entry point.

'Dunno,' I answered. 'Just some slag.'

'Don't get me wrong,' said Len, 'I only ask because I followed her into town from the house. She didn't even know I was there.'

'She ain't fucking surveillance conscious then?' said a voice from behind.

I laughed. Anybody would know Len was there. Over six feet tall, six feet wide, in full kit he weighed over twenty stone, and he had a vertical scar running through the short hair on his head. Len and I had done selection together. Once I had asked him how he came by his scar. He told me that it was an old injury from a night out when he had got drunk. At that point it was nothing more than a small mark. His mates, however, in their drunken stupor, thought he looked remarkably like a money box and kept attempting to put coins in his head. Unconscious and oblivious to pain, Len had no option but to accept his fate, only to wake up later covered in blood and surrounded by small change. The scar he now sported was nothing more dramatic than the legacy of a 'good night out'.

In the hours that followed I got together with Mark, the Blue Team sergeant, and Don, our duty officer. It was time to iron out a plan.

'I favour two covert vans, one front, one back, with a team in each,' I said, pointing to the overhead plans. 'My team will take the rear aspect using the garages as cover. At that point we're on the blind side. Once we bail out with the ladders it's a fifty-yard dash to the back fence. In the dark we should be OK.'

Don nodded. 'What about Blue Team?'

I looked at Mark. 'Where we leave the FUP for the FAP the road splits. We'll carry on turning left into the garages, you turn left at the junction and hold just short of the address.'

This would be the first of many scenarios suggested before the plan was perfected, and was solely for discussion by the SO19 supervisors. Kick it around, see if it's feasible. The second briefing would be with the teams, making sure everybody was aware of their role within the plan. Only when we were happy would I brief the SIO; there was no point in going in half cocked. Once the plan was approved, a 'formal' briefing could be held for everybody involved, including the support services.

Ten minutes later, Don and Mark agreed the plan. Three and a half hours had elapsed since our arrival. Our basic plan now consisted of a rapid entry from both the front and rear of the building. It was to be co-ordinated if possible with one team securing the the upstairs bedrooms and the other the ground floor.

'He's back, he's back,' shouted the DS, interupting the briefing. 'Hurry – we've only got ten minutes at most.'

'Bollocks,' said Don. 'If he's come back he's not aware we've recced the place. The environment hasn't been disturbed, which is good, but we aren't going anywhere until we're properly briefed. If he leaves we'll wait till he comes back.'

Looking somewhat distraught, the DS turned and fled.

'I cannot emphasize how dangerous this man can be,' said the DCI at the main briefing. 'He is now believed to have a firearm, and is likely to take a hostage at the first opportunity. Doctors are standing by with sedatives, and if captured he will be taken directly to Broadmoor.' He went on, 'This is SO19's game. Once they have him secure, those cuffs will not be removed under any circumstances. We have just been updated that he has left the address but is likely to return, any questions?'

Briefing over, we filed out. 'I can't believe one man could be so dangerous,' Len said, walking into the corridor. 'This is bollocks.

Who the fuck does he think he is? I'm going to pull his head off and shit in the hole.'

I looked up, seeing his grinning face. He was joking, I thought for a second. 'Yes you probably could.'

Twenty minutes later we found ourselves at the forward holding area, two minutes' running time from the address. In the darkness the vans disgorged their cargo of men and dogs and we made our way to the cramped room that had been set aside for the wait. I sat on a small table, the extra four stone of assault kit weighing heavily on my shoulders. Awaiting McLeod's return, we had to be ready to go at a moment's notice, so the kit stayed on: helmet, mask, gloves, body armour and weapons. As the minutes passed into hours, inane conversation filled the room, but at the back of our minds we waited for the call and the deployment that would last but seconds. The dog handlers, huddled in a corner, soon became bored – and revelled in silently sending their dogs forward to steal an unsuspecting team man's biscuits brought for the journey. We laughed at their antics, but soon lapsed into our own thoughts and conversations.

'Standby, standby.' The command we had waited to hear shattered the din. 'OP has him into the premises.'

Outside, I heard the distant roar of engines sparking into life. Picking up our weapons we sprinted out, our discomfort vanishing as we entered the dark interior of the vans and pulled down the roller shutters behind.

'Green Team ready for the off?' Don came over the net.

'Ready, Don,' I replied.

'Blue Team ready?'

'Ready,' came Mark's reply.

'OK. Standby, lets roll.'

Banging twice on the side of the van with a gloved fist, I braced myself against the thin aluminium wall as the van jerked forward and picked up speed. It was all down to the drivers now; we had no control over this phase of the operation. I looked around the inky blackness. Nothing save the laboured, heavy breathing of the men inside and the regular panting of our canine companions.

'Fucking hell,' said Pecky, cutting through the darkness. 'I don't remember it being this far. That driver better get it right.'

'Don't worry,' I whispered, 'you lose track when your vision is impaired. Not far now.'

Feeling the van lurch to the left I instinctively knew we had reached the garages; the slowing of the vehicle served only to confirm it. 'Don, FAP now. Move up,' I whispered into the radio. The roller shutter had already begun to rise, and incandescent light was filling the darkness.

'Moving up now,' came Don's muffled reply. I mentally pictured the front aspect of the building and the van moving silently forward. No matter what, in seconds the premises would be contained, with no avenue of escape. This achieved, we desperately needed to get to the man before he got to a potential 'hostage'.

Silence was of the essence. I exited the van, extending the folding stock on my MP5 and jabbing it firmly into my shoulder. The ladder party behind were ready.

Leading off along the side of the van, I saw a middle-aged female unlocking her garage door. Bent double, she looked up sharply, trapped like a startled rabbit in the glare of a lamp, a look of abject horror on her face. Eight men in black, bristling with guns, wearing hoods and helmets, stood before her. 'Evening,' I said as we trotted past towards the fifty yards of open ground and our ultimate objective. (I was later to learn from CID that the woman's two teenage sons had gone with her to park the car. It being dark and a somewhat 'bad' neighbourhood, they felt Mum may need protection – it was their daily routine. Seeing us, however, had caused the two youngsters to lock themselves in the car. As Mum tried in vain to gain access, the boys refused to let her in, leaving her trapped outside to face an uncertain fate. Some protection! Having calmed down, the poor woman had apparently seen the funny side and, like all decent law-abiding citizens, she had wished us well.)

The ladder party broke the open ground at a run. Pushing the PTT switch on my chest, I began a commentary for the team at the front: 'Back fence now, no compromise. Ladders up. One over, two over, still no compromise, four over . . .'

Perching on top of the ladder ready to drop into the yard, I was suddenly hit by white light which cut through the darkness and silhouetted the team by the fence. Inside the house somebody had entered the kitchen, switching on the light and illuminating the small back garden.

'Compromise, compromise,' Pecky hissed, covering the short distance to the back door.

I jabbed at the PTT. 'Compromise, compromise. *Go, go, go!*' I shouted, dropping heavily from the fence on to one knee. Running the length of the garden, I covered in through the kitchen window.

The noise was unbelievable. The two door men had already begun to attack the double-glazed back door. The two large windows erupted, glass cascading across the floor, as those designated to smash and cover hacked away with axes, reaching through and pulling out curtains and runners. A large, pointed shard of glass dropped dangerously from the framework striking Pecky in the chest. Impervious, the assault continued.

Looking at the heavy metal framework of the back door, I could see it was failing to yield to the constant battering. Standing back I shouted, 'Baulked on the door. Window, window, window.' Although the door was to have been our main entry point we had designated windows as secondary, and now we had to gain access at all costs, had to maintain the momentum. Hearing the command, the team instinctively slipped into their new role and three heads disappeared through the wrecked window into the kitchen as they made their way towards the main reception room.

Jumping on to the rabbit hutch, head down, heart pounding. I ducked beneath an ugly piece of glass and on to the now dented stainless steel draining board. Catching my right boot in the net curtain wire, I hit the kitchen floor trailing it behind.

What had seemed like minutes trapped in the garden had in fact been no more than seconds. Looking through the hall I saw the front door lying on the ground, Blue Team streaming up the stairs to the muffled shouts of 'Room clear. Room clear, re-org.' Two males and a female lay trussed up and face down on the living-room floor, a hole where the bay window had been now filled by the masked and helmeted Blue Team cover man, whose task had been to effect a limited entry covering those inside.

I felt good. The op had gone well and, surprisingly enough,

without injury – a feat in itself as all the windows had been smashed.

Digging into the leg pocket of my coveralls, I produced a tatty colour photograph of our prey. 'Turn him over,' I said to Steve, indicating one of the suspects,

Leaning over and grabbing his shoulder, Steve pulled the man round to face me.

I held the photo beside his face. 'Nope,' I said, indicating the other suspect. 'What's your name?' I asked the man with a ponytail.

'Michael,' came the reply.

I held the photograph beside his face, and shook my head. Heading for the hall, I got on the radio. 'Don, we are secure. Bring up CID, but I don't think he's here.'

Within minutes, incident room staff had rushed forward. 'Where is he? Where is he?' shouted the frantic DS.

I pointed. 'Turn him over, Steve.'

A look of pure horror played across the DS's features. 'Fuck it! The OP was a hundred per cent sure it was him.'

I shook my head.

'I just can't believe he got the fucking jump on us again, I just don't.'

I jabbed a finger at him. 'Nobody left this place – our part was slick.'

'Look,' said Don, 'he's got scars in the right places. Let's take them all in, I think it could be him.'

TSG officers in full riot gear were called forward to remove the 'suspect' suspect. Head down, his hands cuffed behind his back, he was led from the address. As he drew level with me, he looked up into my eyes and smiled. 'I'm not going to struggle, guv. Honest.'

Arriving back at south London, I dashed to the incident room.

'Well?'

'Don't know yet. The psychiatric nurse who knows him is going to look.'

I struggled out of my kit in the small upstairs office. The teams were packing up their kit and weapons in silence. The smell of sweat hung in the air; we had been kitted for four hours. Glad to shed my burden, I rubbed my shoulders and again thought how your body aches once the adrenalin rush is over.

A young PC stuck his head through the door. 'DCI would like to see you downstairs, Sarge.'

Throwing the heavy bergen on to my back I quipped, 'Here we go again – they've housed him at another address.'

We sat dejectedly around the large canteen table, the normal banter having vanished. It had been a long day.

'You boys have made me the happiest man alive,' hooted the DCI, entering with a large grin on his face.

'You mean it was him?' I asked in amazement.

'Course it was,' he beamed.

In the corridor outside I could already see the arrangements being made for his removal. The contingency equipment included two sets of handcuffs, a body belt, enough tranquillizer to kill an elephant, and a sergeant with six PCs. 'Dunno what all the fuss is about,' Len smiled. 'He was Jack shit at the end of the day.' We laughed.

The DCI continued: 'Let me just say again how happy I am, Steve. I know you've been out loads of times – you're Green Team, right?' I nodded. 'And the other is Blue?' Again I acknowledged. 'Well,' he went on, 'there'll be a little something coming for both of you.'

'Thanks very much,' I said, catching Mark's eye.

'Oh, and by the way,' the DCI said, turning. The Assistant Commissioner sends his gratitude for a job well done.'

I frowned. The events of the day were indeed puzzling. I knew McLeod was a bad man, but like all bad men he had come quietly in the end. All the resources that were standing by to deal with him after his capture now weighed heavily on my mind . . . And the Assistant Commissioner phoning? So soon after his arrest? At this time of night? Surely there was something more to this man than met the eye. In my eighteen years in the job I have never known anyone to be treated with so much caution – and that included terrorists, murderers and armed robbers! An incident room for one man?

'Oh – and by the way,' the DCI said, leaving the room. 'Of course I doubt he'll ever be released from Broadmoor.'

'What's going on, Don?' I asked the guvnor.

'Fuck knows. They wanted him real bad for some reason. By

173

the way, the DCI left you this,' he said, hoisting a clean, crisp fifty-pound note in the air. 'Said have a drink on him.'

That did it for me. Never have I seen a senior officer shell out fifty pounds of his own money to a bunch of blokes that were only doing their job. It was a very generous gesture, but also a very puzzling one.

'Fuck the ethics,' Len said, reaching into Mark's coat pocket. 'Give me the phone.'

Pressing a button, he grinned. 'Hello Ian, it's Len. We all right for a drink?'

Mark looked at me. 'Good, ain't it – when you've got the number of the local pub stored in the memory of the team's mobile.'

I laughed.

'Look,' Len was saying, 'there's sixteen of us and a fifty-pound note. What am I trying to say? 'I know your licence is until midnight, so don't close before.'

'Mount up, lets go,' I called as we moved to the vehicles at a run, for a harrowing drive back to base. Once there, I left a quick note on the board for the other teams. It read simply: 'The 17th Baddest Man in the World has been captured – by the 16 Baddest Men in the World!' Beside it I stuck McLeod's tattered photograph with a cross through his face. Winking at him, I made my way into the cold night air and headed for the pub.

True to his word, Ian, a good friend of the teams, was waiting. Downing the first pint of lager in one, I thought, I've not had a drink for six hours.

12.30 a.m. Sitting on the last tube home, I couldn't get it out of my head that something was missing. Something we'd not been told, perhaps? I don't know. I'll never know. You're only as good as your last job, and that was mine. It would be two o'clock by the time I got home.

Tomorrow was another day!

11

It Pays to Keep it Clean

Green Team had been great. At the end of my tour I'd been given a magnificent send-off. Then I'd spent Christmas in the States, returning to Black refreshed and ready to go!

And in the months that followed we really started to gel as a team. As the jobs came thick and fast we seemed to handle them with the kind of confidence that can be acquired only through months of training and hard work; I was proud of the boys and the results they'd started to achieve – and thus I was on quite a high one fateful February morning when I entered the Flying Squad offices.

Sipping my hot, strong coffee, I searched the groups of busy detectives for that familiar face.

'Steve, over here!' he shouted in his strong Glaswegian accent. Making my way through the throng, I quickly found his corner, walls adorned with white-boards, maps, photos and plans for the forthcoming briefing.

I took in the heavy build and ruddy complexion of the bearded but smartly dressed detective sergeant. 'How you doing, Gordon?' I smiled, accepting his proffered hand. I'd worked with Gordon a lot over the past year or so. He always organized 'quality' jobs for us and, unlike the majority of Flying Squad officers, he was keen to involve us.

'I've been busy over the past couple of days,' he said, pointing to the large folders of intelligence and plans. 'I reckon it'll go today. Ninety-nine fucking per cent!'

That was good enough for me. If there was an informant he hadn't mentioned it – and I didn't want to know, it was none of our concern. We were brought in only to 'go across

175

the pavement'. Targeting armed robbers (or 'blaggers', as they were commonly known) was the squad's fundamental role, and a challenge they pursued with relish. Unlike many of the guys on SO19, I could understand the reluctance of some squads to call us in. After months or even years of investigations, they typically wanted to be in on the arrest, to witness first-hand the culmination of their painstaking enquiries. It did, however, really grip my shit when I read of Flying Squad officers 'going across the pavement' ill-prepared and with nothing more than revolvers to defend themselves against a heavily armed gang. Like it or not, that was a job for us – and luckily Gordon fully accepted this fact.

'OK. A bit of hush, please!' the DI shouted above the din. Taking our seats, we listened intently, scribbling notes.

Two, possibly three armed suspects were intent on robbing a post office remittance van as it delivered 'cash in transit' to a sub-post office in the Crouch Hill area of North London. Running north to south between the boroughs of Haringey and Islington, this area was considered an ideal plot. Due to a set of pedestrian guard-rails, the van was unable to park directly outside, leaving the custodian a short walk along the crowded street. That walk was considered the ideal opportunity for a determined blagger, the £250,000 the van carried making it all the more worthwhile. I visualized the plot in my mind's eye, having recced it earlier that week with Joe. And would our plan work? Never before had I felt so apprehensive, for I knew the full weight of the repercussions of a full-scale gun battle in a crowded street.

(It has since been mooted in the press from a source close to one of the robbers that he was set up and the police were operating some sort of 'Shoot to Kill' policy. I'd like to take this opportunity to dispel any such nonsense. Every shooting within the department is investigated at the highest level under the direct control of the Police Complaints Authority. Any suggestion of wrongdoing would be dealt with using the full weight of the law. No, 'Shoot to Kill' policies do not and have never existed.

The briefing was as full and comprehensive as anybody could wish. Then it was my turn. Rising, I addressed the audience. 'Now, you've all worked with us before, but unlike many other plots I need to fill you in on a few details. When the attack is called, only SO19 will be going across the pavement. The reasons for this are twofold.' I glanced around the faces. 'First – and call me Mr Paranoid – but the potential for a hostage situation is paramount in my mind. If this happens we'll stand off and attempt to negotiate.'

Muttering broke the pregnant pause. I continued: 'As always, the safety of the public is our main priority, and a gun battle in a confined, crowded space won't do us any favours. The second reason you won't come forward is because I have a sniper on a roof two hundred yards up the road. He has a rifle with telescopic sights and a commanding view of the plot. If there's the slightest suggestion of danger to life, he will deal with it, and we don't want anybody in his way!'

I went on to detail casevac and post-incident procedures, before concluding: 'The dress of the day, for everyone, will be body armour and cunt caps!' They laughed. 'Cunt caps' was the term used by the department for the high-visibility baseball caps donned when operating in plain clothes. Unlike the Americans (and typical of most British police forces) we went for quantity rather than quality. I'd originally heard the term while on Level Two selection, and had asked Kev how they got their name. 'Put one on your head and look in the mirror,' he'd replied.

I had to agree he was right.

Before we had left Old Street that morning, the team had been fully briefed on their roles within the plan, which we called operation Odense. This would negate the need for any complex briefing at the other end. We found this arrangement both practical and time-saving, with each man knowing his job within the greater sphere of things.

'It's going to happen, isn't it?' Bill said excitedly. He'd recently dubbed himself the 'Arctic Fox', due to his many winters in Norway with the Royal Marines.

'Indication's good. I've not felt this way since Emerge,' I said.

Having a separate team briefing after the event was not the norm, but due to the way I (and, judging by the mood, everybody else) felt, I wanted to iron out a few things before we split and went our separate ways.

'I'm concerned about the hostage potential. I can't emphasize that enough. If we are unable to deal with it immediately, then we must have the discipline to stand off and leave it to Joe.'

I turned to the Duty Officer. 'You happy, Andy?'

'Yeah.' He nodded. 'I think we've covered everything. Just watch that alley up the side of the shops, if they get up there we're fucked!'

'You're right,' I said. 'It's scary enough going across the pavement knowing Joe has got a scope on your back and the safety off.'

Picking up the gear, we sought our respective drivers. I had in fact been with Joe the day before at Lippetts, where he had meticulously zeroed in the team rifle and hit a dangling tomato at the end of the range. I knew he was professional enough not to let us down. I also knew the full potential of the .223 round he was using. It was more than capable of punching a hole clean through your body armour.

Settling into the OP in a flat above a shop opposite the post office, which the squad had aquired after approaching the owner, I felt the tension rise. Nigel, Andy and I had been delivered there separately by squad drivers, and now everybody was back together I felt the hair on the back of my neck rise. I knew what was about to happen.

From behind the 'safety' of the net curtains I stared down on to the street below, at the small shops and people going about their business, all oblivious to the fact that they were being watched by men with enough firepower to start a small war.

I knew where the van would stop, where the guard would walk, where the hit would happen. Wiping my sweaty palm on my jeans, I checked comms for the third time that day.

'Joe, you in position?'

'Yeah,' came the non-committal reply. 'I'll stay out of sight until the wagon's on the plot, then get out on to the roof, no probs.'

Nigel sat deep in thought as he fingered the strap of his MP5. 'Not long now,' I said, visualizing the cut-off team parked down the road in a black cab.

I had decided the attack would come from three directions – and as such the lads knew well the potential for a blue on blue – Andy, Nigel and I would come in on the 'blind' side from the OP across the road, hitting the van back and front. If a getaway vehicle was identified I would deal with it by smashing a window and throwing in a smoke grenade (I had decided you couldn't get very far in a car full of smoke). A flounder (squadspeak for black cab) containing Brad, Chris and the Arctic Fox would come in from the north. Joe was on the roof to the south, and just below him in a similar OP were Ninja and Sinex. We were, in effect, strategically placed so that, in the event of a hostage situation where negotiations had failed, the gunman would have only one clear option: towards the front of the van, towards Joe, and to certain death, because by my reckoning you don't go far without a head.

As the minutes dragged slowly by I engaged in the inevitable banter with Nigel. We knew each other well, lived in each other's pockets, and for many periods spent more time at work than at home. Nigel was a friendly, intelligent guy with a wicked streak of humour. He was also a keen family man with a fierce sense of loyalty.

'Standby, standby,' the DI was suddenly yelling from his perch by the window. My heart missed a beat as the adrenalin coursed through my veins. Snatching up his Five, Nigel was at my side.

Hoisting the radio the DI called, 'Red Box on the plot. Repeat, Red Box on the plot!'

This was it. Like it or not this was what we'd been waiting for since we started some six hours before. Racing down a small flight of stairs, we hit street level. I instinctively drew my Glock as we stacked on the door leading out on to the street. Staring out of the frosted glass façade, I could just make out the faint red form of the van parked across the road. Heart now racing, I wondered how busy it would be. Would we cross in time? With all our planning we still had no control over the traffic. The seconds seemed like hours. For the hundredth time that day I checked my equipment. Cunt cap, plasticuffs, field dressing, and finally the Hayley & Weller smoke grenade strapped to my body armour.

I tapped my radio. Nothing! I looked at Nigel quizzically. 'Shit! This is going to blow out!'

Suddenly the radio sparked into life. 'We have two suspects on the plot, one dressed as a police officer, the other all in black. *ATTACK! ATTACK! ATTACK!*'

The OP had spotted both men. Thirty-three-year-old Steven Charalambous, a petty burglar with a string of convictions, wore a plastic police helmet, white shirt, black tie and fluorescent jacket; he also sported a false moustache and was armed with a large black self-loading pistol. Likewise armed, his sidekick, thirty-one-year-old bodybuilder and wine bar owner Loukas Manicou, was dressed totally in black, complete with balaclava.

As they disappeared from view we hit the door, bomb bursting on to the pavement. Negotiating the fast-moving traffic, I sprinted head-down on collision course for the front of the van, Nigel by my side. Expecting to see the custodian heading for the post office, I paused momentarily behind the van. I waited. Nothing! Something had obviously gone wrong – that was apparent. Hearing muffled screams from behind the van, I took the bull by the horns. The position of the van had totally obscured the view from the OP. From his position Joe could see nothing. Nobody had 'eyeball'. Leaving Nigel at the nearside wing and Andy at the rear, I gripped my Glock in both hands and bounded on to the pavement, looking along the nearside of the van. Charalambous, his 'uniform' realistic enough to have fooled the guard momentarily, was standing facing me with the guard as a shield, having dragged him to the rear of the van. In his hand he held the large gun, pointed towards the guard's head. He was screaming obscenities into the poor man's ear. Dropping my knees slightly, I punched the weapon forward with both hands and screamed, *'Armed police! Drop the gun!'*

With a sneer on his face and still holding his captive, Charalambous raised the self-loader, pointing it squarely at my chest. People that have been in similar traumatic circumstances will often tell you that time appears to slow down – and this was certainly my experience. In the split second that followed, I took in not only his expression, but thought how ridiculous he looked in fancy dress. As I waited for the impact, unable to fire for fear of hitting the guard, I wondered whether he would hit the grenade, causing me to explode in the middle of Crouch Hill in a spectacular display of green smoke. I also thought of Joe, high above in his lair behind me, poised, finger on trigger and cross-hairs on my back.

That was enough. In one movement I sprang back behind

cover, accompanied by the sharp *crack* of gunfire. No more than a fraction of a second later, there were screams all around me as more shots followed. I was back on the pavement in an instant, witnessing the tumbling form of the 'joke' cop as he spiralled towards the floor, and away from the guard. Nigel, to my left, had grasped the opportunity. Bringing to bear the MP5 he had instinctively fired a pair. His sense of direction – the ability to hit a target without aiming, taught extensively by SO19 for close-range work – causing the rounds to hit Charalambous in the chest and spinning him. With the weapon in his hand he was still a threat, so Nigel had fired two more rounds at the falling man.

During those vital and chaotic seconds a number of things had taken place.

'*ATTACK! ATTACK! ATTACK!*' boomed the radio in the flounder, which was parked up five hundred yards away.

'Get this fucking thing moving!' Chris screamed at the unfortunate squad man designated to drive, as the cab leapt at speed into the fast-moving traffic.

'Come on, come on, for fuck's sake,' whined Bill. 'It'll all be over by the time we get there.' Caps on, they squatted in the back, MP5s combat-ready, waiting for the opportunity to bail out. Brad had his hand on the door handle as the cab slowed.

CRACK, CRACK! The sound was familiar enough; they instinctively knew it was gunfire.

'Fuck me, it's all over,' Bill shouted.

CRACK, CRACK! 'No it's not!' he yelled. 'Get this thing moving!'

Amid the squeal of brakes they bailed out and hit the pavement at the rear of the van.

The man ran, ran with all of his energy, to escape the madness of that day, the mayhem he had just witnessed outside the small sub-post office in North London. Sinews straining, he ran for his life.

'Stand still, stand still!' Brad screamed, levelling his MP5 at the hapless pedestrian, using his free hand to grab his clothing and drop him to the floor in one swift movement, not realizing the poor bloke was merely fleeing from the confusion of what was to be his most memorable day. Brad was the cut off, and he was doing just that.

CRACK, CRACK! The second pair immediately jerked me back into action. Leaping the body of the fallen guard I levelled my Glock at the impostor, as his helmet fell to the ground. The Glock was inches from his chest, ready to fire; still spiralling he fell, the gun dropping from trembling fingers and skidding across the pavement with a metallic clatter. A resounding thud echoed through the alleyway as he hit the ground, and a look of shock and disbelief covered his pain-filled features, the moustache hanging at a grotesque angle. He lay motionless on his back.

Tunnel vision is a strange phenomenon that can often affect people in what might be termed 'stressful' situations. This was one such event. For two seconds, all eyes were on the shot man, the centre of focus. As a result I had totally forgotten the second bandit. Over the prone figure I instinctively spun, dropping immediately to the kneeling position, weapon up and pointing at the mass of the awesome figure in black, who was standing dumbstruck, weapon raised.

'Get on the floor, on the fucking *floor!*' I screamed, moving fast and at a crouch, catching Andy in my peripheral vision.

He let the weapon fall, staring in disbelief at his fallen partner. Grabbing him roughly, I threw him to the ground and covered, waiting for the team to secure him. To my right, the trembling, cowering figure of the guard crawled for cover.

Now there were more shouts as Flying Squad vehicles screamed on to the plot, urgently disgorging the arrest-and-search teams who, incident tape in hand, started to secure the scene. The whole episode was over in ninety seconds.

I turned to Nigel. 'How's the guard?' he asked nervously. 'Did I hit the guard?'

'The guard's fine,' I replied. 'He just shit himself and fainted. Look, he's crawling away!'

'You sure?' Nigel asked, a look of relief crossing his pale features.

'Course I am. More to the point, how are you?'

He shook his head. 'I'm OK. Why did he do that? Is he some sort of fucking idiot? Why did he point the gun?'

'Dunno,' I replied. 'Instinct, I suppose. It was in his hand and he thought he could escape.'

Nigel was one of the most sensible and stable men I knew, who always went about his duty unflinchingly – and on this occasion he had done a magnificent job. As I had gone wide and right of the vehicle he had gone left, hugging its contours, which gave him a far superior angle. As Charalambous had brought the weapon to bear, he had seen his chance and instinctively fired off a pair. Thanks to his superior sense of direction, both had found their mark, striking the man in the chest. As Charalambous had spun back out of control he had maintained his grip on the gun. Fearing for the lives of the public (and ourselves), Nigel had taken a conscious decision. Still considering the suspect a threat, he had fired a second pair, one grazing the man's chin, the second cutting his tie in half and ricocheting off the alley wall. (It later transpired that it was this last round that had caused the startled pedestrian – whom Brad was now dusting down – to run.)

I called to Ninja; 'Take Nigel to one of the squad motors and stay with him. Nobody touches his weapon and nobody interviews him. I want him well away from the scene.'

'I'm OK,' Nigel said in a steady voice.

'I know you are, and it was a good shoot – but the press will be here in a minute and I don't want you bothered.'

He nodded, taking one last look as Ninja led him slowly from the scene.

Over to my right Andy had already taken charge. One of our men had been involved and our prime concern was his welfare.

'How is he?' I asked Mario, the team medic.

'Bad,' he replied tonelessly, ripping open the bloodstained shirt to reveal two neat bullet wounds and a graze. As he applied field dressings I was already aware of the sound of the evidential camera's auto-wind mechanism, the team and the squad now working in unison. Everthing would be photographed in situ, from empty shell cases to weapons and even discarded field dressings.

I looked into the contorted face of the robber, lying on the ground and screaming with pain, feeling nothing but contempt, glad that it hurt. Only minutes before, this man had levelled a gun in my direction. (The self-loader later turned out to be a replica, although the second suspect's was real enough, loaded with one in the chamber.) His one ambition today was to be counting that money, I thought. Far from his great expectations, he now lay bleeding on the pavement with two hairy-arsed coppers attempting first aid. Still, life's a bitch, and then you die. He was lucky.

The hum of the air ambulance filled the air, and as always the pilot did a brilliant job of landing the machine in a busy street. Running to our location, the doctor and medics set about a fascinating life-saving procedure. Quickly setting up a drip, they handed Chris the bottle, ordering him to hold it high. Without any apparent anaesthetic, they quickly made an incision in Charalambous's side. By inserting a metal instrument resembling a tyre iron, they proceeded to collapse his damaged lung.

I smiled as I looked up at Chris swaying. His face drained of colour he stared intently, unable to tear his eyes from the gruesome, bloody scene. Once more Charalambous gave a blood-curdling scream. 'Fuck this,' Chris said shakily (he had never liked the sight of blood), 'somebody take over!' And handing the bottle to Bill he sat on some nearby steps, fanning himself furiously with his cap. (I later heard rumours from various unenlightened sources that Chris had actually fainted. This is not true. I was there, and can now set the record straight. Chris, you owe me a beer!)

With a whine, the rotors gradually picked up speed, and the helicopter lumbered slowly from the road before soaring off to the London Hospital with its grisly cargo.

Making our way wearily back to the squad office we were met by a SOCO, as was standard proceedure. Unloading our weapons in his presence, he carefully listed and bagged the rounds and weapons in accordance with the SIO's instructions. All the weapons would now be sent away for forensic examination and swabbed to see if they'd been fired. As with everything, the police had to be seen to be whiter than white.

Leaving the squad room amid pats on the back and shouts of 'well done', we drove quickly back to base, and what I considered a well-deserved pint.

Subsequent examination of both the rounds and weapon proved beyond doubt that the shots were fired from Nigel's

MP5. It was retained for evidence, should it be required for examination at later proceedings. One other weapon was also held. Unusually, although it hadn't been fired, it wasn't quite as clean as it should have been (a punishable offence). Once a weapon has been fired then cleaned, it has a tendency to 'sweat', and if subsequently swabbed it might show traces of residue. (Because of this, all weapons should be 'pulled through' with a dry cloth before going out on an operation.) When we first heard about this second weapon, we were desperate to find out who it belonged to. Finally we were told. It was Bill, the 'Arctic Fox', the 'Engineer of Death'. He was fined by the team, and three days later he produced a large cake, inscribed in icing with the words, 'It Pays to Keep it Clean!'

Charalambous made a full recovery. Both he and Manicou (the second man) pleaded guilty at a subsequent hearing at the Old Bailey. Jailing them for five years each, Recorder Anthony Arlidge QC concluded. 'You were both involved in a very serious offence indeed. Next time you can expect to get between fifteen and twenty years!'

But, incredibly, the story doesn't end there. A full inquiry (presided over by the Police Complaints Authority) quite rightly exonerated us from any wrongdoing, and after a period spent on training (as is the normal procedure), Nigel eventually returned to ops. Three years later, in an extraordinary bid to claim a quarter of a million pounds in compensation (funnily enough the amount he had tried to steal), Charalambous sought legal aid from his prison cell, in an attempt to sue the police for unlawful assault, trespass to the person, and excessive and unreasonable force. He also claimed to have been shot at least once while on the ground (untrue). Apart from this ridiculous amount, he claimed an extra £335 for the damage the bullets had caused to his clothing. Legal aid, I'm glad to say, was later withdrawn. A few days later, in what can only be described as a publicity stunt, he escaped from prison, proclaiming his innocence for a crime he'd already admitted. He surrendered late the next day.

At the time of writing he is completing the remainder of his sentence.

12

Terrorism Stops Here

In the wake of Operation Odense, which was hailed a great success, a wave of Flying Squad operations began to wing our way. Perhaps it was the way in which we'd dealt with the suspects under the most traumatic of circumstances. Perhaps they'd finally come to recognize our professionalism – or their own shortcomings! Who knew? Who even cared? The team had a motto: 'A job's a job.' Be they large or small, we revelled in the planning and enjoyed the buzz.

The Flying Squad jobs were usually quite exciting – and now another big one was in the offing. Events have a way of catching up on themselves, and things were about to come to a successful and dramatic conclusion – certainly as far as Black Team were concerned!

Mario, who had left the department for a career in another force, had been replaced by Rick, who'd been attached to the OP on Operation Emerge and had now become a fully fledged member, having worked his way up through the rifle section. Years previously he'd joined the Territorial Army, passed selection, and been 'badged' by 21 SAS. Later however, he found that his SO19 commitments (which constituted his fulltime employment) put a severe strain on his Army activities. Thus he had opted for one of the less élite regiments, and underwent selection for a team. With his large, droopy moustache and short, clipped hair, he looked every inch the part. He also happened to be a whizz when it came to communications. His only drawback (if you could call it such) was the fact that he was a 'kit nut'. I found it hard to believe he could actually move at all when he put his assault vest over his body armour; adorned as it was with

186

every conceivable piece of kit imaginable, it must have weighed a ton! Surely, I often thought, he could never find a use for it all. Nevertheless he persisted, and in time-honoured tradition it earned him a nickname: 'Rick the Kit'!

Another new member to the fold was Neil. Short, muscular and extremely fit, he was a Physical Training and shield control instructor from PT18, the public order specialists. He wore his hair cropped close to his head, and would be the first to admit he resembled the archetypal knuckle-dragger we'd come to expect. However, he was an extremely friendly and competent character.

Neil was a replacement for Brad, who was now on recuperative instructional duties, having been involved in an accident some months previously. It had happened during a late shift one cold winter's evening in Clapham. Standing by at the section house on the common, we'd been called in to assist a Force Intelligence Bureau surveillance team who were up behind a suspect wanted for murder. The intelligence gathered suggested the man was in possession of a handgun, although he favoured (and always carried) a large, flat-bladed knife. The SIO had just finished telling us this when the radio crackled into life. The surveillance officer reported the suspect on foot, heading towards Clapham Common. If he made it, they feared he would be 'lost'.

With no time to brief, we made swiftly for the Rangies and sped off, monitoring the surveillance channel. Racing across the relatively short distance, I quickly briefed the team by radio.

'Bravo, Alpha!'

'Go, go,' was the muffled response.

'Yeah, Bravo, you getting this on the small set? He's south towards the common. Male, black, leather jacket, hood up. Both hands in his pockets. He's well eyes about, repeat eyes about, over!'

Brad's voice came on the net. 'Yeah, Dolph, got that. How do you want to play it?'

I'd already decided. 'The pavement there is quite wide. We should be coming up behind him. Once we ping him we'll drive past and throw the motor across his path. You do the same behind, cutting off his escape. We'll have a stick man in each vehicle!'

'Yeah, received.'

Cruising slowly down the dimly lit street, I scanned my surroundings for the suspect. It was Chris who suddenly pointed frantically to his left. 'It's him! Over there.'

I followed his finger and spotted a lone figure hunched over, his hood up. Battling against the chilly evening breeze, if he had been eyes about he'd certainly lost his unease by now.

'Nice one.' I smiled. 'And no public about. Sweet.'

Ninja tapped me on the shoulder with a three-foot wooden stave. 'Watch his hands.'

The incessant babble on the small set suddenly died. Picking up the radio and tapping the battery, I realized there was nothing wrong with the set – it was purely that the team could sense the hit. The hunters had scented their prey.

'Trojan Alpha?'

'Go, go,' I called.

'Eyeball confirms that is your man. Over to you.'

I acknowledged.

'Bravo, Alpha.'

'Go, go.'

'Bravo, I have control. Confirm our target. Mike India, over.'

'Yes, yes,' Brad's reply, calm and monotone with no hint of anxiety.

'Standby, standby.'

I nodded to Chris. Gunning the powerful four-litre engine, we took off towards our objective a hundred yards ahead. From the footwell I pulled out my MP5 and retracted the stock. Checking the magazine was properly seated I sat with the gun lightly resting on my knees. Checking the wing mirror, I confirmed that Bravo were hanging slightly back. It was a manoeuvre we'd practised many times in the past.

Perhaps oblivious to everything but the biting cold, the suspect paid no attention as we passed some ten feet to his right. Suddenly Chris threw the powerful beast violently to the left, and bouncing up the kerb we came to a bone-jarring halt. My door was open almost before we had stopped.

Frozen with fear, his eyes saucer-wide, the suspect started to react. (As Tony had once said, 'When a man starts to react, that is when he's at his most dangerous.') Turning on his heel he sought escape, but it was a pointless exercise. Behind him his exit was blocked by Bravo, who in a move not dissimilar to ours, had boxed him with clinical professionalism.

'Don't move! Get your fucking hands in the air. *IN THE AIR!*' I screamed, levelling the five at his chest slowly, calmly. In the same instant I was aware of Chris, who on the blind side had exited the driver's door and was now diving across the bonnet. The suspect's hands slowly came out of his pockets. Empty. Chris grabbed his wrist as Ninja stood, baton raised. After a quick, jerky twist, I heard screaming way off to my left. Pay no attention, I thought, Bravo will deal. Seconds later, face down, arms trussed behind him, our target protested his innocence.

Coming out of my almost trance-like condition, I was became aware of the screams of pain getting louder. Chris looked at me quizzically. I shrugged my shoulders. 'What the fuck's that?' I asked, bewildered. 'If he had a third eye watching his back I certainly didn't see him!'

Chris shook his head. 'Nah, he was on his own.'

Peering over the bonnet of Bravo, we saw Brad lying on his back, spreadeagled on the pavement, his white face a mask of sheer pain. He was moaning loudly as a medic tended his foot.

I bent over. 'For fuck's sake, Brad, shut up,' I hissed. 'We're supposed to be hard.'

With sweat beaded on the forehead of his bloodless face, he pointed towards his damaged foot as the medic pulled off his sock.

'Fucking hell.' I whistled at the black, throbbing, mangled piece of meat, no wonder he was in pain. Unable to take my eyes off his foot I asked, 'What happened?'

Sinex huffed. 'He was getting ready to bail out as we went up the kerb. I don't know what happened but somehow the Rangey went over his foot.'

I winced. 'Ouch.'

A TSG carrier screeched to a halt at the kerb. 'Fucking brilliant hit, fellas' the skipper shouted from the window. He looked down at Brad. 'Can we help?'

I smiled. 'Yeah, cheers. He needs a hospital.' I turned to Joe. 'Go with him, Joe. Give us a bell when you know what's happening.'

He nodded – and the moaning para was manhandled roughly into the vehicle.

It later transpired that Brad's foot had been completely crushed by the three-and-a-half-ton Rangey. No wonder he'd been in so much pain. A keen marathon runner, it would be months before he'd be anywhere near fit for duty. Years after he would still suffer as a result.

Later, we picked him up from casualty in the van and headed for base. By now he was a completely different person. Christ knows what they'd given him, but he was sitting in the passenger seat of the van, pipe sticking proudly from his mouth, and his leg dangling lifelessly out of the window against the outside of the door!

Brad was sorely missed (by the rest of the lads), as had been Nigel, who was taken off ops after Odense. Now, however, after the Police Complaints Authority investigation ruling, he was coming back.

It was a genuine pleasure to see his smiling face as he dragged his bergen into the crew room that afternoon. In the following weeks we would need every man we could get!

In late 1992, an Active Service Unit of the PIRA (Provisional Irish Republican Army) waged a new campaign of violence on mainland Britain. By June 1993 the country was reeling from ten bomb atrocities that had rocked the hearts of her major cities. It had started in February, as four blasts around the country had culminated in eighteen people injured in Camden when a litter bin exploded.

Worse was yet to come. In March, the entire nation mourned the senseless loss of two young boys, Tim Parry and five-year-old Jonathan Ball, killed at a dramatic blast in Warrington.

Then the IRA switched tactics, returning to London in an effort to maintain their stranglehold of terror. In April, after a small device exploded outside the Conservative Club in Central London, the City was blasted by a huge explosion deep in the heart of its financial quarter. A lorry packed with explosives had been abandoned in Bishopsgate. The result was more than one billion pounds' worth of damage and the tragic death of freelance journalist Edward Henty. In, June, smaller devices were planted as far afield as Oxford and Tyne and Wear.

Growing criticism was levelled at the police and security services, whose recently promoted head Stella Rimington held a firm belief that the only way to catch terrorists was through surveillance and informants. Unbeknown to the public, the slowly turning wheels of justice were already gathering momentum!

On the thirtieth of June that year, Owen Kelly, the Commissioner of Police for the City of London, announced in a blaze of publicity the implementation of a Belfast-style 'ring of steel' to be thrown around Britain's financial heartland. Armed blockades and mobile road-checks in the City were soon to become a way of life.

One week previously, the intelligence services (MI5 etc., collectively referred to as 'Box'), operating in their own cloak-and-dagger twilight world of informants and moles, had latched on to an IRA main player.

At forty-four years of age, twenty-stone 'enforcer' Robert (Rab) Fryers, brought up in the staunch Republican world of knee cappings and sectarian murder, had been hand-picked to deliver the 'ultimate outrage'. Mockingly referring to the ring of steel as the 'ring of plastic', the IRA godfathers intended to breach its security and detonate a massive blast within.

Leaving Belfast, Fryers was unaware of the team of watchers (Box surveillance) on his tail. With little or no luggage, he boarded the ferry at Larne on the north-eastern tip of the Province.

Docking at Douglas on the Isle of Man, he boarded the ferry shuttle to Stranraer. Then he made for an IRA safe house in Sauchie, near Alloa.

'The plan's been pretty much finalized,' I said to Andy, pulling the briefing package from the drawer of the metal filing cabinet. 'Just need you to look through it and see what you think.'

He nodded. Taking the large brown envelope, he shook its contents on to the table. Something was troubling him, but I knew when not to push. As a punishment for crossing him, Big Joe was currently serving penance by driving a uniformed ARV.

Andy's face cracked into a broad grin. 'Do you think we can pull it off?'

I smiled. 'Yeah, I think so. I've had a good look at the plot, But I'll need two and a half teams and you in control.'

He nodded. 'I've got a mate coming down next week. He'll be observing for a few days; he's thinking of applying for the department.' He paused.

'What rank?' I asked.

'Sergeant.'

I shook my head. Shoving the documents haphazardly back

into the envelope, I slammed the drawer. 'Job-stealing bastard!'

Andy smiled, nodding at the cabinet. 'When's it due to come off?'

'Blagger's day next week.' (Blagger's day is Thursday, due to the large number of wages deliveries usually occurring.) 'But there's a lot to do,' I added.

Andy frowned, scanning the small, empty briefing room to ensure we were alone. Then he hunched over conspiratorially. 'There's a big thirteen [SO13 – anti-terrorist squad] job bubbling. We'll probably be covering it by the weekend. Trouble is, if it goes over, you'll have to be pulled off to cover the blag with another team. I know it's complicated, and most of it's in your head – there's only so much you can put on paper.'

I felt as if I'd been kicked in the guts. So that's what had been bothering him. He knew I'd want to be involved in the Paddy job. On the other hand, I knew he was right, I'd put a lot of effort into the blag, and it was only right I should be there to brief it. 'Well,' I smiled, 'we'll have to make sure it comes off before, won't we?'

Having picked up a powder blue Ford Escort, over the next couple of days (and under the never-sleeping gaze of the watchers) Fryers made numerous dummy runs to the capital. A creature of habit, his route remained the same. M80 from Stirling to Glasgow, A74(M) to Carlisle, M6 to Birmingham's spaghetti junction, where he picked up the M1 to London; leaving his vehicle parked at the end of the motorway near Staples Corner, he would take public transport through the 'ring of plastic' into the City itself. Satisfied, he'd then return to Sauchie.

Andy gave the briefing.

'Sorry to drag you all in. There's a big PIRA job come on top. Thirteen and Box are up behind one of their main players. Things at present are shaping up nicely. They want to bring us in for the hit.' Murmuring ran through the small, tightly packed briefing room. I sat and cursed silently.

Andy outlined the plan. 'This will have to be very fluid. Green and Orange are out on the plot at the moment, covering nights. You'll do days. From now on it's twenty-four-hour cover.' He looked up. Nobody was arguing. 'Same SOP as always. We'll be in gunships with Thirteen's drivers. We'll be up behind the surveillance team, ready to be pulled through. It could be mobile, but most likely an ambush on foot, depending on how far they let it run.'

I cringed. Whoever had the job of calling on the hit would have to time it right, knowing a man has a device but not knowing where he'll plant it. Even with the experienced eyes of the watchers, the suspect could quite easily be lost in a crowded street while carrying his lethal cargo. What if he went to the toilet and came out empty-handed?

Andy continued: 'When we take him it's more than likely he'll have the device to hand. He'll also probably be armed. This man is a top IRA enforcer brought over for one specific mission. Remember that! Parade tomorrow morning four-thirty for a six-thirty handover on the plot. Any questions?'

Silence.

'Steve?'

I nodded. 'Thanks, Andy. OK, fellas, as we're here and earning we'll go through the postings now to save time in the morning. Needless to say, plain clothes, light order body armour and caps . . .'

'Fucking hell,' said Stevie, the tall South Londoner from Green Team. 'Don't think you'll be too busy today. We've been on his arse all night. Nearly as far as Scotland before they turned us back.' He beamed at the adventure.

Having paraded at four-thirty, we were already briefed by the time we had reached the RVP (in the back yard of a small North London nick) well ahead of schedule. It made me laugh – on jobs of this nature everybody wanted to be in on the hit. As a consequence, when it came to changeover time we all got in early and dashed out to the plot. This really pissed off the team you were due to relieve, not only because it was eating into their overtime, but because they feared they might miss out on something they would otherwise have been involved in.

'What happened then?' I asked as we swapped over our kit in the boot of the nondescript Cavalier.

'Ah, they reckoned he wouldn't do anything, so the sweaties took over.' ('Sweaty Sock' was slang for 'jock' or Scotsman. In this case the Scottish police had taken over surveillance.)

Shrugging against the early morning chill, I waved him fare-well. Placing my MP5 in the rear passenger footwell for easy access, I started coughing. Bollocks. As much as I'd dosed myself up with paracetamol, I felt I was definitely sickening for some-thing.

I slumped in the back seat of the inconspicuous-looking gunship. 'It's fucking freezing in here. Can't we do the window up a bit?'

'Sorry, skip,' replied the unconcerned radio operator. 'He's one of these health freaks.' He nodded towards the sleeping driver who, with seat fully reclined, snored peacefully.

'Yeah,' I moaned. 'I know another one of them.' I turned to Chris, my partner for the day. 'You still on that diet?'

'It's not a diet,' he whined indignantly. 'I happen to be in train-ing.' He looked down at my expanding waistline. 'Something all of us might benefit from,' he added sarcastically. It was true.

It was also five forty-five in the morning and I was already incredibly cold. And incredibly bored. I had to pick on somebody. 'Yeah, well if you can run faster than thirteen hundred feet a second [the muzzle velocity of an MP5] you're fucking good!' I had to admit, though, that with all the weights, health food, and what I can only describe as rabbit droppings in sawdust, Chris seemed to be bulking up nicely. The only drawback was that he suffered terrific wind!

Five minutes later I asked, 'How come it's so bloody cold? It's the beginning of July.'

Chris shrugged and chomped on yet another Granny Smith.

When it came to squad jobs I was never really that organized. I don't mean that in a professional sense, purely a domestic one. Many of the team were always prepared, packing cartons of sandwiches the evening before. I for one had always relied on the squad driver's intimate knowledge of all the local greasy spoons, where you could pick up a nice hot egg and bacon banjo, coffee, and a sausage sarnie. Too late I realized my mistake, having posted myself with the only health nut in the department.

I pulled myself deeper into the thin cotton material of my jacket. To my left, Chris farted. 'Oh, for God's sake,' I shouted. 'That's outrageous. Can't you get out and do that?'

'Fuck off. It's freezing out there,' came his sleepy reply.

Using my sleeve, I rubbed condensation from the window and

peered out. The Granada parked alongside vibrated gently as the engine idled. Exhaust plumes billowed lazily, hanging in the cold early-morning air. I knew the heater would be on full-blast. Lying back, their heads turned to one side, slept the driver and operator. Mouths open, their tongues lolled grotesquely.

A faint ethereal glow emanated from the back of the car. Curious, I switched my gaze. Rick stared blankly ahead, totally oblivious to his surroundings and my supreme discomfort. In one hand he held an egg sandwich from which he took a large bite and chewed slowly. In our car I slavered as my stomach groaned with hunger. Steam rose from the piping hot cup of coffee in his other hand. His gaze never faltered as he took yet another tantalizing bite. Lifting my head slightly, I sought the source of the light. To my utter amazement the bastard was actually watching breakfast TV on a small colour set plugged in to the car's cigarette lighter!

I slumped dejectedly into the seat in an effort to stave off the cold. Sleep would not come easily. Popping a couple of paraceta- mol, I grimaced as I swallowed them dry. Perhaps I could change partners, I thought, excitedly looking across at Rick. To my left, Chris farted again.

As the day progressed, so my cold grew worse. With Fryers safely in Scotland there was nothing for us to do but stand by. The early, watery sun brought some respite from the cold, but by the time the night team relieved us, all I wanted was my pit.

The next morning I returned with a vengeance. After two more paracetamol and a very large Scotch, I had slept like a baby. Bounding energetically into the briefing room, packed lunch under my arm, I was raring to go. Looking up from his seat, Chris raised his eyebrows to the ceiling. And took another mouthful of sawdust.

Monday passed like all the others. This time I'd brought a Jack Higgins thriller to while away the hours, and I was interrupted only occasionally by a trumpeting fart from my colleague and friend. Half-way through the afternoon I was jerked awake from an uncomfortable slumber by the familiar sound of a pager. All four of us reached down to our belts in unison and checked the screens. Only mine flashed up a message. The one I had been dreading. Unable to put it off any longer, I got out of the car and trotted over to Andy's gunship, tapping on the window.

'Job's on for Thursday,' I stated flatly. 'Ninety-nine per cent.'

Andy sighed. 'Sorry, mate. But nothing's happening here. It could go on for ever.'

I nodded. 'Can I hold out for as long as possible? If I leave a note for the early turn skipper on Wednesday, he can make a few calls and jack everything up.'

He thought for a while. 'OK. So long as it's sorted. By the way, my mate Bob starts with us on Wednesday.'

'Cheers, guv,' I mumbled, and hands in pockets I made my way dejectedly back to the car. Fucking great! I thought bitterly. If this comes off, some skipper not even in the department will be in on the hit while I'm working my bollocks off elsewhere!

By Tuesday, though, I was looking forward to Thursday. At the handover, Stevie reported that Fryers had made a journey by train and was still in Scotland. With frustrating monotony, I sat in the back of the gunship with Chris's arse for company. 'This is shaping up to go nowhere,' I complained.

Chris agreed. 'Do you think that blag will come off on Thursday?'

I nodded. 'So they say. I'm actually looking forward to a decent job for a change. This one is bollocks!'

Wednesday – and the big day loomed nearer. Getting to Old Street early, I left a long, complicated list of things to arrange – and prayed I wouldn't be let down. Reaching the plot, we were greeted by an excited Stevie, who couldn't wait to give us a rundown. 'He's back,' he beamed. 'Don't know what he's up to, but it's close. He's not very smart. Spent the night in a motel in Hertfordshire. Drank ten pints of Guinness and sung Republican songs. Doubt if you'll get much response today,' he said happily. I sighed. It was 6 a.m.

Andy's mate Bob introduced himself. He seemed a nice enough bloke, but it was hard to get over that twinge of jealousy. 'Bob will be in the control vehicle with me,' Andy told me. 'If it comes off, I'll hand control over to you.'

I nodded. Fat Chance!

Fryers surfaced early, only this time with a sense of purpose. It was seven-thirty before we really knew anything had changed.

'Steve!' Andy called urgently. 'Inside.'

Frowning, I left a sleeping Chris and clambered out of the gunship to follow Andy into the building where I found him in hurried discussion with the SO13 DI.

I nodded. 'All right, guv?'

'Steve, it looks like this is it!' Andy whispered seriously.

The DI nodded. 'We think he's going to lay it down this morning somewhere in the City. We've more intelligence coming in, but we favour him parking up and jumping a bus.'

I stood there, dumbfounded. A feeling I'd never experienced before (or for that matter since) coursed through my body. Anger, hate, adrenalin . . . a sense of purpose? Perhaps it was a combination of all four.

I looked at Andy, my mouth dry. 'I'd like a final scrum down with the lads, guv. We may get split up, and I want them to know exactly how we'll play this at the end of the day.'

'OK,' he said, turning to the DI. 'But be quick. We may get the off any time now.'

Nodding, I turned and left.

'Oh, and Steve!'

I turned again. 'Yes, guv?'

'They need your car on the surveillance. You and Chris will have to split.'

Thinking back to the gas-filled interior I smiled. 'No probs. I'll double up with Nigel in the flounder.'

By eight o'clock things were beginning to shape up nicely. All thoughts of cold or hunger now vanished as we concentrated on the job in hand. Sitting in the back of the roomy black cab, I tapped the mags of the MP5 reassuringly. I knew they were loaded, knew they were seated – I'd checked them twice already – but there was no room for mistakes. We now realized that it would almost definitely fall on us to take him somewhere in the street, and I was more than conscious that any sudden movement he might make would be interpreted by us as hostile. From what we'd been told, we strongly believed he would be carrying a bomb of some description. Whether or not it was primed was another matter.

During the heads-down session with the lads, I had decided we would place the suspect face-down next to the package, covering him from a safe distance with a ninety-three. The reasons for this, I had argued, were twofold: it would give us time to clear any public from the area (with a sniper covering the suspect through a scope, any false move whatsoever would cause the sniper to 'deal'); and if the bomb was primed (or for that matter booby trapped) it would give us time to think, and the suspect wouldn't

197

be too comfortable lying next to it. As a result he might want to tell us its condition.

The radio snapped me back to the present. 'Steve, Andy.' His voice sounding distant from the control vehicle.

'Go, go.'

'Yeah, he's on the move, heading back towards Cricklewood. There's a large car park five hundred yards from the plot. We're going to move up and hold. Over.'

I pressed the Send button. 'Yes, yes. Two seven to all Trojan units – mount up!'

Pulling the heavy side door of the cab shut, I leaned over the partition. 'Cricklewood please, driver,' I grinned. Nigel chuckled as we eased our way into the slow-moving rush-hour traffic.

We tried to get lost in the car park, but with six gunships of all makes and colours it wasn't easy. The best we could hope for was to lie low, stay in our vehicles and hope we were far enough away from the plot should any third eye decide to sweep it (another thing particular to this part of London, with its large Irish population, was that it was extremely Zulu).

Suddenly, as if on cue – it happened. The thing we'd all been dreading. A BMW, three up, cruised slowly into the car park and started driving aimlessly around. 'Bollocks,' I cursed at Nigel. 'Get down.'

Half lying across the seats, we disappeared from view, leaving the driver to sit nonchalantly reading his newspaper.

The radio was alive with traffic. 'Were they ours?', 'Were they theirs?' Nobody knew. As the car drove slowly up and down through the ranks of parked vehicles, it suddenly dawned on everybody that they could be nothing more than opportunist car thieves, looking for a tasty motor to screw! It would have been foolish to show out, more so to call the uniforms, so all we could do was sit, watch, and wait.

Suddenly, as they passed another team car, their back-seat passenger made eye contact with one of the team. It was enough to spook him. There was a hurried exchange between the three occupants, then to the accompaniment of screeching rubber they quickly left.

The next ten minutes or so were strangely quiet. Andy and Bob in the control vehicle had the advantage of the big set, and were listening in on the surveillance. In the back of the flounder, Nigel and I received only snippets relayed through the small partition by the driver.

'Well, this is it,' Nigel smiled.

I nodded, about to make some smart remark.

'Standby, standby.'

This *was* it. The atmosphere was electric.

'Steve? Andy.'

'Go, go.'

'He's standing at a bus stop at the shops. Crest Road. 46 BP 34. Fat man, dark jacket and jeans. He has a holdall. Confirm it *is* a bomb.'

Every valve in my body opened wide as adrenalin rushed through to my brain. Senses heightened, I was fully alert. 'Yes, yes. Understood.'

Andy paused. 'I have control. I have control. Over to you, Steve!'

The flounder at the head of the convoy, we left the car park. Opposite me sat Nigel, hand on the door, ready to go.

Pulling into Oxgate Lane, the slow-moving convoy slid cautiously towards the junction of Coles Green Road. Turning right, the driver called over his shoulder, 'I think it's down here, fellas.'

Looking over to my left I saw our man. Standing calmly at the bus stop, bag over his shoulder. He hadn't seen us. With a convoy this long it seemed a miracle, but like us he was concentrating solely on the job in hand.

We'd overshot. 'That's him,' I hissed, pointing wildly.

To my amazement, the driver ignored me and continued his route.

'He's at the bus stop. *GO, GO, GO!*' I screamed into the small set. My only hope now was that some of the other gunships hadn't yet turned right. '*YOU CUNT!*' I shouted. 'Stop this fucking motor!'

Nigel was out, moving fast, and I joined him. Rounding the corner, we saw the man on his knees, arms raised high, the bag conspicuous on the pavement beside him. It never ceased to amaze me how quickly IRA operatives reacted when challenged, almost instinctively. This time he surrendered.

Darting across the road I hit cover. 'Look at me! Look at me!' screamed Sinex from behind a wall. In the blink of an eye we'd regained control of what could quite easily have been an absolute disaster. Sinex and Ninja, taking up the initiative, had ordered their driver on, bailed out and taken him. Rick, the sniper, was now in position with the ninety-three, spreadeagled on the pavement. Down the road was the cordon, and Chris clearing the crowd of onlookers.

SILENCE.

Nothing stirred. Satisfied, I quickly ran across to Sinex. 'On your knees.' I called.

Rising on all fours, the suspect crawled as directed five yards away from the device. Sinex called for the SOCOs with their white sterile overalls necessary to preserve forensics.

'Rab' Fryers, top IRA enforcer, lay prone.

'Is that thing primed?' I said.

He stared at me in defiance, then grinned arrogantly.

The bomb contained two and a half kilos of Semtex, together with two litres of petrol. Had it detonated, its napalm-like effect would have claimed many innocent lives. Already, the police in Scotland were rounding up his companions. For his part, 'Rab' Fryers would later receive a twenty-five-year sentence at the Old Bailey.

Manhandling him to his feet, the SOCOs frogmarched him away. As he passed defiantly by, I smiled and pointed to my face, uttering those immortal words:

'Terrorism stops here!'

Epilogue

As a result of numerous injuries sustained in a police career spanning some nineteen years I was unable to continue the fight. With the fondest of memories I was forced to retire on medical grounds in December 1996.

That same month the first woman – ever – passed selection for a specialist firearms team. She knows who she is, and I wish her the very best. In January 1997 Tony returned to the department in a move long overdue.

With no respite, SO19 operations continue to hurtle along at breakneck speed. When you turn out your light and sleep safely in your bed, spare a thought for the van gliding silently to a halt. Think of the fast-moving shadows, and listen for the barking of dogs, then breathe a sigh of relief. For out there, cloaked under the cover of darkness, risking their lives for you on a daily basis – are the men in Black!

Steve Collins
April 1997

Glossary

ACPO	Association of Chief Police Officers
Across the pavement	Term used for confronting robbers in the commission of an offence
AFO	Authorized Firearms Officer
ARV	Armed Response Vehicle (uniformed)
ASU	IRA Active Service Unit or Air Support Unit
Assaulter	Term for SO19 SFO member kitted for hostage rescue or rapid entry
AWAC	Airborne Warning and Control system
Baby	Portable ram used by SO19
Bergen	Large army backpack issued to SO19
Birdshot	Shotgun round containing a large number of lead balls, now predominantly used for clay pigeon shooting
Blagger	Armed robber (slang)
Blat	Fast drive (slang)
Blue on blue	Accidental contact by friendly forces
Bod	Body armour
Box	MI5 security services, or security van (i.e. Blue Box)
Carabiner	Metal clip used in abseiling
Carrying	Armed
Casevac	Casualty evacuation
CID	Criminal Investigation Department

Clusterfuck	Term describing situation where everything goes wrong
CROPs	Covert Rural Observation posts
CRW	Counter Revolutionary Warfare
CS	Chemical irritant (often referred to as gas)
CTR	Close Target Reconnaissance
D6	Title of the first Metropolitan Police firearms unit
D11	Name given to D6 after internal reshuffle
DA	Deliberate Action
DC	Detective Constable
DCI	Detective Chief Inspector
DEA	(American) Drug Enforcement Administration
Deemed	Placed in a mental institution
DI	Detective Inspector
Dig-out	Early-morning raid by SO19
Double German	Double-width ladder for house assaults
Double tap	Term used for firing two rounds of ammunition almost simultaneously, usually without aiming
DPG	Diplomatic Protection Group
Dragon light	Powerful rechargeable lamp
DS	Detective Sergeant
Emerge	Operation Emerge
End-ex	End exercise
Enforcer	Portable hand-held ram used by SO19
ER	Emergency reaction
Eyeball	Surveillance speak for visual contact
FAP	Final Assault Position
Federation	Police Federation (Police Officers' Union)
Fed Rep	Federation Representative
Ferret	Shotgun cartridge containing CS irritant
FHA	Forward Holding Area

FIB	Force Intelligence Bureau
Flash crash/bang	Slang for stun grenade
Flounder	Squad speak for black cab
Flop	Safe house
FME	Forensic Medical Examiner
Forward control	SO19 control point within a cordon
FUP	Forming-Up Point
Ghostbusters	Metropolitan Police Property Service Dept
GIGN	French paramilitary unit Groupment d'Intervention de la Gendarmerie Nationale
Grain	The weight of the head of a bullet – as in 158 grain
Grot	Sleeping bag
GSG9	German paramilitary unit Grenzschutz Gruppe 9
Gunship	Vehicle for carrying firearms officers on an operation (usually unmarked)
Happy Bag	Squadspeak for robber's bag containing firearms etc.
Hatton round	Shotgun round made of wax and powdered lead for shooting off door hinges, etc.
Head of Shed	Boss
Hit	Term used by SO19 for calling on an attack
Hooley	Hooligan Bar – a jemmy with a spike at one end
IED	Improvised Explosive Device
India	Suspect
IR	Information room or infra-red
JSP	Jacketed soft-point (as in the head of a round)
Jump off	Vehicle or premises near to a plot where a team can wait to attack

LAS	London Ambulance Service
Lay visitor	Member of the public who, as part of a scheme, visits prisoners held in police custody
Level 1/2	Part of the PT17 two-tier team system
LOE	Limit of Exploitation
LUP	Lying-up Point
Meanie	Slang for stun grenade
Met	Metropolitan Police
Mike India	Move in – radio instruction
Minster	Operation minster
MOE	Method of Entry
Mutual aid	Providing of assistance to other forces
Multi-burst	Slang for stun grenade
Net	Radio network
Odense	Operation Odense
OIC	Officer in Charge
OP	Observation Post
Pink card	Authority to draw firearms
PIP	Post-Incident Procedure
PIRA	Provisional Irish Republican Army
Plasticuffs	Nylon ties used for handcuffing prisoners
Player(s)	Suspect(s)
Plot	Scene of an operation (i.e. robbery plot)
Plod	Uniformed police officer
PNG	Passive Night Goggles
Pongo (Percy)	Navy term for a soldier, insinuating they fail in their personal hygiene (where Percy goes the pong goes)
PTT	Press To Talk switch
Posse	Black gang associated with Yardies
PR	Personal Radio
PT17	Forerunner of SO19 (Personnel and Training)
PT18	Shield Training instructors (or

commonly referred to as knuckle-draggers)

Rapid entry	Fast entry into premises to preserve evidence
Rapid (10 shot)	A distraction device simulating machine-gun fire
RCS	Regional Crime Squad
Re-org	Reorganization phase of an operation
Resi	Standard S6 respirator worn by SO19
RIP round	Round Irritant Personnel (a shotgun round containing CS that will penetrate a door before dispersing)
RVP	Rendezvous Point
SAS	Special Air Service
SBS	Special Boat Service
Scanner	Device used for monitoring police radio
Seated	Ensuring a weapon's magazine is correctly engaged
Sectioned	Placed in a mental institution
SFO	Specialist Firearms Officer
Shot	Authorized firearms officer
SIO	Senior Investigating Officer
Sit rep	Situation report
Slaughter	Safe premises where stolen goods drugs can be divided
Slot/Slotted	To shoot somebody
SOP	Standard Operating Procedure
SOCO	Scene of Crime Officer
SO11	Met Police surveillance unit
SO13	Anti-terrorist squad
SO19	Met Police tactical firearms unit
SP TEAM	SAS (special projects) team
SPG	Special Patrol Group
Stave	A 3-foot wooden truncheon
Stick	Stave, or small file of men
Stickman	Team member armed with a stave
Stronghold	Position within a building containing a suspect

Suits	CID
Strapping	Filling in on a team
Tenure	A policy introduced to change officers engaged on specialist duties
Thief-taker	Police officer with a good arrest record
TI	Target Indication
Tooled up	Armed
Trojan	Callsign for armed SO19 units
Trojan horse	Covert vehicle concealing an SO19 team
Trumpton	Fire brigade
TSG	Territorial Support Group
Up behind	Slang for surveillance on a suspect
U101	Pager message for emergency
Woodentop/Woody	Term used by plain-clothes for uniformed Officer
X-ray	Hostage-taker
Yankee	Hostage
Yardie	Jamaican Mafia
Zulu	Hostile

Police Weapons

Browning	9 mm self-loading pistol issued to PT17 Level One teams. Subsequently replaced by the Glock 17
Glock 17	Austrian-made 9 mm self-loading pistol with a magazine capacity of 17 rounds. Standard issue to SO19
MP5	Heckler & Koch 9 mm carbine. The A3 version, with retractable stock, is issue to SO19 SFO teams
93	Heckler & Koch 93 .223 rifle used for sniper/containment

Kurtz	Fully automatic Heckler & Koch 9 mm short-barrel machine-gun
Model 10/19	Smith & Wesson .38 six-shot revolvers
Remington 870	Pump-action shotgun, also available in the sawn-off version. Extremely versatile weapon for use with Hatton rounds or delivering CS etc.
SD	Silenced version of the H & K MP5

Weapons available to SO19 Specialist Teams (see plate no. 12)

1.	Steyer 7.62 mm sniper rifle
2.	Heckler & Koch (Kurtz) sub-machine-gun
3.	Heckler & Koch 93 .223 sniper rifle
4.	Heckler & Koch MP5 (SD) silenced version
5.	Night sight
6.	Glock 9 mm self-loading pistol
7.	Heckler & Koch MP5 (A2) fixed stock
8.	L1A1 66 mm CS launcher
9.	Heckler & Koch MP5 (A3) retractable stock
10.	L67 baton gun
11.	Remington 870 12-bore pump-action shotgun (sawn-off version for 'Hatton' rounds)
12.	Remington 870 12-bore pump-action shotgun with folding stock

Selection of MOE Equipment (see plate no. 13)

1. & 2.	Various sized sledgehammers with carrying ropes for slinging over body armour

3.   Metal bar for posting through letterbox of an outward-opening door – the chain is attached to an armoured vehicle and the door pulled from the frame (prototype designed by the author)

4.   'Baby' – a manual battering ram

5.   'Hooley' – hooligan bar

6.   Metal spike

7.   Crowbar

8.   'Enforcer' – this ram replaced the outdated 'Baby'

9.   This shows the ingenuity of team members in solving a problem. Made from a crowbar, it is designed so the spike punches through the metal and glass mesh of a fire door. Pulling back sharply, the hook catches the emergency exit bar and opens the door.

10.   Various sized axes for windows

11.   Bolt croppers

12.   Two-man 'Baby'

Personal Equipment of an SFO member (see plate no. 11)

1.   Heavyweight overt body armour of kevlar construction with upgraded ceramic plate

2.   Bergen

3.   Lightweight covert undershirt body armour for plain-clothes operations

4.   Plasticuffs and cutters

5.   Ballistic helmet and goggles

6.   High-visibility baseball cap donned during plain-clothes ambushes

7.   Boots (team members normally choose

	their own design although these are issue)
8.	Goretex waterproof suit
9.	Beret (normally only now worn on ceremonial or instructional duties)
10.	Coveralls
11.	Northern Ireland padded gloves
12.	Ear defenders
13.	Leg protectors
14.	Abseil/fast rope gloves
15.	Covert radio rig
16.	Respirator case
17.	Heckler & Koch MP5 (A3)
18.	Glock SLP
19.	Abseil harness
20.	Belt rig
21.	Maglight torches – the smaller has an infra-red filter for PNG work
22.	Standard S6 respirator